LIFE IN HAWAII

Titus Coan

Titus Coan was born in Killingworth, Connecticut on February 1, 1801. He graduated from Auburn Theological Seminary after two years study, and was ordained in 1833. He was sent to explore Patagonia for a year on his first missionary effort. In 1834 he married Fidelia Church, sailed for Hawaii, and was stationed at Hilo. It was here that he made his life's work, and served for nearly 48 years. After learning and mastering the Hawaiian language, he won the confidence of the Hawaiians and converted thousands to Christianity. He later established churches and trained native converts to act as missionaries among their own people.

In addition to his missionary labors, he added a great deal to our knowledge of volcanic eruptions. He corresponded and worked with geologist James Dwight Dana, performed many observations and explorations of the volcanic activity on Hawaii, and published in the *American Journal of Science* and the *Missionary Herald.* He is best known for his books *Adventures in Patagonia* (1880) and *Life in Hawaii* (1882). Titus Coan died in his home on Hilo, December 1, 1882.

Scriptoria Books

The word "scriptoria" literally means "places for writing." Historically, scriptoria were writing rooms, areas set apart in some monasteries for the use of scribes, or copyists of the community, to faithfully create or reproduce books by hand. Their work was exacting, and great care was taken to ensure a high degree of copy fidelity.

Scriptoria Books continues in the traditions set forth in these communities long ago. Each new Scriptoria publication has been transcribed word for word from an original text, then edited, formatted, typeset, and proofread through each revision. Our procedures are not automated. Our books are not facsimiles; they are carefully created new editions of classic works.

LIFE
IN
HAWAII

AN AUTOBIOGRAPHIC SKETCH
OF MISSION LIFE AND LABORS
(1835-1881)

REVISED 2ND EDITION

TITUS COAN

Scriptoria Books

Life in Hawaii: An Autobiographical Sketch of Mission Life and Labors (1835-1881); Revised 2ND Edition

The Revised 2ND Edition of Life in Hawaii: An Autobiographical Sketch of Mission Life and Labors (1835-1881) was transcribed, edited, and typeset by Scriptoria Books. Necessary corrections to the original text and index (including: misprints, punctuation, spelling, and citations) have been incorporated into this edition. Original source published by Anson D. F. Randolph & Company, New York, 1882.

Life in Hawaii : An autobiographic sketch of mission life and labors (1835-1881) / by Titus Coan. -- Revised 2nd edition.
p. cm.
Includes index
ISBN 9780615880068 (pbk)
1. Missions -Hawaii 2. Hawaii -Description
I. Coan, Titus (1801-1882).

Scriptoria Books
Mesa, Arizona USA

www.scriptoriabooks.com

You shall love the Lord your God
with all your heart, with all your soul,
with all your strength, and with all your mind,
and your neighbor as yourself.

Luke 10:27

Titus Coan

CONTENTS

NOTE

THE task of reading the proofs of the following sketches has fallen to one whose recollections include more than a few of the scenes and events described. It seems to him that this record of mission life and labors will appeal to all those who have followed the wonderful changes wrought in Hawaii during a life time, from the period of "the great awakening" until now. The accounts of visits to the Marquesas Islands have their own independent interest. Still more, the greatest volcano in the world is in Mr. Coan's parish, and other readers will turn to the chapters on its eruptions for vivid and faithful descriptions of the most imposing volcanic phenomena on record.

T. M. C.

PREFACE

A PILGRIM of four-score years, standing near the margin of the Border Land, essays to give a sketch of his life—and why?

Because many personal and Christian friends have long urged it as a duty to my beloved Master to leave my testimony behind me of His faithfulness and grace.

To publish my autobiography was far from my thoughts.

It is a difficult, delicate, and dangerous task. One does not choose to publish his own follies and sins, and surely it is not modest for one to proclaim his own goodness. I will, therefore, only say in the words of the great Apostle, "Unto me, who am less than the least of all saints, is this grace given, that I should preach among the Gentiles the unsearchable riches of Christ."

Let me then ask, if in reading this narrative there shall seem to be the weakness of egotism or of vain boosting, that the fault may lie at the door of the writer, or be pardoned on account of the great difficulty of relating one's own experiences and observations without often repeating the pronoun *I*.

On the other hand, if it shall appear that during a ministry of almost half a century a blind man has been led into the light, a lame man has been helped to walk in the Way of Life, a leprous soul has been washed in the Fountain opened for sin and uncleanness; if a heathen has found the true God, and cast away his dead idols, if a fierce cannibal has been persuaded to cease to eat the flesh of his enemies, and taught to trust the Son of Man for pardon, or if some who were dead in trespasses and sins have been raised to life by the quickening power of the Gospel, then let God have all the glory.

T. C.

He Lived By Faith.

He Still Lives.

Believest Thou This?
John 11:26

This simple inscription appears on a marble slab above the grave of Titus Coan, given as a gift from his people on Hilo.

1

Parentage, Childhood, and Early Years – Militia Service – Asahel Nettleton – Three Years in Western New York – Sickness – Home Again – Auburn Seminary.

MY father was Gaylord Coan, of Killingworth, Middlesex Co., Connecticut. He was a thoughtful, quiet, and modest farmer, industrious, frugal, and temperate, attending to his own business, living in peace with his neighbors, eschewing evil, honest in dealing, avoiding debts, abhorring extravagance and profligacy, refusing proffered offices, strictly observing the Sabbath, a regular attendant on the services of the sanctuary, a constant reader of the Bible, and always offering morning and evening prayers with the family. He was born Aug. 4, 1768, and died Sept. 24, 1857, in his 90th year.

My mother was Tamza Nettleton, sister of Josiah Nettleton and aunt of Asahel Nettleton, D.D., the distinguished Evangelical preacher. She was the tender, faithful, and laborious mother of seven children, six sons and one daughter. Of these I was the youngest.

While still in the vigor of womanhood, she was cut down Jan. 14, 1818, by typhus fever, aged 58. Her death left the house desolate, and the loss was deeply mourned by all the children.

After this our father married Miss Platt, of Saybrook, by whom he had one daughter, who died at the age of eighteen.

I was born on the first day of February, Sunday morning, 1801, in the town of Killingworth, Conn. My physical constitution was good, my health was perfect, and my childhood happy.

From the age of four to twelve I was sent to the district school, where the boys and girls were drilled in Webster's spelling book, The American Preceptor, writing, arithmetic (Daball's), Morse's geography, Murray's grammar, and the Westminster Shorter Catechism. Days and weeks and years went quietly along, with the usual experiences of joyous childhood. Spring, summer, autumn, and winter each had their peculiar charms, their duties and diversions, and I moved along the stream with only now and then a ripple.

Once, when a boy of about seven years, I had a memorable experience. My father was to be absent during the day, and in the morning he said to me, "Titus, go straight to school today." When he left, some boys came along and persuaded me to play truant. Off we started, and spent the day in as much pleasure as we could enjoy, with some twinges of guilt and fear. At 4 P.M., the time for the school to close, I managed to fall in with the children who were returning home.

Evening came—my father returned. We had supper and prayers. My conscience throbbed a little, and I prepared for bed early. When ready in my night-robe to leap into bed, my father called me to him. I trembled, but obeyed. Sitting quietly in his chair, he laid me, face downward, across his knees, took up a small birch rod and said, "Well, Titus, you are all ready now for the reward of disobedience— you did not go to school." He then gave me a few salutary touches with the birch, and I stole off to bed. That was one of the best lessons of my childhood. It made a distinct impression upon me which I could not forget. It worked through my skin and my flesh, and went into my heart. I never played truant again.

Yes, I did get one more lesson which cooled my blood and made me thoughtful. A deep millpond lay between my home and the schoolhouse. In the winter this pond was often frozen over, and my father warned me not to venture upon the ice on my way to school. One morning when I was nine years old, a mate of my age went with me to school. As we came to the pond we agreed to have a little slide. We went on halfway across the pond, I leading, and Julius following. Coming to the deepest part of the pond, the ice broke suddenly under me and I went under the water, but found no bottom. I rose to the surface in the same place where I went down, and screamed for help. My companion stood aghast and feared to come near. I threw up my hands and caught hold of the ice, but it broke before me. Again and again I struggled to find firm hold, but still the treacherous ice gave way until I nearly despaired of life. At length, however, I came to firmer ice, and clung to it as with a death grasp, calling on Julius for help. The timid boy approached slowly until his hand reached mine; and with his help and God's mercy I was delivered from a watery grave. But it was midwinter, and I was sadly chilled. To avoid freezing we ran all the way, a half mile, to the schoolhouse, where we found a roaring fire and the master not there. I stood by the fire, turning round and round, and smoking like a sparerib, until the master came, when I took my seat and shivered until noon. The intermission being one hour, I improved it to dry my clothes, and went home at evening, charging my schoolmate never to tell any one of this event. He kept his promise until I came to the Hawaiian Islands, and then he told the story. This was another lesson which I report with thanks to the Lord for sparing my life, and as a warning to all children to "Obey their parents in the Lord that their days may be long."

But it is not necessary to enlarge on "the scenes of my childhood," though diversified, and very many of them "dear to my heart."

Nor will I take time to tell all my childhood's faults; and as for its virtues, I have nothing of which to boast.

When about thirteen I worked with my father on the farm during the summer months, and attended school in the winter. The next year I was a pupil in a select school at the house of my honored and excellent pastor, the Rev. Asa King. In this school I spent two happy winters, while my summers were passed on the farm, or in fishing on Long Island Sound, or for shad in early spring in the Connecticut River.

Not satisfied with my knowledge of English grammar derived from Murray and unskilled teachers, I had private lessons from a teacher fresh from a grammar school in the city of New York, and under his instructions gained a more satisfactory insight into the construction of my mother tongue than from all my winter's study in what seemed to me dry Murray.

I also read eagerly such worthy books as I was able to buy or borrow; few indeed, compared with the overwhelming flood of literature of the present time. I read history, rhetoric, astronomy, philosophy, logic, and the standard poets. I joined an Academy in East Guilford, now Madison, where I studied with delight geometry, trigonometry, surveying, etc., under the instruction of the Principal, an active graduate of Yale College.

At the age of eighteen I was called to teach a school in the town of Saybrook, and from this time onward my winters were occupied in teaching in Saybrook, Killingworth, and Guilford, until I left New England for Western New York.

When the time came for me to enter the militia ranks, according to the laws of the State, I enlisted in a company of light artillery whose regiment had been commanded by Col. Bray during the war of 1812-15, and in which one of my brothers had served in the garrison of my native town during that war.

In this company I was at once chosen sergeant, and in about two years was promoted, receiving first the commission of 2d Lieut., then that of 1st Lieut.

I had been dazzled, while a boy, with the tales of military and naval exploits, with the flashing of sabers, the waving of plumes, and with the beauty of uniforms. It had been my delight to watch the evolutions of cavalry, artillery, and militia regiments on days of drill and of general review. I had seen the proud warships of Britain driving the fishing-boats, the sloops, schooners, brigs, barks, ships, all the floating commerce of Long Island Sound, into our rivers, lagoons, bays, creeks, and harbors. I had seen the flashes and heard the thunder of their guns; had been wakened at midnight by the alarm-bells of the town, and the quick fire of the garrison. I had heard of Canada, of Buffalo, of the Northern and Southern Lakes, of the Potomac, of Washington, of New Orleans, and of the peace with its joyful celebrations, and its thunder-notes of gladness rolling over the land.

Afterward, when all this died out, and a more rational, a calmer and purer peace spread over land and sea, there came a change in my military feelings and aspirations.

While absent from my native town, a memorable season of religious interest was awakened among all classes in Killingworth.

The Rev. Asahel Nettleton, whose fame as an evangelical preacher has spread over the land, was invited to return to the place of his birth, to preach the Gospel to his kindred and townsmen. He came, and the "Power of the Highest" came with him. Our pastor, Mr. King, was heart and soul with him. Sinai thundered the law, and Calvary cried pardon to the penitent. "The axe was laid at the root of the trees" and the winnowing fan was seen in the hand of the Eternal. Conversions multiplied. Profanity was hushed. Revelry ceased. "Young men" became "sober-minded." The fiddle and the midnight dance were superseded by the "Village Hymns," the "Songs of Zion," the quiet sanctuary, and the tender, the loving, and the happy prayer-meeting. All things became new. I heard the fame of them, but was absent. In childhood, tender and anxious religious thought had often filled my eyes with tears, and my heart with throbs. I had prayed under the shadows of rocks and lone trees, but no man knew my spiritual wants or met them. I regretted my absence from Killingworth while my kind pastor and own beloved cousin were thus leading thirsty souls to the Fountain of Life. I returned just in time to see 110 of my companions and neighbors stand up in the sanctuary and confess the Lord Jehovah to be their Lord and Saviour, and pledge themselves to love, follow, and obey Him.

I was thoughtful and sober, but passed on much as usual in the ordinary affairs of life.

In the spring of 1826, with a friend and my sister, I left my native home in a private carriage, and went via Middletown, Hartford, Stockbridge, Albany, and Schenectady to Rochester, taking the Erie Canal at Schenectady and leaving our friend to go on in the carriage.

I had then four brothers in Western New York; the oldest, the Rev. George Coan, had received that summer a call from the Presbyterian church at Riga, in Monroe County, to become its pastor. This call he accepted, and at the same time I was engaged to teach the large school near the church. Here I often met excellent pastors of the surrounding churches, whose preaching, religious conversation, and personal friendship awakened afresh the pious longings of my soul. Most of these pastors are now in heaven, and I know of but one who is still living, and now more than fourscore years old. His letters of love still come to me fresh as the dews of Mount Zion.

During this summer of 1826 I often rode by a schoolhouse in a western district of Riga, and through the windows I saw a face that beamed on me like that of an angel. The image was deeply impressed, and is still ineffaceable.

On inquiry, the young lady proved to be Miss Fidelia Church, of Churchville. I often saw her sunlit face in the choir on the Sabbath, for she was a sweet singer, but I did not make her acquaintance for many months.

During the summer of 1827, after the close of my winter-school, I opened a select-school in Riga, and Fidelia applied for admittance. In this I rejoiced greatly, for it gave me a good opportunity to mark the character of her mind, which proved bright and receptive, and to become acquainted with her moral and social characteristics.

I was called again to teach the central school during the winter of 1827-28, and though I had not yet united with the visible Church, I was elected and urged to become superintendent of the Sabbath-school, which I reluctantly accepted under the firm resolve to spend the remainder of my days, not in doubting and inactivity, but in doing what I could to bless my fellow mortals, and to honor God. And in this resolution, which formed an era in my life, I was greatly helped, comforted, and established, so that duty done for Christ was a sweet and joyous pleasure.

On the 2d day of March, 1828, I was received to the fellowship of the Presbyterian church in Riga, then under the pastoral care of my brother. Although I had now publicly devoted myself to the service of the Master, my profession was not yet chosen.

Soon after this union with the church, I visited Medina, a young and promising village west of Albion, in Orleans County, where one of my brothers was established in mercantile business. As this brother had long urged me to connect myself with him in his business, I went to look into it and to consider his offer. I spent the summer and winter with him.

Here work for the Master opened before me. The town was new, the inhabitants were from different parts, and of various professions and religious opinions. But notwithstanding this, there was much harmony in the village, so that, if a Methodist, a Baptist, a Presbyterian, an Episcopalian, or a Congregational minister came along and was invited to preach, a large portion of the people united harmoniously in listening to the Gospel; and when there was no clergyman, the layman professors kept up Sabbath services in reading sermons, and with exhortation and prayer. I was appointed Sunday-school superintendent, and this with visiting the sick, attending funerals, and assisting the brethren in religious services, opened just such a field of labor as I needed.

As winter approached I was again pressed into school-teaching, spending outside hours with my brother in the store.

Still I had not chosen my lifework. Four paths lay before me. My brother wished me to become his partner in the mercantile business. A good physician in Rochester, and several in other places, advised me to become a physician, offering to teach me free of charge. Some said I was made for a school teacher, and many clergymen and Christian laymen urged me to go into the Gospel ministry.

What should I do? What could I do? The subject pressed heavily upon my mind and heart. I said that teaching is pleasant in youth, but for *life* it would not satisfy me. As for the medical profession, I was not adapted to it, and I dared not make the trial. But how of the sacred ministry? I felt utterly unfit and unworthy—my natural talent, education, piety, were all unequal to the exalted calling. As Moses, Isaiah, and Jeremiah shrank from the offices of legislator and prophet, so I from being an ambassador of Christ, yet I was willing to work hard as a layman, and even longed to go as a servant among the heathen, to help the honored missionaries. Thus my spirit labored under a burden which none but God knew, and to find relief, I decided to be an active and devoted layman; to return to Connecticut, finish up my business there, and then settle down to a mercantile life in Medina.

In April, 1829, I left Medina for the East, and in Bergen met, by agreement, an old and faithful friend, the Rev. H. Halsey, who had been chosen by his Presbytery a representative to the General Assembly of the Presbyterian Church, which was to meet in Philadelphia the coming May. With him I agreed to visit Philadelphia, attend the sessions of the General Assembly, and then go on to Connecticut. We took the canal-boat at Rochester, and on the next day I had a shake of ague, followed by a fever. We had no doctor and no medicines, and I kept quiet, thinking to brave it out.

On the next Saturday we reached Syracuse, my ague shakes becoming more positive. We left the boat and went to Onondaga Hollow, spending the Sabbath and Monday with the Principal of an Academy, who was brother-in-law to Mr. Halsey. Here the ague was heavy and I had little comfort.

On Tuesday we went on to Albany, and thence by steamer to New York; my chills and fever growing all the while more and more intense. Here I gave up going to Philadelphia, parting reluctantly with my companion. Taking passage up the Sound, I went to Madison, where I had friends. I was then so prostrated I could go no farther, and was laid at once on a bed of weakness, from which I did not rise for four months. A good physician and kind friends ministered to me daily, but the disease held me fast until I was wasted to a skeleton, so that I could not sit in an easy-chair without fainting while my bed was being made. This was a time for reflection.

When the cold winds of autumn came, the disease relaxed, and I was taken carefully in an easy carriage to my father's house, only seven miles distant. Here I was ill until the last of October. I then rose through the mercy of God, and was offered the school where my cousin Nettleton and where all my brothers and sisters had been taught their A B C.

During all that winter there was a cheering revival in the town and in my school, and many of my pupils were hopefully born again. This was the best year of my life up to that time. It was the turning point, the day of decision. It was the voice of God to me. I could no longer doubt. I had purposed and the Lord had disappointed. I had chosen, but He had other work for me. I said, Lead me, Saviour. Tell me where to go and what to do, and I will *go* and *do*.

On my return to Western New York I had a free consultation with many ministerial friends, and all advised me to pursue a short course of preparatory study, and enter Auburn Theological Seminary.

I had formed a pleasant acquaintance with the Rev. Lewis Cheeseman, while he was pastor of a church in Albion. He then seemed like a young Apollos, fervid, eloquent, and impressive. He had now settled in Byron and was preaching with great power and success. He invited me to study and labor with him, as an interesting work of grace was in progress, not only in Byron, but in Rochester and many other towns of that region.

Accordingly I spent the summer of 1830 in his family, studying and laboring in the revival; sometimes meeting the Rev. Charles Finney.

In the autumn an earnest invitation came to me from the Rev. David Page and the church in Knoxville, to come and labor there. I accepted the invitation, and spent the winter and spring in that place, continuing my classical studies, and assisting the pastor, and conducting evening meetings in surrounding villages. The religious interest was widespread, the meetings were full and solemn, consciences were tender, and many were turned to the Lord.

On the first day of June, 1831, I entered the middle class of Auburn Theological Seminary.

The faculty then consisted of the Rev. Doctors Richards, Perrine, and Mills, all noble men and fine scholars.

Here the months and seasons flowed pleasantly along, and I was very happy in my studies, in the society of the students and in the instructions of the professors. Every Sabbath morning I went with other students to teach the convicts in the Auburn State Prison, numbering seven or eight hundred, and for a year or more I had the office of Superintendent of the prison Sunday-school. This work was very interesting, as I had personal access to every class and to every individual. Many confessed to deeds and purposes of great depravity, and some professed a radical change of heart. About 200 professed conversion. A few of these I afterward met in Rochester and Albany, of gentlemanly bearing, and in citizen's dress. I did not recognize the men whom I had known in the convict's garb, until they gave me their names. I was rejoiced to find them members of Sunday-schools and churches, in good business, and happily settled in life.

On the 17th of April, 1833, I was licensed to preach the Gospel by the Presbytery of Cayuga County, at a meeting in Auburn.

I was then invited to preach during the summer vacation in one of the churches in Rochester, while the pastor was absent as a delegate to the General Assembly of the Presbyterian Church in Philadelphia.

At the close of the vacation, as I was about to return to Auburn, the elders of the church in which I had labored put the following paper into my hands:

Rochester, *July* 8, 1833.

Rev. Titus Coan:

Dear Sir:—In behalf of the First Free Presbyterian Church and Congregation of Rochester, we present you this testimonial of our entire satisfaction of your ministerial labors among us during the absence of our beloved pastor, Rev. Luke Lyons, who was called from us to attend the General Assembly of the Presbyterian Church in Philadelphia.

You may rest assured that we shall remember you in our prayers, and may the Lord abundantly reward you for your labors of love among us, guide you by His counsel, and make you eminently useful in promoting the Redeemer's Kingdom in whatever situation you may be placed.

We are, dear sir, your friends and brethren in Christ our Lord.

(Signed), A. W. Riley,
Elisha Ely,
Nathan Lyman,
Manly G. Woodbury.

It was but a few days after my entrance upon my last term at the Seminary, when a letter from the Rev. Rufus Anderson, Secretary of the A.B.C.F.M., called me to Boston to be ordained, and to sail on a mission of exploration to Patagonia, on which expedition I embarked on the 16th of August, 1833. An account of this trip may be found in my "Adventures in Patagonia."

2

Marriage - Embarkation for Hawaii - Santiago, Callao, and Lima in 1835 - Arrival in Honolulu - Passage to Hilo - Our New Home - First Labors.

ON returning from Patagonia I landed in New London, Conn., May 7, 1834. During all the long months of my absence in the South, not a word had come to me from friends, nor had any tidings from me reached the land of my birth. There had been many fond recollections and tender heart-longings, and quires of paper had been filled, but no breath of heaven, no bird of the air had wafted these yearnings, these burning thoughts from North to South, and from South to North. Over the Atlantic or the vast continent no answer had come to anxious inquiries, no echo to calls of love.

But the perils of the sea and of the howling wilderness of savages were now past, and I was in the land of liberty, of light, and of Christian love.

I went to Boston and reported; to Killingworth, to surprise with joy my aged and mourning father; and to Middlebury in Vermont to find the one whom I had chosen, and who had waited patiently and without change of object or of purpose, for seven long years to welcome this glad day.

She was then teaching with the dear mother Cooke, in the Middlebury Female Seminary.

She went with me to her father's house in Churchville, where on the 3d of Nov., 1834, we were married in the church on Monthly Concert evening. On Nov. 4th we left for Boston, visiting friends in New York and Connecticut by the way.

On the 23d of November we received our instructions as missionaries to the Sandwich Islands, in Park Street church, together with Miss Lydia Brown, Miss Elizabeth Hitchcock, Mr. Henry Dimond and wife, and Mr. and Mrs. Edwin O. Hall.

On the same occasion a company of twelve missionaries, destined to Southeastern Africa, received their instructions. The house was packed and the occasion was one of great interest.

On the 5th of December, 1834, we embarked on board the merchant ship *Hellespont*, Capt. John Henry, and bade farewell to Boston, to hundreds of dear and precious friends, to our dear country, not expecting ever to see them again. On the 6th we awoke and looked in vain for land. City, hills, mountains, had sunk in the ocean, and nothing outside of the dancing *Hellespont* was seen but the ethereal vault and the boundless blue sea.

We plunged into the Gulf Stream and were handled roughly by current and wind and foaming wave. The wild winds howled, the clouds thickened and darkened, and the tempest raged.

Our good ship labored, plunged, rose, trembled, plunged and rose again amidst the foaming billows, shaking off the feathery spray like a sea-lion, and rushing along her watery way with grandeur. In the night her shining pathway was all aglow with countless, sparkling brilliants. Our voyage soon became pleasant. The weather was favorable, the captain attentive and kind, the officers faithful, and the crew obedient and respectful. Our seasickness vanished, our skies brightened, and we were a happy family, daily becoming better acquainted with each other. Miss Brown was a maiden lady from New Hampshire, of true devotion to the work of the Lord. She was appointed to the Islands to teach the women of Hawaii domestic duties, such as carding, spinning, weaving, etc., in connection with a civilizing Christianity. Miss Hitchcock was also a maiden lady, well educated and pious. One of her brothers was already an active missionary on the Islands, and she was going out to assist in teaching. She afterward married Mr. Edmund H. Rogers, a missionary printer.

Mr. Dimond came as a bookbinder. His good wife was Miss Ann Anner, of New York City. Both of them are now living. Mr. E. O. Hall was a printer from Rochester, N. Y.

He also found his wife in New York City, a Miss Williams, a devoted lady. Mrs. Hall died a few years ago.

This united circle held morning and evening devotions, and our days were spent in reading, writing, and social intercourse. On Sabbaths when the weather was favorable we had preaching, at which service the captain, officers, and crew were present.

But I need not detain the reader with a third voyage in the Atlantic. Enough to say that we passed pleasantly along to the South, sinking the Northern constellations one by one, and raising the Southern, seeing no Equatorial line, no Neptune, and no land until the hills of Terra del Fuego lifted their snowy heads upon us above the clouds. I had longed to see the wild coast of Patagonia and the Falkland Islands, where only a year before I had roamed with the savage tribes, or found more comforts among the whalers and sealers of those southern islets. But we passed between the Continent and the Islands, descrying neither.

My heart mourned for this land of Patagonia, a land on which the shadows of death had always rested, and where no day had yet dawned.

We passed through the Strait of Le Maire, and with all sails set, in a balmy and bright summer day sailed very near the dreaded Cape Horn.

Only a day after we had set our studding sails and spread all our canvas, a stormy wind took us far toward the Southern Cross and the ice mountains of the Antarctic. But in a few days, more favoring gales hurried us Northward again, and on the 8th of March the joyful sound of "land ho!" thrilled all on board, and the lofty Cordillera chain stood out in grandeur before us. It was Chili, and the city of Valparaiso was in sight. We came into the roadstead, dropped anchor, furled sails, congratulated one another, and blessed the Lord for a safe passage thus far.

As the *Hellespont* was to remain in port about twenty days, Mr. Dimond and I engaged a carriage and driver, and made a trip to Santiago, the capital of Chili, about 100 miles inland and near the foothills of the Andes. Our ride was very exhilarating. This city is one of the most beautiful in South America, well watered from the mountain snows, and well shaded with trees. On our way we passed over high hills and broad plains. The roads over these hills were wide and cut in zigzag lines, with ample terraces or resting-places at the angles. On ascending one of these lofty hills at early dawn, we descried the heads of two men, recently severed, each nailed to a high post at different places, and grinning ghastly upon us. Our driver told us that these men were highway robbers and murderers; that they had, on going up this hill, perpetrated the vilest of crimes, killed a husband and his wife, with two children, stolen their baggage, clothes, and horse, and thrown the dead bodies into a deep ravine below; and for these horrid crimes their heads had been made beacons of warning to all who passed along this road.

We left Valparaiso on the 27th of March, and anchored in the harbor of Callao, Peru, on the 6th of April, 1835. Here we spent twenty-one days, giving us opportunity of going on shore as often as we desired, of visiting Lima, of attending the gorgeous ceremonies of Passion Week, of looking into the grand Cathedral and their splendid churches, and of noticing the monuments of art, and the scars of revolution in that renowned, but often suffering, desecrated, and vandalized city.

With the courteous Bishop of Lima, we went through the Cathedral, he bowing and crossing himself as he passed by the various pictures and statues, telling us of the guardian care of the different saints over the city.

We left Callao on the 27th of April, saw the mountains of Hawaii on the 5th of June, and on the 6th landed in Honolulu. The Hawaiian mission was then in session, and on the arrival of the *Hellespont*, the mission appointed a committee of three to meet us on board, while the meeting was adjourned, and a large part of the members with wives and children came down to the wharf to welcome us, and to escort us to the house of the Rev. Hiram Bingham. The welcome was warm and warmly reciprocated, and the meeting was joyful. It seemed to us *apostolical*. We regarded these veteran toilers with a feeling of veneration. Some looked vigorous and strong, others seemed pallid and wayworn. Here were the fathers and mothers in Israel, and here the brothers and sisters, with flocks of precious children. We rejoiced that we were permitted to be numbered with this honored and happy family. We all united in a hymn of praise and thanksgiving to God, and then knelt in prayer.

The new reinforcement united in the daily meetings of the mission until the closing of its sessions, when we went forth to our appointed stations; my wife and I to Hilo, Hawaii, with Mr. and Mrs. Lyman.

We embarked at Honolulu, in the schooner *Velocity*, falsely so-called, on the 6th of July. The schooner was small, a slow sailer, dirty, crowded with more than one hundred passengers, mostly natives, and badly managed. The captain was an Irishman given to hard drinking.

We sailed from Honolulu on Monday. The sea was rough and nearly all of the passengers were very seasick. Our first port was Lahaina, eighty miles from Honolulu, where we were to land Mr. and Mrs. Richards, Dr. and Mrs. Chapin, Mr. and Mrs. Spaulding, and other families. On Wednesday morning the captain announced that the land just ahead was Maui, and that we should all land in about an hour at Lahaina, where we might rest a day, bathe, eat grapes and watermelons, and be refreshed for the rest of the voyage, about 150 miles further.

But the poor captain's eyes were dazed, and he had lost his reckoning. We had gone about in the night and we were back at Honolulu! This fact came upon us with a shock of agony. After such seasickness as some of us had never before endured, the dreadful thought came over us, "Shall we ever reach our homes on this vessel and with this master?" Many of us had tasted neither food nor water from Monday to Wednesday, and all had lain crowded on a dirty deck, exposed to wind, rain, and wave, and how could we live to reach our destination? But there was no alternative. We said *go*, and the dull *Velocity* went about and headed again for Lahaina, where we landed passengers, and on the 21st we saw the emerald beauty of Hilo, and disembarked with joy and thanksgiving.

Hundreds of laughing natives thronged the beach, seized our hands, gave us the hearty "*Aloha*" and followed us up to the house of our good friends, Mr. and Mrs. Lyman, who were with us to comfort and inform us all the way.

The bay of Hilo is a beautiful, spacious, and safe harbor. The outline of its beach is a crescent like the moon in her first quarter. The beach is composed of fine, volcanic sand, mixed with a little coral and earth. On its eastern and western sides, and in its center, it is divided by three streams of pure water; it has a deep channel about half a mile wide, near the western shore, sufficiently deep to admit the largest ship that floats. Seaward it is protected by a lava reef one mile from the shore. This reef was formed by a lateral stream of lava, sent out at right angles from a broad river of molten rocks that formed our eastern coast. This reef is a grand barrier against the swell of the ocean. Lord Byron, who visited Hilo, when he brought home the corpses of King Liholiho and his queen, gave the name of "Byron's Bay" to this harbor, but that name is nearly obsolete.

The beach was once beautifully adorned with the cocoa palm, whose lofty plumes waved and rustled and glittered in the fresh sea-breeze. Beyond our quiet bay the broad, blue ocean foams or sleeps, with a surface sometimes shining like molten silver, tumbling in white foam, or gently throbbing as with the pulsations of life.

Inland, from the shore to the bases of the mountains, the whole landscape is "arrayed in living green," presenting a picture of inimitable beauty, so varied in tint, so grooved with water channels, and so sparkling with limpid streams and white foaming cascades, as to charm the eye, and cause the beholder to exclaim, "This *is* a scene of surpassing loveliness."

Behind all this in the background, tower the lofty, snow-mantled mountains, Kea and Loa, out of one of which rush volcanic fires. At the first sight we were charmed with the beauty and the grandeur of the scene, and we exclaimed, "Surely the lines are fallen to us in pleasant places, and we have a goodly heritage."

We were satisfied, yes more, we were *delighted*, with our location, and to this day we bless the Lord that He inclined the minds of the mission to assign us to this field of labor. In this, as in all the past, we see the guiding hand of Him who has promised to "direct the steps" of all who "commit their way to Him."

Hilo had then but one framed house. It was a low, two-story building in the style of a New England farm-house, built and occupied by the Rev. Joseph Goodrich, a good and faithful missionary of the A.B.C.F.M.

Mr. Lyman's home, into which we were received, was a small, stone house, with walls laid up with mud, and a thatched roof. Each family had but one room about fifteen feet square.

Mr. Goodrich, with his family, left Hilo in November for the United States, not to return, and we were advised to occupy his house, which with later additions and improvements has been our habitation ever since.

Mr. Lyman soon built a comfortable house near us, and the old stone-and-mud hut was devoted to a schoolroom.

By the advice of the Lymans, who had been two years in Hilo, and whose experience and wise counsel were of great use to us, we at once began teaching a school of about a hundred almost naked boys and girls, being ourselves pupils of a good man named Barnabas, who patiently drilled us daily in the language of his people. By reading, trying to talk, teach and write, we crept along, without grammar or dictionary, the mist lifting slowly before us, until at the end of three months from our arrival, I went into the pulpit with Mr. Lyman, and preached my first sermon in the native language. Soon after, I made a tour with him into Puna, one wing of our field, and then through the district of Hilo, in an opposite direction. These tours introduced me to the people for whom I was to labor, and with whom I had a burning desire to communicate freely, and helped me greatly in acquiring the language.

The General Meeting at Honolulu in June had advised Mr. Lyman and myself to establish a boarding-school for boys, leaving to us the question as to which of us should be the principal of the school, and which the traveling missionary.

He chose the school as his chief work, and I the pastoral and preaching department. Our labors, however, were not separated for a long time, he preaching always when I was absent on tours, and often when I was at home; we always worked in harmony. After a year or two, the school being enlarged and important, Mr. Lyman requested the mission to accept his resignation of the joint pastorate of the church and to appoint me as the sole pastor. This was done harmoniously, and we have labored side by side until the present day, mutually assisting, and rejoicing in the success of all departments of the service.

Under the efficient care of Mr. and Mrs. Lyman the school has been a great success. Its department of manual labor is an important feature in the institution. It has given a very valuable physical training to the boys, imparting to them skill and health, and making the school nearly self-supporting. The young men are well dressed, neat and manly in their appearance, and give evidence of an elevation above the common masses around them. In all, the Seminary has graduated about one thousand pupils. Many of them are among the most useful members of society, and some of them have become legislators, judges, teachers, Christian ministers, foreign missionaries, etc.

Mr. Lyman, feeling obliged through declining health to resign his office as Principal, the Rev. W. B. Oleson was appointed in September, 1878, as his successor.

3

The Field – The People – Hilo District – Crossing the Torrents – Perils of a Canoe Voyage – Puna District.

THE field in which I was called to labor is a belt of land extending by the coastline 100 miles on the northeast, east, and southeast shore of Hawaii, including the districts of Hilo and Puna, and a part of Kau.

The inhabited belt is one to three miles wide, and in a few places there were hamlets and scattering villages five to ten miles inland. Beyond this narrow shore belt there is a zone of forest trees with a tropical jungle from ten to twenty-five miles wide, almost impenetrable by man or beast. Still higher is another zone of open country girdling the bases of the mountains, with a rough surface of hill, dale, ravine, scoriaceous lava fields, rocky ridges, and plains and hills of pasture land. Here wild goats, wild cattle, with hogs and wild geese feed. Still higher up tower Mauna Kea and Mauna Loa, nearly 14,000 feet above the sea, the former being a pile of extinct craters, often crowned with snow, and the latter a mountain of fire, where for unknown ages earthquakes that rock the group and convulse the ocean have been born, and where volcanoes burst out with awful roar, and rush in fiery rivers down the mountain sides, across the open plains, through the blazing forest jungle and into the sea. All but the narrow shore belt is left to untamed bird and beast, and to the wild winds and raging fires of the mountains, except when bird-catchers, canoe-makers, cattle-hunters, or volcano visitors are drawn thither by their several interests from the shore.

The population of this shore belt was probably at that time about 15,000 to 16,000, almost exclusively natives. Very few foreigners had then come here to live. Several missionaries had resided in Hilo for short periods, but none had settled here permanently except Mr. and Mrs. Lyman. Occasional tours had been made through Hilo and Puna, and the Gospel had been preached in most of the villages. Schools had also been established through the districts and a goodly number could read and write. Some pupils were in the elements of arithmetic, and many committed lessons in the Scriptures to memory.

Forms of idolatry were kept out of sight, but superstition and ignorance, hypocrisy and most of the lower vices prevailed. The people were all slaves to their chiefs, and no man but a chief owned a foot of land, a tree, a pig, a fowl, his wife, children, or himself. All belonged to his chief and could be taken at will, if anger or covetousness or lust called for them. I have seen families by the score turned out of their dwellings, all their effects seized, and they sent off wailing, to seek shelter and food where they could. "On the side of the oppressor there was power, but the poor man had no comforter."

Hilo, the northern wing of this field, is a district including about thirty miles of its shoreline. It is covered with a deep rich soil, clothed with perennial green of every shade, watered with the rain of heaven, and grooved by about eighty water channels that run on an angle of some three degrees, leaping over hundreds of precipices of varied heights, from three or four feet to 500, and plunging into the sea over a cliff rising in height, from the sand beach of the town, to 700 or 800 feet along the northern coastline.

For many years after our arrival there were no roads, no bridges, and no horses in Hilo, and all my tours were made on foot. These were three or four annually through Hilo, and as many in Puna; the time occupied in making them was usually ten to twenty days for each trip.

In passing through the district of Hilo, the weather was sometimes fine and the rivers low, so that there was little difficulty in traveling. The path was a simple trail, winding in a serpentine line, going down and up precipices, some of which could only be descended and ascended by grasping the shrubs and grasses, and with no little weariness and difficulty and some danger.

But the streams were the most formidable obstacles. In great rains, which often occurred on my tours, when the winds rolled in the heavy clouds from the sea, and massed them in dark banks on the side of the mountain, the waters would fall in torrents at the head of the streams and along their channels, and the rush and the roar as the floods came down were like the thunder of an army charging upon the foe.

I have sometimes sat on the high bank of a streamlet, not more than fifteen to twenty feet wide, conversing with natives in the bright sunshine, when suddenly a portentous roaring, "Like the sound of many waters, or like the noise of the sea when the waves thereof roar," fell upon my ears, and looking upstream, I have seen a column of turbid waters six feet deep coming down like the flood from a broken mill-dam. The natives would say to me, "*Awiwi! awiwi!* o paa oe i ka wai"—"*Quick! quick!* or the waters will stop you."

Rushing down the bank I would cross over, dry-shod, where in two minutes more there was no longer any passage for man or beast. But I rarely waited for the rivers to run by. My appointments for preaching were all sent forward in a line for thirty or sixty miles, designating the day, and usually the hours, when I would be at a given station, and by breaking one of these links the whole chain would be disturbed. It therefore seemed important that every appointment should be kept, whatever the inconvenience might be to me. In traveling, my change of raiment was all packed in one calabash, or large gourd, covered by the half of another; a little food was in a second calabash. With these gourds one may travel indefinitely in the heaviest rains while all is dry within. Faithful natives carried my little supplies.

I had several ways of crossing the streams.

1st. When the waters were low, large rocks and boulders, common in all the water-channels, were left bare, so that with a stick or pole eight or ten feet long, I leaped from rock to rock over the giddy streams and crossed dry-shod: these same poles helping me to climb up, and to let myself down steep precipices, and to leap ditches six to eight feet wide.

2d. When the streams were not too deep and too swift I waded them; and

3d., when not too deep, but too swift, I mounted upon the shoulders of a sturdy aquatic native, holding on to his bushy hair, when he moved carefully down the slippery bank of the river, leaning upstream against a current of ten knots, and moving one foot at a time, sideways among the slimy boulders in the bottom, and then bringing the other foot carefully up. Thus slowly feeling his way across, he would land me safe with a shout and a laugh on the opposite bank. But this is a fearful way of crossing, for the cataracts are so numerous, the waters so rapid, and the uneven bottom so slippery, that the danger of falling is imminent, and the recovery from a fall often impossible, the current hurrying one swiftly over a precipice into certain destruction. Both natives and foreigners have thus lost their lives in these streams, and among them three of the members of the Hilo church who have traveled and labored and prayed with me.

I once crossed a full and powerful river in this way, not more than fifty feet above a cataract of 426 feet in height, with a basin forty feet deep below, where this little Niagara has thundered for ages. A missionary brother of another station seeing me landed safely, and knowing that this crossing would save about six miles of hard and muddy walking, followed me on the shoulders of the same bold native that took me over. But before he had reached the middle of the rushing flood, he trembled and cried out with fear. The bearer said, "Hush! hush! be still, or we perish together." The brother still trembling, the native with great difficulty managed to reach a rock in the center of the river, and on this he seated his burden, commanding him to be quiet and sit there until he was cool (he was already drenched with rain and river-spray), when he would take him off, which he did in about ten minutes and landed him safely by my side.

This mode of crossing the streams, however, was too dangerous, and I soon abandoned it.

A fourth mode was for a sufficient number of strong men to form a chain across the river. They made a line, locking hands on the bank; with heads bending upstream entering the water carefully, and moving slowly until the head of the line reached good foothold near the opposite bank. With my hands upon the shoulders of the men I passed along this chain of bones, sinews, and muscles and arrived in safety on the other side.

The fifth and safest, and in fact the only possible way to cross some of these rivers when swollen and raging, was to throw a rope across the stream, and fasten it to trees or rocks on either side; grasping it firmly with both hands, my feet thrown downstream, I drew myself along the line and gained the opposite bank. This I sometimes did without removing shoes or garments, then walked on to my next station, and preached in wet clothes, continuing my travels and labors until night; when in dry wrappings I slept well, and was all ready for work the next day.

I was once three hours in crossing one river. The day was cold and rainy, and I was soaked before I entered the stream. This was so wide at the only possible crossing point, that we were unable to throw a line across, even with a weight attached to the end of it. The raging, roaring, and tossing of the waters were fearful, and the sight of it made me shudder. Kind natives collected on both banks by scores, with ropes and courage to help. The fearful rapids, running probably twenty miles an hour, were before us. Fifty feet below us was a fall of some twenty feet, and about 100 yards further down was a thundering cataract, where the river was compressed within a narrow gorge with a clear plunge of about eighty feet.

Our natives tried all their skill and strength, but could not throw the line across. At length a daring man went upstream close to a waterfall, took the end of the rope in his teeth, mounted a rock, calculated his chances of escape from the cataracts below, and leaped into the flood; down, down he went quivering and struggling till he reached the opposite shore only a few feet above the fall, over which it must have been a fatal plunge had he gone. But by his temerity, which I should have forbidden, had I known it in season, a passage was provided for me.

After years had passed, and a little had been done toward making roads, I purchased a horse, and tried to get him over these streams by swimming or hauling him over with ropes. Twice when I attempted to go over in the saddle, his foot caught between two rocks in the middle of the stream, and horse and rider were saved only by the energy and fidelity of the natives.

Once in going up a steep precipice in a narrow pass between a rocky height on one hand and a stream close on the other, my horse fell over backward and lay with his head down and his feet in the air, so wedged and so wounded that he could never have escaped from his position, had not a company of natives for whom I sent came to the rescue and extricated the poor, faithful animal from his rocky bed. I escaped instant death by sliding out of the saddle upon the narrow bank of the stream, before the back of my horse struck between the rocks. He was so hurt that I was obliged to leave him to recover.

In order to save time and escape the weariness of the road and the dangers of the rivers, I sometimes took a canoe at the end of my tours to return home by the water. This trip required six to eight hours, and was usually made in the night.

On three occasions my peril was great. One description will suffice for all; for although the difficulties and escapes were at different points along a precipitous and lofty sea-wall, yet the causes of danger were the same, viz.: stormy winds, raging billows, and want of landing-places.

About midway between our starting-place and Hilo harbor, we were met by a strong headwind, with pouring rain and tumultuous waves in a dark midnight. We were half a mile from land, but could hear the roar and see the flashing of the white surf as it dashed against the rocky walls. We could not land, we could not sail, we could not row forward or backward. All we could do was to keep the prow of the canoe to the wind, and bail. Foaming seas dashed against our frail cockleshell, pouring in buckets of brine. Thus we lay about five hours, anxious as they "who watch for the morning." At length it dawned; we looked through the misty twilight to the rockbound shore where "the waves dashed high." A few doors of native huts opened and men crawled out. We called, but no echo came. We made signals of distress. We were seen and numbers came down to the cliffs and gazed at us. We waved our garments for them to come off to our help. They feared, they hesitated. We were opposite the mouth of a roaring river, where the foam of breakers dashed in wild fury. At last four naked men came down from the cliff, plunged into the sea, dived under one towering wave after another, coming out to breathe between the great rolling billows, and thus reached our canoe. Ordering the crew to swim to the land, they took charge of the canoe themselves because they knew the shore. Meanwhile men stood on the high bluffs with kapa cloth in hand to signal to the boatmen when to strike for the mouth of the river. They waited long and watched the tossing waves as they rolled in and thundered upon the shore, and when at last a less furious wave came behind us, the shore men waved the signals and cried out, "*Hoi! hoi!*" and as the waves lifted the stern of our canoe, all the paddles struck the water, while the steerer kept the canoe straight on her course, and thus mounted on this crested wave as on an ocean chariot, with the feathery foam flying around us, we rode triumphantly into the mouth of the river, where we were received with shouts of gladness by the throng who had gathered to witness our escape. Then two rows of strong men waded into the surf up to their arm-pits to receive our canoe and bear it in triumph to the shore.

Praising the Lord for His goodness, and thanking the kind natives for their agency in delivering me, I walked the rest of the way home.

The district of Puna lies east and south of Hilo, and its physical features are remarkably different from those of the neighboring district.

Its shoreline, including its bends and flexures, is more than seventy miles in extent. For three miles inland from the sea it is almost a dead level, with a surface of *pahoehoe* or field lava, and *aa* or scoriaceous lava, interspersed with more or less rich volcanic soil and tropical verdure, and sprinkled with sand-dunes and a few cone and pit-craters. Throughout its length it is marked with ancient lava streams, coming down from Kilauea and entering the sea at different points along the coast. These lava streams vary in width from half a mile to two or three miles. From one to three miles from the shore the land rises rapidly into the great volcanic dome of Mauna Loa (Long Mountain). The highlands are mostly covered with woods and jungle, and scarred with rents, pits, and volcanic cones. Everywhere the marks of terrible volcanic action are visible. The whole district is so cavernous, so rent with fissures, and so broken by fiery agencies, that not a single stream of water keeps aboveground to reach the sea. All the rainfall is swallowed by the 10,000 crevices, and disappears, except the little that is held in small pools and basins, waiting for evaporation. The rains are abundant, and subterranean fountains and streams are numerous, carrying the waters down to the sea level, and filling caverns, and bursting up along the shore in springs and rills, even far out under the sea. Some of these waters are very cold, some tepid, and some stand at blood heat, furnishing excellent warm baths. There are large caves near the sea where we enter by dark and crooked passages, and bathe by torchlight, far underground, in deep and limpid water.

Puna has many beautiful groves of the cocoa-palm, also breadfruit, pandanus, and ohia, and where there is soil it produces under cultivation, besides common vegetables, arrowroot, sugar-cane, coffee, cotton, oranges, citrons, limes, grapes, and other fruits. On the highlands, grow wild strawberries, cape gooseberries, and the ohelo, a delicious berry resembling our whortleberry.

On the shoreline of the eastern part of Kau, adjoining Puna, were several villages, containing from 500 to 700 inhabitants, separated from the inhabited central and western portions of the district by a desert of unwatered lava about 15 miles wide, without a single house or human being. These villages were occasionally visited by the Rev. Mr. Forbes, then stationed in South Kona; but to reach them required a long, weary walk over the fields of burning lava, and at his request,

I took them under my charge, thus extending the shoreline of my parish ten miles westward.

4

First Tours in Hilo and Puna - The Work of 1837-38 - Spontaneous Church-building - The Great Awakening - The Volcanic Wave - Pastoral Experiences and Methods - The Ingathering.

I MADE my first tours of Hilo and Puna during the latter part of my first half year on Hawaii. In 1836 I had gained so much in the language as to be able to converse, preach, and pray with comfort and with apparent effect on my audiences.

On my arrival in Hilo, the number of church members was twenty-three, all living in the town. A considerable portion of our time was then devoted to the schools. Mr. and Mrs. Lyman were heartily engaged in the boys' boarding-school. Mrs. Coan was already teaching a day-school of 140 children, and I a training-school of 90 teachers to supply the schools of Hilo and Puna.

Giving a vacation to my pupils, I set off Nov. 29, 1836, on a tour around the island. This was made on foot, with the exception of a little sailing in a canoe down the coast of Kona. My companions were two or three natives, to act as guides and porters. On reaching the western coast of Kau, I visited all the villages along the shore, preaching and exhorting everywhere. The people came out, men, women, and children, in crowds, and listened with great attention. Here I preached three, four, and five times a day, and had much personal conversation with the natives on things pertaining to the kingdom of God.

On reaching the western boundaries of Puna, my labors became more abundant. I had visited this people before, and had noticed a hopeful interest in a number of them. Now they rallied in masses, and were eager to hear the Word. Many listened with tears, and after the preaching, when I supposed they would return to their homes and give me rest, they remained and crowded around me so earnestly, that I had no time to eat, and in places where I spent my nights they filled the house to its entire capacity, leaving scores outside who could not enter. All wanted to hear more of the "Word of Life." At ten or eleven o'clock I would advise them to go home and to sleep. Some would retire, but more remain until midnight. At cock-crowing the house would be again crowded, with as many more outside.

At one place before I reached the point where I was to spend a Sabbath, there was a line of four villages not more than half a mile apart. Every village begged for a sermon and for personal conversation. Commencing at daylight I preached in three of them before breakfast, at 10 A.M. When the meeting closed at one village, most of the people ran on to the next, and thus my congregation increased rapidly from hour to hour. Many were "pricked in their hearts" and were inquiring what they should do to be saved.

Sunday came and I was now in the most populous part of Puna. Multitudes came out to hear the Gospel. The blind were led; the maimed, the aged and decrepit, and many invalids were brought on the backs of their friends. There was great joy and much weeping in the assembly. Two days were spent in this place, and ten sermons preached, while almost all the intervals between the public services were spent in personal conversation with the crowds which pressed around me.

Many of the people who then wept and prayed proved true converts to Christ; most of them have died in the faith, and a few still live as steadfast witnesses to the power of the Gospel.

Among these converts was the High Priest of the volcano. He was more than six feet high and of lofty bearing. He had been an idolater, a drunkard, an adulterer, a robber, and a murderer. For their *kapas*, for a pig or a fowl he had killed men on the road, whenever they hesitated to yield to his demands. But he became penitent, and appeared honest and earnest in seeking the Lord.

His sister was more haughty and stubborn. She was High Priestess of the volcano. She, too, was tall and majestic in her bearing. For a long time she refused to bow to the claims of the Gospel; but at length she yielded, confessed herself a sinner and under the authority of a higher Power, and with her brother became a docile member of the church.

During this tour of thirty days I examined twenty schools with an aggregate of 1,200 pupils.

After my return, congregations at the center increased in numbers and in interest. Meetings for parents, for women, for church members, for children, were frequent and full. Soon scores and hundreds who had heard the Gospel in Kau, Puna, and Hilo, came into the town to hear more. During all the years of 1837-38, Hilo was crowded with strangers; whole families and whole villages in the country were left, with the exception of a few of the old people, and in some instances even the aged and the feeble were brought in on litters from a distance of thirty or fifty miles. Little cabins studded the place like the camps of an army, and we estimated that our population was increased to 10,000 souls. Those who remained some time, fished, and planted potatoes and taro for food. Our great native house of worship, nearly 200 feet long, by about eighty-five feet wide, with a lofty roof of thatch, was crowded almost to suffocation, while hundreds remained outside unable to enter. This sea of faces, all hushed except when sighs and sobs burst out here and there, was a scene to melt the heart. The word fell with power, and sometimes as the feeling deepened, the vast audience was moved and swayed like a forest in a mighty wind. The word became like the "fire and the hammer" of the Almighty, and it pierced like a two-edged sword. Hopeful converts were multiplied and "there was great joy in the city."

Finding the place of our worship "too strait" for the increasing multitudes, our people, of their own accord and without the knowledge of their teachers, went up into the forest three to five miles, with axes, and with ropes made of vines and bark of the hibiscus, cut down trees of suitable size and length for posts, rafters, etc., and hauled them down through mud and jungle, and over streams and hillocks to the town. Seeing a very large heap of this timber, I inquired what this meant. The reply was, "We will build a second house of worship so that the people may all be sheltered from sun and rain on the Sabbath. And this is our thought; all of the people of Hilo shall meet in the larger house, where you will preach to them in the morning, during which time the people of Puna and Kau will meet for prayer in the smaller house, and in the afternoon these congregations shall exchange places, and you will preach to the Puna and Kau people; thus all will hear the minister."

Several thousands, both men and women, took hold of the work, and in about three weeks from the commencement of the hauling of the timber, the house was finished and a joyful crowd of about 2,000 filled it on the Sabbath.

Neither of the houses had floors or seats. The ground was beaten hard and covered from week to week with fresh grass.

When we wished to economize room, or seat the greatest possible number, skilled men were employed to arrange the people standing in compact rows as tight as it was possible to crowd them, the men and women being separated, and when the house was thus filled with these compacted ranks, the word was given them to *sit down*, which they did, a mass of living humanity, such perhaps as was never seen except on Hawaii.

During these years my tours through the extended parish were not given up. Nearly every person left in the villages came to the preaching stations. There were places along the routes where there were no houses near the trail, but where a few families were living half a mile or more inland. In such places, the few dwellers would come down to the path leading their blind, and carrying their sick and aged upon their backs, and lay them down under a tree if there was one near, or upon the naked rocks, that they might hear of a Saviour. It was often affecting to see these withered and trembling hands reached out to grasp the hand of the teacher, and to hear the palsied, the blind, and the lame begging him to stop awhile and tell them the story of Jesus. These pleas could not be resisted, for the thought would instantly arise, "This may be the *last time*." And so it often was, for on my next tour some of them had gone never to return. It was a comforting thought that they had been told of "the Lamb of God who taketh away the sin of the world," and to feel a sweet assurance from their tears of joy and eager reception of the truth that they had found "Him of whom Moses and the Prophets wrote."

Time swept on; the work deepened and widened. Thousands on thousands thronged the courts of the Lord. All eastern and southern Hawaii was like a sea in motion. Waimea, Hamakua, Kohala, Kona, and the other islands of the group, were moved. Reporting and inquiring letters circulated from post to post, and from island to island. One asked another, "What do these things mean?" and the reply was, "What indeed?" Some said that the Hawaiians were a peculiar people, and very hypocritical, so debased in mind and heart that they could not receive any true conception of the true God, or of spiritual things; even their language was wanting in terms to convey ideas of sacred truth; we must not hope for evangelical conversions among them. But most of the laborers redoubled their efforts, were earnest in prayer, and worked on in faith. Everywhere the trumpet of jubilee sounded long and loud, and "as clouds and as doves to their windows," so ransomed sinners flocked to Christ.

I had seen great and powerful awakenings under the preaching of Nettleton and Finney, and like doctrines, prayers, and efforts seemed to produce like fruits among this people.

My precious wife, whose soul was melted with love and longings for the weeping natives, felt that to doubt it was the work of the Spirit, was to grieve the Holy Ghost and to provoke Him to depart from us.

On some occasions there were physical demonstrations which commanded attention. Among the serious and anxious inquirers who came to our house by day and by night, there were individuals who, while listening to a very plain and kind conversation, would begin to tremble and soon fall helpless to the floor. At one time, when I was holding a series of outdoor meetings in a populous part of Puna, a remarkable manifestation of this kind occurred. A very large concourse were seated on the grass, and I was standing in the center preaching "Repentance toward God and faith in the Lord

Jesus." Of a sudden, a man who had been gazing with intense interest at the preacher, burst out in a fervent prayer, with streaming tears, saying: "Lord, have mercy on me; I am dead in sin." His weeping was so loud, and his trembling so great, that the whole congregation was moved as by a common sympathy. Many wept aloud, and many commenced praying together. The scene was such as I had never before witnessed. I stood dumb in the midst of this weeping, wailing, praying multitude, not being able to make myself heard for about twenty minutes. When the noise was hushed, I continued my address with words of caution, lest they should feel that this kind of demonstration atoned for their sins, and rendered them acceptable before God. I assured them that all the Lord required was godly sorrow for the past, present faith in Christ, and henceforth faithful, filial, and cheerful obedience. A calm came over the multitude, and we felt that "the Lord was there."

A young man came once into our meeting to make sport slyly. Trying to make the young men around him laugh during prayer, he fell as senseless as a log upon the ground and was carried out of the house. It was some time before his consciousness could be restored. He became sober, confessed his sins, and in due time united with the church.

Similar manifestations were seen in other places, but everywhere the people were warned against hypocrisy, and against trusting in such demonstrations. They were told that the Lord looks at the heart, and that "repentance toward God and faith in the Lord Jesus" were the unchangeable conditions of pardon and salvation, and that their future lives of obedience or of disobedience would prove or disprove their spiritual life, as "The tree is known by its fruit."

But God visited the people in judgment as well as in mercy. On the 7th of November, 1837, at the hour of evening prayers, we were startled by a heavy thud, and a sudden jar of the earth. The sound was like the fall of some vast body upon the beach, and in a few seconds a noise of mingled voices rising for a mile along the shore thrilled us like the wail of doom. Instantly this was followed by a like wail from all the native houses around us. I immediately ran down to the sea, where a scene of wild ruin was spread out before me. The sea, moved by an unseen hand, had all on a sudden risen in a gigantic wave, and this wave, rushing in with the speed of a race-horse, had fallen upon the shore, sweeping everything not more than fifteen or twenty feet above high-water mark into indiscriminate ruin. Houses, furniture, calabashes, fuel, timber, canoes, food, clothing, everything floated wild upon the flood. About two hundred people, from the old man and woman of threescore years and ten, to the newborn infant, stripped of their earthly all, were struggling in the tumultuous waves. So sudden and unexpected was the catastrophe, that the people along the shore were literally "eating and drinking," and they "knew not, until the flood came and swept them all away." The harbor was full of strugglers calling for help, while frantic parents and children, wives and husbands ran to and fro along the beach, calling for their lost ones. As wave after wave came in and retired, the strugglers were brought near the shore, where the more vigorous landed with desperate efforts and the weaker and exhausted were carried back upon the retreating wave, some to sink and rise no more till the noise of judgment wakes them. Twelve individuals were picked up while drifting out of the bay by the boats of the *Admiral Cockburn*, an English whaler then in port. For a time the captain of the ship feared the loss of his vessel, but as the oscillating waves grew weaker and weaker, he lowered all his boats and went in search of those who were floating off upon the current. Had this catastrophe occurred at midnight when all were asleep, hundreds of lives would undoubtedly have been lost. Through the great mercy of God, only thirteen were drowned.

This event, falling as it did like a bolt of thunder from a clear sky, greatly impressed the people. It was as the voice of God speaking to them out of heaven, "Be ye also ready."

Day after day we buried the dead, as they were found washed up upon the beach, or thrown upon the rocky shores far from the harbor. We fed, comforted, and clothed the living, and God brought light out of darkness, joy out of grief, and life out of death. Our meetings were more and more crowded, and hopeful converts were multiplied.

Even the English captain, who spent his nights in our family, and his intelligent and courteous clerk, professed to give themselves to the Lord while with us, and both kneeling with us at the family altar, silently united in our morning and evening devotions, or cheerfully led in prayer. The captain was a large and powerful man, bronzed by wind and wave and scorching sun. He had been long upon the deep, had suffered shipwreck, had been unable to reach his London home for more than three years, and had been given up as dead by all his friends. Under this belief his wife had married another, when he surprised her by his return, and she gave him joy by returning to him. He gave us an interesting account of his eventful life, and confessed that he had enjoyed very few religious privileges and had thought little of God or the salvation of his soul. He now accepted the offer of life through Christ, with the spirit of a little child.

On returning to the ship he immediately told his officers and crew that he should drink no more intoxicants, swear no more, and chase whales no more on the Lord's day, but, on the contrary, observe the Sabbath and have religious services on that holy day.

Though thousands professed to have passed from death unto life during the years 1836-37, only a small proportion of these had been received into the church. The largest numbers were gathered in during 1838-39. I had kept a faithful note-book in my pocket, and in all my personal conversations with the people, by night and by day, at home and in my oft-repeated tours, I had noted down, unobserved, the names of individuals apparently sincere and true converts. Over these persons I kept watch, though unconsciously to themselves; and thus their life and conversation were made the subjects of vigilant observation. After the lapse of three, six, nine, or twelve months, as the case might be, selections were made from the list of names for examination. Some were found to have gone back to their old sins; others were stupid, or gave but doubtful evidence of conversion, while many had stood fast and run well. Most of those who seemed hopefully converted spent several months at the central station before their union with the church. Here they were watched over and instructed from week to week and from day to day, with anxious and unceasing care. They were sifted and re-sifted with scrutiny, and with every effort to take the precious from the vile. The church and the world, friends and enemies, we're called upon and solemnly charged to testify, without concealment or palliation, if they knew aught against any of the candidates.

From my pocket list of about three thousand, 1,705 were selected to be baptized and received to the communion of the church on the first Sabbath of July, 1838. The selection was made, not because a thousand and more of others were to be rejected, or that a large proportion of them did not appear as well as those received, but because the numbers were too large for our faith, and might stagger the faith of others. The admission of many was deferred for the more full development of their character, while they were to be watched over, guided, and fed as sheep of the Great Shepherd.

The 1,705 persons selected had all been gathered at the station some time before the day appointed for their reception. They had been divided into classes, according to the villages whence they came, and put in charge of class leaders, who were instructed to watch over and teach them.

The memorable morning came arrayed in glory. A purer sky, a brighter sun, a serener atmosphere, a more silvery sea, and a more brilliant and charming landscape could not be desired. The very heavens over us and the earth around us seemed to smile. The hour came; during the time of preparation the house was kept clear of all but the actors. With the roll in hand, the leaders of the classes were called in with their companies of candidates in the order of all the villages; first of Hilo district, then of Puna, and last of Kau. From my roll the names in the first class were called one by one, and I saw each individual seated against the wall, and so of the second, and thus on until the first row was formed. Thus, row after row was extended the whole length of the house, leaving spaces for one to pass between these lines. After every name had been called, and every individual recognized and seated, all the former members of the church were called in and seated on the opposite side of the building, and the remaining space given to as many as could be seated.

All being thus prepared, we had singing and prayer, then a word of explanation on the rite of baptism, with exhortation. After this with a basin of water, I passed back and forth between the lines, sprinkling each individual until all were baptized. Standing in the center of the congregation of the baptized, I pronounced the words, "I baptize you all into the name of the Father, and of the Son, and of the Holy Ghost. Amen."

The scene was one of solemn and tender interest, surpassing anything of the kind I had ever witnessed. All heads were bowed, and tears fell. All was hushed except sobs and breathing.

The nature of the Lord's supper and the reasons for its observance were then explained, and the bread and cup distributed among the communicants.

This was a day long to be remembered. Its impressions were deep, tender, and abiding; and up to the present time, the surviving veterans of that period look back to it as the *day of days* in the history of the Hilo church.

At this period the ecclesiastical year of the mission began on the 1st of May. The reports of the churches were made up to the 30th of April, 1838. I find in the records of Hilo church, the..

Number received during year ending April 30, 1838, . .	639
" " " " " " " 1839, . .	5,244
" " " " " " " 1840, . .	1,499

During the following decade ending in 1850, the number received was 2,348

And for the decade ending in 1860, ... 1,445

The whole number received on profession to 1880,				12,113
"	"	"	" by letter,	812
"	"	"	dismissed,	3,546
"	"	"	deceased,	8,190
"	"	"	of marriages,	3,048
"	"	"	of children baptized,	4,370

Those received from the district of Kau, when there was no settled pastor there, were afterward dismissed to the church which was organized and placed under the care of the Rev. J. D. Paris.

In order to keep every member under my eye, and to find ready access to each, I prepared a book ruled thus:

Date	*Name*	*Residence*	*Dismissed by Letter*	*Received by Letter*	*Excommunicated*	*Died*	*Children Baptized*
1838 July 1	Kapule. . .	Waiakea	. . .	. . .	. .	Mar. 1841	Abenera, Joane
Sept. 2 1837	Lonoakeawe	"	To Hana, June, 1840	. . .	. .	. . . . . .	. . . .

By simple signs males and females were distinguished. This is important here, because the same name is often used interchangeably for the sexes.

For many years I always took this book with me in my tours, and called the roll of the church members in every village along the line. When any one did not answer the roll-call, I made inquiry why. If dead, I marked the date; if sick, visited him or her, if time would allow; if absent on duty, accepted the fact; if supposed to be doubting or backsliding, sent for or visited him; if gone to another part of the island, or to another island, I inquired if the absence would be short or perpetual, and noted the facts of whatever kind.

Our young men often shipped for whaling voyages. Noting these cases, I would watch for their return, and then visit them, inquiring whether they chased whales on the Lord's day, used intoxicants, or violated other Christian rules of morality; and I dealt with them as each case demanded.

Some church members removed to other districts or islands without letters of dismissal. The names of these I used to send to the pastors whither they had gone, requesting them to look after these absent ones, and receive them to their communion, reporting to me.

As hundreds of our people went from place to place to visit friends or on business, to learn whither they had gone, to follow them with letters, and to see them properly cared for, became an important but arduous labor. The Hawaiians are not nomads, but they are fond of moving, and curiosity or the call of friends leads very many of them to wander over many parts of the group. During my annual visits to Honolulu, on occasion of the General Meeting of the Mission held there in May or June, I often gave public notices in the churches that I would meet any of my people who were there, at a given hour on Sunday, and a company of fifty to a hundred would assemble at the hour appointed.

Our Confession of Faith is the Bible, and each individual in the Hilo church promises, with his hand on the Sacred Book, to abstain from all that is forbidden, and to obey all that is commanded therein. We advise them to abstain from the use of tobacco, ava (a narcotic root), and from all intoxicants. Like all savages, they were almost to a man addicted to the use of these articles, especially of tobacco, and we supposed that it would be next to impossible to persuade them to abandon these habits. But the Lord came to our help. All over Hilo and Puna, during that mighty work of the Spirit, multitudes pulled up all their tobacco plants and cast them into the sea or into pits, and thousands of pipes were broken upon the rocks or burned, and thousands of habitual smokers abandoned the habit at once and forever. I have been surprised at the resolution and self-denial of old men and women who had long indulged in smoking, in thus breaking short off. Some, however, went back to the old habit, and some used the article secretly. I have never excommunicated or suspended members for this indulgence, but have taught them, by precept and example, a better way. Mr. and Mrs. Lyman, and nearly every missionary brother and sister on the islands, were united with me in this matter.

In all cases we found that those who would not relinquish smoking were the more troublesome members of the church, giving more doubtful evidence of love to Christ, and oftener running into other excesses which called for church discipline.

5

Mrs. Coan's School for Girls - Common Schools - Medical Work - The Sailors' Church - Sunday Work - Visits of Foreign Vessels - The U.S. Exploring Expedition.

IN the year 1838, Mrs. Coan opened a boarding-school for native girls. This was to be self-supporting in part, but to receive such aid in labor, food, kapas, mats, etc., as parents and friends chose to render.

As soon as the plan was made known to the church and people they rallied cheerfully, went into the woods, hauled down timber by hand, and with great promptness erected and thatched a comfortable building on our premises. A floor was laid over about one-fourth of the building, on which was placed a table, and a few chairs for the teacher and visitors.

On each side of the remaining three-fourths of the house was a row of little open cells, partitioned from each other by mats, and furnished with beds of straw or dried grass, and with mats and kapas for coverings. In the space between these rows of compartments was a plain table, with seats, bowls, spoons, etc., for the pupils. The number of little girls in the school was twenty, their ages from seven to ten years. Arrangements were made with the people living in and near the town, that they should bring in weekly supplies of food and fish for the girls. Taro, potatoes, bananas, and fish were then abundant and cheap, and the people provided willingly. At length they set apart a parcel of ground and appointed each monthly concert day as a time when they would cultivate that ground and thus supply the food necessary for the school.

Little gifts of money were sometimes made by strangers who came to Hilo, by officers of whale-ships and men-of-war; or a piece of print or brown cotton was given, and thus the real wants of the school were supplied. No application to the A.B.C.F.M., or to any Board, or to an individual was ever made for help. Mrs. Coan toiled faithfully from day to day, in spite of pressing family cares, teaching her charges the rudiments of necessary book knowledge, and of singing, sewing, washing and ironing, gardening, and other things. Most of the girls became members of the Hilo church, and we had hope that all were the children of God. The school was sustained about eight years, and sent out a company of girls, who, for the most part, did honor to their instructions, and who were distinguished among their companions for neatness, skill, industry, and piety. As domestic cares increased and her strength was weakened, the faithful teacher at length felt compelled to give up her charge.

For a time I had the supervision of the common schools, numbering not less than fifty, and containing about 2,000 pupils. My duties were to furnish them with books, slates, and pencils; to visit them on my tours, to attend their examinations, and make a tabular record of numbers, readers, writers, etc. For want of writing-paper or a full supply of slates, the children would prepare square pieces of the green banana-leaf, and with a wooden style or slate-pencil form letters and thus learn to write.

At the central station and on all my tours I was thronged with the sick and afflicted multitudes, or their friends, begging for remedies for almost all kinds of diseases. So numerous were the applications for medicines, and so varied and sad were the spectacles of disease, that it became a task for the skill and the whole time of a well-read and experienced physician. I had a fair collection of medical books, and these were consulted as much as was possible in connection with my other labors, but my regret was that I could not visit the sick as I wished, or pay them the attention they needed.

When at last, in 1849, a good physician, Charles H. Wetmore, was sent to our relief, my heart rejoiced. I immediately resigned my medical functions, turned over my medicine-chest and drugs to him, and blessed the Lord that I was not doomed to wander "forty years in the wilderness of powders and pills." This kind and faithful doctor with his excellent wife have been our nearest neighbors ever since their arrival.

I was also greatly relieved of the care of the common schools by Mr. and Mrs. Abner Wilcox, lay missionaries, who came to us as teachers and remained in Hilo several years.

Previous to our arrival, when whale-ships and other vessels were in the harbor of Hilo, the officers and crews received kind attentions from the missionaries at this station. The Reverends Joseph Goodrich, Jonathan Green, Sheldon Dibble, and D. B. Lyman, and their wives, had entertained many of these sons of the deep, given them reading-matter, and sought to promote their spiritual interests.

We were at once ready to help in this important work. Masters, officers, and sailors were made welcome to our house; books and tracts were provided for them to take to sea, and a religious service was held for them every Sunday afternoon.

For many years this service was held in one of the houses of the missionaries. Finally, we fitted up the old stone-building, our first home, for a bethel, and added a library of about 200 volumes, with periodicals.

My regular services on the Sabbath were: a Sunday-school at 9 A.M.; preaching at 10:30; at 12 M. a meeting for inquirers; at 1 P.M. preaching; and at 3 P.M. preaching in English to seamen, and English-speaking residents and visitors. When ships were in port we often had a full house, and not a few hearers professed a determination to forsake all sin and to live godly lives. Of some we afterward learned, either by their own letters or otherwise, that they had kept their vows and united with Christian churches, and that some had become ministers of the Gospel.

Several masters and officers gave up Sabbath whaling, and instead held religious meetings with their men on the Lord's day.

Very precious friendships were formed with many of these seamen, which friendships continue to this day. We have found noble specimens, not only of generosity and fine natural talent among this class of men, but also many choice Christians.

Not a few national ships have visited Hilo, from the tender or schooner up to the sloop-of-war, the frigate and the great seventy-four-gun line-of-battle ship, as the *Collingwood* and *Ohio*.

The largest of these ships represented the United States of America, the next Great Britain, then France, Russia, Germany, and Denmark. We have had more than seventy-five of these war-ships of different nationalities in our harbor, and of all classes of vessels about 4,000. The approximate number of seamen who have visited Hilo during our residence here we put at 40,000.

In this labor for seamen I have been led to correspond with the American Bible, Tract, Peace, Temperance, and Seamen's Friend Societies, and have obtained Bibles and tracts in the English, French, German, Spanish, Portuguese, Swedish, Danish, and Chinese languages; which with many thousands of tracts have been distributed among these vessels. Some of this "bread cast upon the waters" has been found again according to the promise.

In 1840, Charles Wilkes, commander of the United States Exploring Expedition, arrived in Hilo bay in the flagship *Vincennes*. Here with an admirable corps of scientists he spent three months in explorations, measurements, observations, etc. Parties of officers and scientific gentlemen were detailed to visit different parts of the island, some to ascend the mountains, and some to survey the shore, making collections, drawings, and observations in all the branches of the natural history of the Islands. The commander called for 300 young and vigorous men to take him, with the materials of a wooden house and all the apparatus of a large observatory, with food, fuel, water, beds, etc., to the summit of Mauna Loa, where he and his attendants were to spend twenty or thirty days in taking observations.

Other parties required large numbers of men to carry baggage, instruments, etc., and to act as guides and assistants in making surveys and collecting a large amount of specimens.

Parties of natives thus employed needed to be recruited often on account of fatigue and exhaustion, and for the lack of shoes and warm clothing to endure the hard travel and the rains, cold, and snows of the mountains. Some died of cold. It is supposed that about one thousand of our strongest men were brought into this service, and with small pay, during these three months. Some parties of men were required to travel and work on Sunday as on other days. All this had a demoralizing effect upon the poor natives. They had been accustomed to rest from all physical toil, and to worship on the Lord's day. Our congregations were much reduced in numbers. There was no little murmuring among the people at this new state of things, and for years the moral tone of the church and community could not be fully restored to its cheerful and normal state.

This was a trial of faith, and a fan to winnow the church, but most of our Christians stood fast, and although it checked the progress of the revival, the loss to the church was less than might have been feared.

The visit of the expedition to Hilo afforded us an opportunity to form an acquaintance with many worthy gentlemen, several of whom we met again in the United States in 1870-71. Among these we met and received as a very welcome guest the then youthful James D. Dana, one of the scientific corps, now so distinguished in various departments of natural science, and honored as a Christian philosopher. The friendship then formed has been increased by years and can never wane.

6

Mauna Loa – Kilauea – The Eruption of 1840 – The River of Fire – It reaches the Sea at Nanawale – Lava Chimneys – Destruction of a Village.

IT is widely known that the Hawaiian Islands are all of volcanic origin. They are the summits of mountains whose bases are far down in the sea. Their structure is plutonic, and the marks of fire are everywhere visible. They are scarred with hundreds and hundreds of pit and cone craters, most of which are extinct.

Mauna Loa is a vast volcanic dome, subject to igneous eruptions at any time, either from its extended summit or sides. Prof. Dana estimates that "there is enough rock material in Mauna Loa to make one hundred and twenty-five Vesuviuses."* About midway from its summit to the sea on the eastern flank of the mountain and on a nearly level plain is Kilauea, the largest known active crater in the world. The brink of this crater is 4,440 feet above the sea level; its depth varies from 700 to 1,200 feet, and its longer diameter is about three miles. Grand eruptions have issued from it in past ages, covering hundreds of square miles in different parts of Puna and Kau.

The first eruption from Kilauea which occurred after my arrival in Hilo, began on the 30th of May, 1840. To my regret, I was then absent at the annual General Meeting of this mission in Honolulu, a meeting which I have always attended. I therefore record a portion of the facts as given by the natives and foreigners who saw the eruption, adding my own observations on a visit to the scene after my return from Honolulu.

There had been no grand eruption from this crater for the previous seventeen years, so that the lavas in the crater had risen several hundred feet, and the action had, at times, been terrific.

* *Am. Journal of Science*, May, 1859, p. 415.

The volcano is thirty miles by road from Hilo, and under favorable conditions of the atmosphere we could see the splendid light by night, and the white cloudy pillar of steam by day. It was reported that, for several days before the outburst, the whole vast floor of the crater was in a state of intense ebullition; the seething waves rolling, surging, and dashing against the adamantine walls, and shaking down large rocks into the fiery abyss below. It was even stated that the heat was so intense, and the surges so infernal, that travelers near the upper rim of the crater left the path on account of the heat, and for fear of the falling of the precipice over which the trail lay, and passed at a considerable distance from the crater. Kilauea is about half in Puna and half in Kau, and all travelers going from Kau to Hilo by the inland road pass the very brink of this crater.

The eruption was first noticed by the people of Puna, who were living only twenty miles from it. The light appeared at first like a highland jungle on fire; and so it was, for the fiery river found vent some 1,200 to 1,500 feet below the rim of Kilauea, and flowing subterraneously in a N.E. direction, for about four miles, marking its course by rending the superincumbent strata and throwing up light puffs of sulphurous steam, it broke ground in the bottom of a wooded crater about 500 feet deep, consuming the shrubs, vines, and grasses, and leaving a smouldering mass instead.

The great stream forced its way underground in a wild and wooded region for two miles more, when it again threw up a jet of fire and sulphur, covering about an acre. At this point, a large amount of brilliant sulphur crystals continued to be formed for several years.

Only a little further on, and an old wooded cone was rent with fissures several feet wide, and about half an acre of burning lava spouted up, consuming the trees and jungle. This crevasse emitted scalding vapor for twenty-five years.

Onward went the burning river, deep underground, some six miles more, when the earth was rent again with an enormous fissure, and floods of devouring fire were poured out, consuming the forest and spreading over perhaps fifty acres. And still the passage seaward was underground for about another six miles, when it broke out in a terrific flood and rolled and surged along henceforth upon the surface, contracting to half a mile, or expanding to two miles in width, and moving from half a mile to five miles an hour, according to the angle of descent and the inequalities and obstructions of the surface, until it poured over the perpendicular sea-wall, about thirty feet high, in a sheet of burning fusion only a little less than one mile wide.

This was on June 3, 1840. It reached the sea on the fifth day after the light was first seen on the highlands, and at the distance of only seventeen and a half miles from Hilo. As this grand cataract of fire poured over the basaltic sea-wall, the sights and sounds were said to be indescribable. Two mighty antagonistic forces were in conflict. The sea boiled and raged as with infernal fury, while the burning flood continued to pour into the troubled waves by night and by day for three weeks. Dense clouds of steam rolled up heavenward, veiling sun and stars, and so covering the lava flow that objects could not be seen from one margin to the other. All communication between the northern and southern portions of Puna was cut off for more than a month.

The waters of the sea were heated for twenty miles along the coast, and multitudes of fishes were killed by the heat and the sulphurous gases, and were seen floating upon the waves.

During this flow, the sea-line along the whole breadth of the fire-stream was pushed out many yards by the solidified lavas, and three tufaceous cones were raised in the water where ships could once sail. They were formed of lava-sand made by the shivering of the mineral flood coming in contact with the sea, and standing in a line 200, 300, and 400 feet above the water, with their bases deep down in the sea. These dunes have been greatly reduced by the waves thundering at their bases and the winds and storms beating upon their summits. One of them, indeed, is now entirely obliterated.

During this eruption most of the foreign residents in Hilo, and hundreds of Hawaiians of Puna and Hilo, visited the scene where the igneous river plunged into the sea, and they described it as fearfully grand and awe-inspiring.

Imagine the Mississippi converted into liquid fire of the consistency of fused iron, and moving onward sometimes rapidly, sometimes sluggishly; now widening into a lake, and anon rushing through a narrow gorge, breaking its way through mighty forests and ancient solitudes, and you will get some idea of the spectacle here exhibited.

When the eruption was at its height night was turned into day in all this region. The light rose and spread like morning upon the mountains, and its glare was seen on the opposite side of the island. It was also visible for more than a hundred miles at sea; and at the distance of forty miles fine print could be read at midnight.

The brilliancy of the light was said to be like a blazing firmament, and the scene one of unrivaled sublimity.

No lives were lost during this eruption. The stream passed under and over an almost uninhabited desert. A few small hamlets were consumed, and a few patches of taro, potatoes, and bananas were destroyed, but the people walked off with their calabashes, kapas, and other chattels to seek shelter and food elsewhere. During the eruption some of the people of Puna spent much of their time in prayer and religious meetings, some fled in consternation, and others wandered along the margin of the lava stream, at a safe distance, marking with idle curiosity its progress, while others still pursued their daily avocations within a mile of the fiery river, as quietly as if nothing strange had occurred. They ate, drank, bought, sold, planted, builded, slept, and waked apparently indifferent to the roar of consuming forests, the sight of devouring fire, the startling detonations, the hissing of escaping steam, the rending of gigantic rocks, the raging and crashing of lava waves, and the bellowings, the murmurings, the unearthly mutterings coming up from the burning abyss. They went quietly on in sight of the rain of ashes, sand, and fiery scintillations, gazing vacantly on the fearful and ever-varying appearance of the atmosphere illuminated by the eruption, the sudden rising of lofty pillars of flame, the upward curling of ten thousand columns of smoke, and their majestic gyrations in dingy, lurid, or parti-colored clouds.

While the stream was flowing it might be approached within a few yards on the windward side, while at the leeward no one could live within a great distance on account of the smoke, the impregnation of the atmosphere with pungent and deadly gases, and the fiery showers that fell on all around, destroying all vegetable life.

Sometimes the intense heat of the stream would cause large boulders and rocks to explode with great detonations, and sometimes lateral branches of the stream would push out into some fissure, or work into a subterranean gallery, until they met with some obstacle, when the accumulating fusion with its heat, its gases, and its pressure would lift up the superincumbent mass of rock into a dome, or, sundering it from its surroundings, bear it off on its burning bosom like a raft upon the water. A foreigner told me that while he was standing on a rocky hillock, some distance from the stream, gazing with rapt interest upon its movements, he felt himself rising with the ground on which he stood. Startled by the motion, he leaped from the rock, when in a few minutes fire burst out from the place where he had been.

On returning from Honolulu I soon started for Puna, with arrangements to make as thorough explorations and observations on this remarkable eruption as my time would allow. I spent nearly two days on the stream. It was solidified and mostly cooled, yet hot and steaming in many places. I went up the flow to where it burst out in volume and breadth from its subterranean chambers and continued on the surface to the sea, a distance of about twelve miles, making the entire length of the stream about thirty miles. In a letter published in the *Missionary Herald* of July, 1841, I called it forty miles, but later measurements have led me to correct this and some other statements made on first sight.

I found the place of final outburst a scene where terrific energy had been exerted. Yawning crevasses were opened, the rocks were rent, and the forests consumed; the molten flood had raged and swirled and been thrown high into the air, and there had been a display of titanic fury which must have been appalling at the time of the outbreak.

In pursuing its course the stream sometimes plunged into caverns and deep depressions, and sometimes it struck hills which separated it into two channels, which uniting again after having passed the obstruction, left islands of varied sizes with trees scorched and blasted with the heat and gases.

Along the central line of the stream its depth could not be measured accurately, for there was no trace of tree or ancient rock or floor. All was a vast bed of fresh, smouldering lava. On the margins, however, where the strata were thinner, I was able to measure with great accuracy. In passing through forests, while the depth and heat of the middle of the stream consumed everything, on the margins thousands of green trees were cut down gradually by the fusion around their trunks; but this was done so slowly that the surface of the stream solidified before the trees fell, and on falling upon the hot and hardened crust, the tops and limbs were only partly consumed, but all were charred, and the rows and heaps were so thick and entangled as to form *chevaux-de-frise* quite impassable in some places. But the numerous holes left in the hot lava bed by the gradual reduction of the trunks to ashes afforded the means of measuring the depth of the flow. With a long pole I was enabled to measure from a depth of five to twenty-five feet. Some of these trunk-moulds were as smooth as the calibre of a cannon. Some of the holes were still so hot at the bottom as to set my pole on fire in one minute.

I had seen fearful ragings and heard what seemed the wails of infernal beings in the great crater of Kilauea, but I had never before seen the amazing effects of a great exterior eruption of lava, and I returned from this weary exploration, after a missionary tour through Puna, with a deepened sense of the terrible dynamics of the fiery abyss over which we tread.

Since then, in crossing and recrossing the wild highlands of my parish I have found in the consumed openings of forests a new class of volcanic monuments, consisting in numerous stacks of lava chimneys standing apart on the floor of an ancient flow. These chimneys measure from five to twenty-five feet in height, and five to ten feet in diameter. I gazed at them at first sight as the work of human art, not knowing that they were cylindrical. On climbing them I found that they were hollow, and that they were as clearly tree moulds as the holes I had measured in the flow of 1840.

Then came the question, how were they formed? The solution soon came—that an ancient eruption had passed through this forest at the height of many feet above the present surface, the fiery river surrounding large trees, but while it consumed all smaller growths, the waves subsided to their present level before these trunks were fully consumed, thus leaving partially-cooled envelopes of lava adhering to them. These moulds or chimneys now stand as monuments of the volcanic action of an unknown age.

Here I leave this subject for a while, purposing to return to it.

In early years Hawaiian hospitality was generous, and on my tours among the natives I found them ready to provide liberally, according to their ability, for me and the helpers who accompanied me. To this good feeling there was one notable exception. There was a small village about eighteen miles from Hilo, where I had taken special pains to tame and Christianize the people. They rarely provided even a cup of cold water until I arrived and begged them to go to a somewhat distant spring to fetch it; and for this I would have to wait two hours, perhaps, while parched with thirst, burning with the heat of a midday sun, and weary with walking over long miles of scorching lava fields. On one occasion, returning from a circuit tour of more than a hundred miles, I stopped at this place and preached and conversed with the villagers. I had been absent from home over two weeks and had consumed all the food I had taken with me, except a little stale biscuit. I had nothing for the two good men, members of the Hilo church, who had traveled all the distance with me. Evening closed in, and I asked the occupants of the house and some of the neighbors who had come in if they could not furnish my two companions with a little food before they slept. The answer was, "We have no food." "Perhaps you can give them a potato, a kalo, a breadfruit, or a cocoanut." They answered as before, "We have *nothing* to eat, not even for ourselves." So, weary and hungry, we lay down upon the mats for the night, and when we were supposed to be asleep, we heard the family under the cocoanut trees eating heartily, and conversing in an undertone that we might not hear them.

After years of kind instructions with the hope of leading them to appreciate the love of God and the value of a true Christianity, they remained the same hardened beings. My patience and desire to lead them to "the Lamb of God" continued; but thinking of what the Saviour said to His disciples about "shaking off the dust of their feet," I resolved on a trial, hoping to win them into a better way.

In a meeting when "the *hearers* but not the *doers* of the word" were assembled, I said to them, "These three years have I come seeking fruit on this fig-tree, and find none. I will, therefore, leave you to reflect on what you have heard from the Lord; and, whenever you repent and desire to hear the Gospel again, send for me and I will hasten to you with joy." But they never sent. Time passed on and down came the fiery torrent of which I have written, and covered the village, consuming the cocoa-palm grove, the potato and banana patches, with the thatched meeting-house and schoolhouse, leaving nothing but a blackened field of lava. The people took their little all and fled.

They settled near the borders of the lava stream, and in the year 1853 the small-pox fell among them (the only place in Puna where the disease went), and a large part of them died. There was no physician within eighteen miles, and the poor creatures knew not what to do. Some bathed in the sea to cool the burning heat, and perished, and some crawled out into the jungle and there died, and were torn and partly eaten by swine. They had fled from the devouring fire only to meet, if possible, a more painful doom, and it reminds one of the words of Jeremiah uttered against the stubborn Moabites: "He that fleeth from the fear shall fall into the pit, and he that getteth up out of the pit shall be taken in the snare."

That the small-pox should find them and no one else in Puna seems remarkable; but these are the facts. A number of these villagers were visiting in Honolulu when the fearful disease raged there. They thought to escape it by returning home, but unknown to them the destroyer had already seized them and they perished in their wild, secluded jungle.

I visited this scene of sorrow and desolation, gathered the stricken remnant of the sufferers, spoke words of condolence, and encouraged them to come with their sins and sorrows to the Saviour. They seemed subdued, welcomed their pastor, and were, I trust, "saved yet so as by fire."

7

More Church-building - Commodore Jones's Visit - Progress of Conversions - The Sacraments under New Conditions.

OF church buildings we had at one time not less than fifty, and of schoolhouses sixty or more. These were all built by the free will of the people, acting under no outward constraint. Some of these houses would accommodate 1,000 persons, others 500, 300, and 150, according to the population for which they were erected. They were, of course, built in native style, on posts set in the ground, with rafters fastened with cords, and the whole thatched with the leaf of the pandanus, the sugarcane, or dried grass. They were frail, needing rethatching once in three to five years, and rebuilding after about ten years. They were usually well-kept, and with open doors and holes for windows, they were light and airy.

In this list I do not include the great buildings at Hilo.

A mighty wind having prostrated our large meeting-house, we commenced, during the winter of 1840-41, to collect materials for our first framed building. All the men who had axes went into the highland forest to fell trees and hew timber. When a large number of pieces were ready, hundreds of willing men and women, provided with ropes made of the bark of the hibiscus, with light upper garments, and with leggins of the Adam and Eve style, such as never feared mud and water, went to bring down these timbers. Arranged by a captain in two lines, with drag-ropes in hand, ready to obey the command of their chosen leader, they stood waiting his order. At length comes the command, "Grasp the ropes; bow the head; blister the hand; go; sweat!" And away they rush, through mud and jungle, over rocks and streams, shouting merrily, and singing to measure. Then comes the order, "Halt, drop drag-ropes, rest!" This is repeated at longer or shorter intervals according to the state of the ground.

I often went up to the woods, on foot of course, and grasped the rope, and hauled with the rest to encourage and keep them in heart. We had no oxen or horses in those days, for the days were *primitive*, and the work was pioneer work. The trees, the jungle, the mud, the streams, and the lava-fields were all primordial.

When the materials were brought together, we employed a Chinese carpenter at a reasonable price, to frame and raise the building, all his pay to be in trade, for "the golden age" had not yet dawned on Hawaii. The natives, men and women, soon covered the rough frame with thatching. There was no floor but the earth, and the only windows were holes about three feet square left in the thatching on the sides and ends. This was the first framed church edifice built in Hilo, and in this building, capable of seating about 2,000 people, we first welcomed Commodore Thomas ap Catesby Jones, of the frigate *United States*, with his officers and brass band. The courteous commodore and his chaplain consented to deliver each an address of congratulation and encouragement to the people for their ready acceptance of the Gospel, and for their progress in Christian civilization. He alluded to a former visit of his to Honolulu by order of the United States Government, to investigate certain complaints made by a class of foreign residents against the American missionaries, stating that on a patient and careful hearing of the parties, the missionaries came out triumphantly, and their abusers were put to shame.

Our people at this time had never heard the music of a brass band, and the commodore kindly gave them a treat. After playing several sacred songs which delighted the natives beyond all music they had before heard, the band, at a signal from the commodore, struck up "Hail Columbia." An electric thrill rushed through the great congregation, and all sprang to their feet in amazement and delight. Since then they have become familiar with the music of the United States', the English and French navies.

Perhaps the most perfect band we have heard in Hilo was that of the Duke of Edinburgh, who visited us in the steam frigate *Galatea* in 1869.

When our first framed church building became old and dilapidated, we decided on replacing it with an edifice of stone and mortar. But after a year's hard toil in bringing stones on men's shoulders, and after having dug a trench some six feet deep for the foundations without coming to the bedrock, we, by amicable agreement, dismissed our mason and engaged two carpenters.

The cornerstone was laid November 14, 1857, and the building was dedicated on the 8th of April, 1859. The material was good, and the workmanship faithful and satisfactory. The whole cost was $13,000.

It was then the finest church edifice on the islands. On the day of the dedication, there was a debt on the house of some $600, and it was our hope and purpose to cancel the debt on that day. But the day was stormy, the paths muddy, and the rivers were without bridges. Things looked dark, but we were happily surprised to see the people flocking in from all points until the house was crowded to its utmost capacity.

Prayers and a song of praise were offered, but we had resolved, by the help of God, not to dedicate the house until the debt was paid to the last farthing. So the people were called on by divisions, according to their villages, to come forward with their offerings; and this was done with such promptness, such order, and such quietness that we soon counted and declared a contribution of over $800. When the result was announced, a shout of joy went up to heaven.

The debt was paid, the house was dedicated, $200 were left in the treasury, and the people went home rejoicing and praising the Lord. On the 27th a contribution of more than $400 was taken, making our dedication offerings $1,239. Our treasury for the meeting-house has never been empty, though we have expended several thousand dollars more in purchasing a large bell, in painting and repairing the house, and in keeping it and the grounds neat and in good condition.

It was an affecting scene to see the old and decrepit, the poor widow, and the droves of little children come forward with their gifts which they had been collecting and saving for months, and offering them with such cheerful gladness to the Lord.

In 1868 an awful earthquake tore in pieces stone walls and stone houses, and rent the earth in various parts of Hilo, Puna, and Kau. Had we built according to our original plan and agreement with the mason, "our holy and beautiful house" would have become a heap of rubbish, and our hearts would have sunk within us with sorrow. How true that "a man's heart deviseth his way, but the Lord directeth his steps."

It was my habit to get all the help that could be obtained from converts, and this was much. As the company of disciples increased, "they went everywhere preaching the word." The Lord ordained them, not man. In every hamlet and village there were found some who were moved by the Holy Ghost, and to whom the Spirit gave utterance; and it was joyfully true that "where the Spirit of the Lord was, there was liberty," not to dispute and wrangle, not to speak vain and foolish things, not to lie and deceive, but to utter the truth in love, without the shackles of form and superstition, but with the freedom granted by Christ.

How true the promise, "My people shall be willing in the day of my power." Willing to give up their sins, their enmity, their vile practices, their pipes, their *ava*, and all their intoxicants; to forgive and be forgiven; to return every man to the wife he had abused, and every wife to the husband she had forsaken; to pay their old debts; to labor with their hands for the supply of their physical wants; to see that their children were in school, in religious meetings; to see that prisons were emptied and churches filled, and that the poor, the sick, the blind, and the lame were not forgotten; to see that the call of love and the offers of life were heard by all. The objects called for laborers, and they were ready at call. Sometimes ten, twenty, or forty men were sent out, two and two, through all Puna and Hilo, into all highways, hedges, jungles, and valleys, to "seek and to save the lost," the sick, the ignorant, the stupid, the timid, or the "remnant of the giants" in idolatry. And they were drawn out by hundreds into the light of the Gospel and the love of the Saviour. There was no retreat among the hills or in the forests where these helpers did not come, and no place where I did not precede, accompany, or follow them. The women also toiled earnestly for souls. They met, prayed, read the commission of the Great Prince, and went out two and two into all the villages, exhorting, persuading, weeping, and praying, and their influence was wonderful for good. They were taught by the Word and the Spirit, and understood their work. With these helpers every village became a guarded citadel of the Lord, and there were few lurking-places for the enemy, no dark passages by which he might make approaches to the camp of the saints.

So far as we could learn, there was not a house or a cabin in all these districts where the voice of morning and evening prayer was not heard; and in most places Scripture lessons and hymns were rehearsed, and efforts, often very rude and inartistic, were made to sing the praises of God.

Previous to the great revival I had been pained at the cold and formal prayers of the natives. All had seemed mechanical and heartless, and in grief I had said, "I do not feel satisfied with this praying, it seems but a thoughtless and unfeeling rehearsal of a lesson." But when the Spirit fell upon the people, all this was changed. Some of the most unlettered and weak became mighty and prevailing wrestlers like the patriarch Jacob. "The feeble among them were like David, and the house of David as the angel of the Lord." They took God at His word, their faith was simple and childlike, unspoiled by tradition or vain philosophy. They went "boldly to the throne of grace," and yet with eyes melted with tears, and hearts yearning with love for souls.

Often have I seen a whole assembly moved to tears and tenderness by the prayers and wrestlings of one man. They plead the promises with no apparent shadow of a doubt, and the answer often came speedily. Is it not recorded for the assurance of faith that "Before they call I will answer, and while they are yet speaking I will hear"? They were praying with melting fervor for the Spirit, and He came, sometimes like the dew of Hermon or the gentle rain, and sometimes "like a rushing mighty wind," filling the house with sobbing and with outcries for mercy.

Controversies among Christians always sadden me. Our warfare is against sin and Satan; and Heaven's "sacramental host" should never fall out by the way, or spend an hour in their conflict with Hell in fighting with one another.

Grasping and defending *vital truths*, and allowing kind and courteous discussions of outward forms, the whole Church of Christ should clasp hands and march shoulder to shoulder against the common foe. The many and different church organizations, with their external rites, rules, and preferences, never offend me where there is "the unity of the spirit in the bonds of peace." All Christians are bound by the supreme law of heaven to love one another, not to bite and devour, nor to indulge in "envy and strife."

I believe in the beautiful rite of baptism, not as essential to salvation, but as a sign and seal of faith in Christ.

I believe that the mode and the amount of water are indifferent, and that every thinking man is at liberty to choose for himself so as to satisfy his own conscience before God, whether by immersion, pouring, or sprinkling; nor do I believe that the Bible warrants dogmatism, division, or non-communion on this subject. For myself I prefer sprinkling, not so much from the many discussions I have heard, or the arguments I have read on the subject, as from the facts in my experience.

Granting that this rite is designed to be *universal* as is the Gospel, Matt, xxviii. 19, I have often found it impossible to baptize by immersion. I have found in parts of Hawaii, one, two, and five miles from the sea, and as far from any pool of water sufficient to immerse even the head, men, women, and children so old or so sick that they could not be carried to any water fountain to be immersed; some ready to die, and begging me with tears to baptize them and administer to them the emblems of the body and blood of the Lord Jesus. They accepted Christ with good evidence of faith and love, and welcomed His messenger with tears of joy and gratitude.

And now let me ask with Peter, "Can any man forbid water that these should not be baptized?"

Similar considerations apply to the communion of the Lord's supper. I have been in situations where it seemed a duty and a privilege to administer this sacrament, but could get neither bread nor wine. Of course this led to reflection. Shall I omit the sacrament? Shall it be postponed for months, with the probability that some of these aged and wasting forms will be laid in the dust within a few days or weeks? Which is of the greater importance, the ordinance or the articles used to symbolize and call to remembrance the death of the Lord Jesus? Do not the food we eat and the water we drink sustain our mortal bodies, and does not faith in the Saviour's broken body and shed blood give life to our souls? The argument seemed to me logical and conclusive. And on further reflection that the bread we now use differs from that used when the ordinance was first instituted, and that much of the wine of this age is a poisoned mixture, the conclusion was further strengthened that neither our bread nor our wine was essential to our acceptable observance of the Lord's supper.

We use bread at the Hilo churches, and for the cup a preparation without alcohol or any poisonous drug; but in making my distant tours we used the food and drink which sustains the life of the people, whether bread-fruit, taro, or potato, and water.

8

Arrival of Catholic Missionaries - Admiral de Tromelin - Proselytism - Controversies with the Priests - Arrival of the Mormons - The Reformed Catholics - Bishop Staley - Lord George Paulet.

THE pioneer Catholic missionaries arrived in 1827, and were rejected by the rulers.

This company was led by Rev. Alexis John Augustine Bachelot, who was commissioned by Pope Leo XII. as "Apostolic Prefect of the Sandwich Islands." They landed without permission and refused to depart, under the delusion that the Pope as the Vicegerent of Heaven had dominion over all earthly principalities and powers, as if the earth were his footstool. Then followed a long struggle, in which arrogance, intrigue, and duplicity were freely exercised, and which conflict has continued until this day. One step of aggression followed another until the power of the French Government was invoked by the priests, and in 1839 Captain Laplace, commander of the French frigate *l'Artémise*, appeared and made charges and demands which, it was then supposed, meant a seizure of the Islands. But the Lord spared us.

Failing in this attempt, the French sloop-of-war *Embuscade*, Captain Mallet, appeared in 1842 with fresh charges and demands, threatening the king and the life of the kingdom. Fortunately royal commissioners had been dispatched to England and France with plenary powers to settle all difficulties amicably with these Governments, especially with the French. Of course Captain Mallet had nothing to do, as the case had been appealed to the supreme power.

In August, 1849, the French frigate *La Poursuivante*, Admiral de Tromelin, came into Hilo with a French bishop and consul on board, who made a pleasant and polite call at our house. From here the Admiral sailed for Honolulu, where he brought new charges of grievances because the French priests and the Catholic religion had been dishonored.

He went so far as to land his marines, and with martial music and waving flag, enter the fort at Honolulu, throw down the guns from the walls, fill up an old well, break up a few calabashes, etc. The fort had no garrison, the gates were wide open, and there being no resistance, it is reported that the gallant Admiral said to his officers and marines: "Let us go on board; they won't fight, and there is no glory in this." I relate the story as it was told me.

Rumors were afloat that the United States Commissioner then in Honolulu had agreed, under the earnest request of the King and nobles, to run up the United States flag as a signal of a protectorate so soon as a hostile gun was fired from the frigate. It is supposed that the Admiral felt that he had gone too far, and could not grasp the prize, and therefore withdrew from the bloodless conflict, since which time we have had no more threatening from the French Government, but have had to meet what looks like Jesuitical tactics on all sides.

I have here given only a hasty sketch of the introduction of Catholicism into these Islands, and for more detailed information I will refer the reader to the histories of the Rev. Hiram Bingham and James J. Jarves, Esq. These histories were written mostly at the times and place of the troubles, and they present a fair and truthful statement of the facts. Mr. Bingham's history also affords a very full and interesting view of the mission of the A.B.C.F.M. from the year 1820 to 1845.

Of this persistent aggression of the Catholics, Hilo and Puna have had their full share. Priests were early stationed in these and the adjoining districts, and they at once took a bold and defiant stand. These emissaries confronted me everywhere. I often heard of them as having gone just before me on my tours. They appointed meetings near by my appointments, and at the same hour; they even came to my congregations in anger to command some of their claimed neophytes to leave the house.

Everywhere they perplexed and vexed the simple natives by telling our best and most tried Christians that they were outside the true Church and on their way to perdition. They taught the people that the Protestants were all heretics and deceivers, that their ordinations were invalid, their pretended marriages adultery, and their teachings delusive.

They also appealed to the selfish and baser feelings of the natives to carry their point, encouraging them in the cultivation and use of tobacco, and assuring them that if they would turn Catholics they would never be called on to give to the priests, to assist in building churches, to contribute at monthly concerts, or be taxed in any way to support religion. Thus they gained weak followers. But when the priests changed their policy and began to call on their proselytes for help in building churches and supporting their teachers, many of the natives saw the duplicity and left them at once.

When a church member was under discipline or had been suspended for notorious sins, he was often sought and received into the Catholic church. Liars, thieves, drunkards, adulterers, were flattered with the belief that all would come out well with them if they were only in the *true Church!*

This "daubing with untempered mortar," and crying "Peace, peace, when there was no peace," was a bold and impudent opposition to sound church discipline, encouraging delinquents to harden themselves in sin. It became "a refuge of lies," a hiding-place of transgressors, a snare to catch souls.

This determined and unrelenting attack of the papal powers upon the church of Hilo and Puna greatly increased the cares and labors of the pastor. I delivered more than thirty public lectures on the history, character, and predictions of the papacy, besides continuous and unwearied private efforts with those who were perplexed by the sophistry of the priests. And I had the comfort of knowing that many of my people became more than a match for the priests in faith and argument.

A priest one day assailed one of the native Christians by asserting that all the American missionaries came to the Islands to get money.

"Ah!" said the native, "you believe that, do you?" "Most certainly," said the priest. "Well, your belief is most marvelous. We Hawaiians think that those who are in search of gold and silver avoid such poor people as we are and go where money is plenty. It is most strange that you should believe that Mr. Bingham, Mr. Thurston, and others came here to get money when there was no money in this country. Do you think them such *fools?*"

Another good old native was accosted one day thus: "Are you one of Mr. Coan's disciples?" to which he replied, "I am one of the disciples of Christ." "What is the *true Church?*" asked the priest. "Why do you priests cast the second commandment out of your catechism?" In a flurry—"The second commandment, the second commandment! I was not talking about the second commandment. I asked you *what is the true Church?*" Good old Paul replied again: "And why do you cast the second commandment out of your catechism?" "What, what! what do you mean—I tell you I am not talking about the second commandment, but about the *true Church*" Steady to his point, Paul coolly and emphatically repeated again, "Why do you cast the second commandment out of your catechism? "Turning on his heels the Jesuit went off exclaiming, "Paul, you are an old stubborn fool." But he never assailed him again.

Another priest meeting Barnabas saluted him with much politeness, and offering a little flattery, began to express great desire that they both might escape delusion and find the one and only way to heaven. Then he began with the usual opening question: "What is the true Church?" Barnabas calmly replied, "The true Church of God is composed of all true believers who love and obey the Lord Jesus, of every age and name and nation on earth and in heaven." This comprehensive truth began to ruffle the priest, and he tried to parry the point of the Spirit's sword by syllogistic logic, saying, "There can be *only one* true Church." Barnabas saw the premises, and anticipating the reasoning and conclusion, he cut the matter short. "I have answered your question, and now, as you and I both have enough to do, I bid you good-morning"—and as he left the priest he heard him murmuring, "Poor deluded and stubborn heretic."

One of their most audacious acts remains to be recorded. I had once visited Mr. Paris, at Kau, on the occasion of transferring those members of my church from that district to the care of Mr. Paris.

On Monday I was returning toward Hilo. When near the center of Kau, as I was passing a Catholic church under the foothills of Mauna Loa, I was stopped by about two hundred Catholics, headed by a French priest, who challenged me then and there to a debate. This was in a narrow pass along the road which was so completely obstructed by the collected Catholics as to prevent my passing on. The challenge I respectfully declined, and as it was late in the afternoon, and I had some eight or ten miles of rough road to travel before I slept, I begged the mob to open the road, and suffer me to pass peacefully on my way. This the priest refused, commanding the people to keep the passage blocked, and with lifted hands and clenched fists, he declared that this Coan, this opposer of the Catholics, should never pass until he had accepted the challenge for debate. Again and again I calmly declined, and asked for a passage through the crowd. The priest became furious and his whole frame trembled with excitement, while the people around him seemed fierce as wolves.

Not being able to proceed, I dismounted and tried to elbow my way through, leading my horse. The priest kept right before me, with hands quivering, and voice roaring: "*Who* is the head of the Church? *Who is the head of the Church?*" For a time I made no reply, but quietly tried to work my way along, till at last I spoke out in full and clear tones, "The Lord Jesus Christ, He is the Head of the Church." Immediately the priest roared out at the top of his voice, "That is a lie, Peter is the head of the Church."

Several faithful natives were with me, watching with intense interest the scene. When this assertion of Peter's headship thundered from the priest, one of the men named Sampson, a bold and powerful man, could hold in no longer, and with the voice of a giant, and the arm of Samson of old, he cried out, "Clear the road, and let my teacher pass," and with the word came the act; with his strong arms he scattered the mob to the right and left, and I followed on through the passage thus opened. As I mounted my horse and rode quietly on, the howling crowd shouted: "He flees! he flees! He is a coward."

Some of the leaders of this mob afterward left the Catholics, and repented with tears.

This priest, recognizing me upon the road one day afterward, at once turned into the bushes, rather than to meet me. I never met him again, and it was not many months before the strong young man was dead.

Not many years after the introduction of the papal priests came a drove of Mormon emissaries. These spread themselves in squads all over the group like the frogs of Egypt.

They made an early descent upon Hilo. At first they employed flattering words. They called at once on me, asserted their divine commission, affirmed the heavenly origin of their order, enlarged on the new and sure revelations made to Joe Smith and his successors, the prophets, and invited me to join them, assuring me that I would then see the full-orbed light of truth, whereas I had only seen its faint dawn. "You are a good man," said they, "and have done what you could; but we have come to teach you the way of God more perfectly, and if you will unite with us and come into this new light, your people will all soon be born again, *i. e.*, be dipped in water, and then by the laying on of hands they will receive the Holy Ghost, and all the signs will follow." I asked, "What signs?" They replied, "Speaking with tongues, healing the sick, and all miracles." I then said, "Let us take up the '*signs*' in order, and see if you Mormons have them. Can you cast out devils?" "Yes." "But, if testimony is true, many of your people, like other sinners, act as if the devil were still in them. 'They shall speak with tongues.' Can you do it?" "Oh, yes, we can at Utah." "And why not here, where you need the gift more? And why do you ask for a teacher of the native language? Do you believe you could handle poisonous serpents, and drink deadly things with impunity?" "We can heal the sick." "And so can I. But do not Mormons die?" "Oh, yes." "Can you raise the dead?" "The Mormons at Salt Lake can do it." "Well, if you will go with me to a fresh grave near by, and raise a dead body to life, I will join you today." This silenced them on miracles and signs. And when I produced my copy of "The Book of Mormon," and showed them I knew more than they about the doctrines of the faith to which they were trying to make me a proselyte, they were confounded, and went away despairing of my becoming a convert.

But for years numbers of this deluded sect traveled over these districts, using all their powers of persuasion, not excepting lying and deceit, to draw the people after them. When once they succeeded in making a disciple they would quarter themselves in his house until he had cooked the last pig, goat, or fowl, and until his taro, potatoes, and bananas were gone, all the while boasting of their great love, and comparing themselves with the American missionaries, who they said came here to get salaries and to oppress the people.

I met the Mormons often on my tours, and had abundant evidence from repeated conversations, and from the testimony of the most reliable members of the church, of their ignorance, bigotry, impudence, and guile.

Finding that they could not prevail by flattery, they assumed a bold front, denounced the American missionaries as false pretenders, deceivers, and blind guides, without baptism, without ordination, and without credentials from heaven. One of their number came into our congregation on a Sabbath, and when I arose at the close of the service to dismiss the assembly, the Mormon arose, and with a loud voice gave notice that he would preach immediately. The great congregation moved quietly toward the church door, when he placed himself in the doorway to prevent their egress, demanding in loud, boisterous language that they all remain and hear "*the true gospel.*" Steadily the crowd moved to the door, and pressing the arrogant intruder aside, returned to their homes.

Though numbers of low characters at first turned after the Mormons, the sect soon ran out here, and now they have neither church, or school, or meetinghouse in all Hilo and Puna.

The entrance of Bishop Staley into the Hawaiian Islands with his corps of priests and sisters has gone into history. Receiving the title of "Lord Bishop of Honolulu," he contemplated the supplanting of the American missionaries, the conversion of the foreign residents and natives to his faith, and the establishment of one grand Episcopal Diocese over all the islands of the group.

The whole scheme was planned, and he soon began to move with his clergy for its execution.

Having established several stations in Hawaii and other islands of the Archipelago, he came to Hilo with one of his clergy.

Ignoring practically the church which had long been established here under its present pastor, and all who had labored to gather and to guide the flock, he walked boldly in as if by divine right, appointed his meetings to preach in the English and Hawaiian languages, and announced that he would at once establish two congregations, one of Hawaiians, and one of English-speaking residents.

In the further pursuance of his scheme, he appointed two boards of trustees or agents, one composed of members of my church, and one of foreign residents. These agents he instructed and empowered to open subscriptions, collect funds, proselyte the people, and make all necessary arrangements for buildings and for gathering congregations. He then presented the appointed curate of Hilo, and engaged board and lodging for him.

All this was done as if by royal authority, and without condescending to confer with or to know the incumbent pastor and his associate laborers. The arrangements having been completed, his lordship returned to Honolulu, taking the curate-elect with him to get his baggage, with the promise that he should return immediately to exercise his priestly functions for the cure of souls, and as the only authenticated messenger of Heaven to the benighted and perishing heathen of Hilo. They came, they saw, they went, but they did not soon return.

It was found that there was one factor in the plot which the shrewd bishop had overlooked, and that was the *will* of the people of Hilo. They had somehow imbibed the doctrine of "Free Agency," which implies will and choice and personality.

The bishop's theory was smooth and perfect, but its practical execution was so clogged by friction that it failed of success. Letters followed Bishop Staley to Honolulu stating that neither of his boards had secured a proselyte or a dollar, that his agents did not act, and that all things were going on in the old way. This was a damper surely, and it might be an extinguisher.

But the bishop rallied and appeared again in Hilo; appointed meetings as before, and wished to know the reasons for the inactivity of his Hilo agents. His efforts were of no avail. The people could not see what allegiance they owed to a lord and bishop created in London, or why they should forsake their "own and their fathers' friends," to whom under God they owed all they knew of civilization and of Christian truth.

The Reformed Catholics have never established a church in Hilo, and it is not known that they have a single convert here.

We wish to be liberal and to labor in loving harmony with all who love our Lord and Saviour, and who pray heartily for His coming and kingdom, but we pity all who are exclusive, and who vainly set themselves up as the only true Church.

During the year of 1843, the English corvette *Carysfort*, Lord George Paulet commanding, made two visits to Hilo.

This young Briton had seized the reins of the Hawaiian Government, hauled down the national flag, dethroned the king, and established what he called a Provisional Government. The country was in confused agitation, and a dark cloud veiled our political sky.

When he arrived he went in person to our prison, commanding the keeper to open the doors, discharge the prisoners, and give him the keys. The guilty offenders and criminals feeling that their hour of triumph had come, rushed out jubilant, and went whither they desired.

Lord George soon called on us, and introduced himself as the savior of the country. He was a young, jolly, and sanguine man, of pleasant manners and very sociable. He seemed at ease, yet self-conscious. "Well," said he, "you are now under the British flag; how do you like it?"

"Well, sir, we choose to be under the Hawaiian."

"No, no! but the English Government is strong, and your protection is sure." "True, but we desire that this weak and small people should be free and independent. It is a right which should not be taken from them without just cause."

"Well, well, but you would rather be under the flag of England than of France?" "That may be, but we choose the flag of the country for which we have labored." "You could not live under the Hawaiian flag. The French were determined to take your islands as they took Tahiti. I knew it, and I hastened hither before them and saved the country, and you ought to thank me."

All this was spoken in great good humor and self-satisfaction, and his lordship shook hands and bowed a pleasant good-morning.

He returned to Honolulu, and our native police went immediately in search of the prisoners he had set free and returned them to the prisons. Hearing of this, and that the same thing had occurred in Lahaina, he hastened back with all canvas spread, landed with bodyguard and side arms, went to the prison and opened again its doors, setting the inmates free. He then inquired for the native judge who had countermanded his orders by returning the prisoners to jail, and hastened in person to his house, as the natives said, "*piha i ka huhu*," filled with wrath.

But the wide-awake judge having had a hint of his coming, and not caring to end his judgeship in prison, stole out at the back door and could not be found.

The commander, to hold the fort, organized a police mostly of foreigners of a certain class, some of whom had, I think, seen the inside of a prison, and others who might be fair candidates for such a place, and giving them strict orders to see that his commands were executed, he left Hilo for the second and last time. Our new police were greatly magnified by their office, and were somewhat haughty and imperious during their brief authority.

Lord George appointed his officers, civil and military, over all the Islands, enlisted and drilled soldiers among the natives and foreigners, and taught them rebellion against their lawful sovereign.

After five months of "torment," the time of the reign of the locusts in the Apocalypse, the flagship of the good Admiral Thomas arrived in Honolulu. The English flag was removed from all its staves, the Hawaiian was raised in all our ports, and the commander of the proud *Carysfort* was ordered to salute the royal signal he had dishonored. To this day it waves and flutters over an independent kingdom, and the *Carysfort* with her lordly commander has been seen no more in our waters.

9

Isolation of the Mission Families – Sufferings on the Inter-Island Voyages – Their Dangers – Parting with our Children – School Discussions and Festivals – Native Preachers – Cheerful Givers – Changes and Improvements.

IN the early years of the mission, the trials of separation were often severe. Hawaii was not only far from all the outer world, but our islands were separated one from another by wide and windy channels, with no regular and safe packets, and no postal arrangements, or regular means of communication.

Add to this, many parts of the islands were so broken by ravines, by precipices, and dangerous streams, and so widely sundered by broad tracts of lava, without house, or pool of water to refresh the weary and thirsty traveler, and without roads withal, that social intercourse was impossible without great toil and suffering.

As to beloved friends and kindred in the far-off fatherland, it seemed like an age before we could speak to them and receive answers.

I think it was eighteen months before we received answers to our first letters sent from Hilo to the United States, a period long enough for revolutions among the nations as well as in families.

All our flour, rice, sugar, molasses, and many other articles of food, with clothing, furniture, medicines, etc., came in sailing vessels around Cape Horn, a voyage of four to six months, so that our news became old and our provisions stale before they reached us, while our stationery might be exhausted, our medicines expended, our flour mouldy and full of worms, before the new supplies arrived. Many a time have we been obliged to break up our barrel of hardened flour with an axe, or chisel and mallet.

But, after all, our inter-island communication was often our more severe trial. A few old schooners, leaky and slow, mostly owned by native chiefs, floated about, sometimes lying becalmed under the lee of an island for a whole week, in a burning sun, with sails lazily flapping, boom swinging from side to side, and gaff mournfully squeaking aloft.

These vessels were usually officered and manned by indolent and unskilful natives, who made dispatch, cleanliness, safety, and comfort no factors in a voyage. They would often be four and even six weeks in making a trip from Honolulu to Hilo and back, a total distance of some 600 miles. They knew nothing of the motto, "Time is money." So long as they were supplied with fish and poi, all was well. They would sometimes lash the helm while they went to eat, then lie down and sleep. We have often found our vessel in this condition at midnight, captain and all hands fast asleep, and the schooner left to the control of wind and wave, and without a lamp burning on board. In addition some vessels were without a single boat for help in the hour of peril.

The cabins being small and filthy, the missionaries slept on deck, each family providing its own food and blankets, and all exposed to wind, heat, storm, and drenching waves which often broke upon the deck. Upon a schooner of forty to sixty tons, there might be one hundred natives with their dogs and pigs, stoutly contesting deck-space with them; and often fifty members of missionary families, parents and children together. These were the families on Molokai and Maui, with, in many cases, those of the several stations on Hawaii. The crowd was distressing, and the sickness and suffering can never be told. Mothers with four or five children, including a tender nursling, would lie miserably during the hot days under a burning sun, and by night in the rain, or wet with the dashing waves, pallid and wan, with children crying for food, or retching with seasickness. I have seen some of these frail women with their pale children brought to land, exhausted, upon the backs of natives, carried to their homes on litters, and laid upon couches to be nourished till their strength returned.

Does any one ask why these delicate mothers left their homes to suffer thus nigh unto death?

The answer is this. For the isolated mission families to visit one another at will, was out of the question. Once a year, provision such as described was made to bring all together in Honolulu, in what was styled "General Meeting." So strong was the social and Christian instinct, that nearly every parent and child would brave the dangers and submit to the sufferings of these terrible passages, rather than deny the intense heart-longings for personal intercourse with their fellow-laborers "in the kingdom and patience of Jesus Christ."

We all went with our households and were received cordially by our dear brethren and sisters in Honolulu, where in consultation on the things pertaining to the mission work, in prayer and praise and in social intercourse, we usually spent three or four weeks. Daily meetings were often held with the children, when with united endeavors we sought to lead them to Him who has said: "Suffer little children to come unto me." And many of those little ones dated their deepest religious impressions from those meetings.

Through the providential care of Him who was with us, no lives were lost in all these dangerous voyages of the early members of the mission. Two of these leaky, ill-managed vessels were, as we suppose, sunk in the night while attempting to cross the channel from Maui to Hawaii, with about two hundred natives on board, eighty of whom were my church members. Not a spar, not a box nor a bucket from these vessels has been seen from that day to this.

It is probable that the helm was lashed, and that captain and all hands were asleep when a squall struck the sails, capsized the vessel, and all were plunged without warning into the dark abyss of waters.

On one of these lost vessels my second daughter had engaged passage to return from Honolulu to Hilo, in company with our neighbor, Judge Austin, and his wife and children. By a sudden impulse and just before the embarkation, the party changed their minds and took passage on another schooner bound to the western coast of Hawaii, where they were safely landed, making their way thence to Hilo by land, a distance of about seventy-five miles. Had they taken the ill-fated schooner, we should never have seen our daughter and our neighbors again on earth.

Another trial of painful character has been borne by the missionaries in the sending of their tender offspring away from their island home to the fatherland. Surrounded by the low and vulgar throng of early mission days, with no good schools, and loaded with cares and labors for the native race, most of the missionaries have felt it a duty to their children to seek for them an asylum in a land of schools and churches and Christian civilization. The struggle of parting has sometimes been agonizing on both sides. Often the child would plead piteously to be suffered to remain, while at the same time the mother's heart yearned over her darling one; but a stern sense of duty nerved her to the sacrifice, and with a last kiss of farewell she would commit her son or daughter to the care of the ship-master, and turn away with a crushed heart to spend sleepless hours in prayers and tears.

Ah! how many of these mothers remember these heart-struggles with a melting agony, and how many of those scalding tears the Father of Mercies has known, with the prayers that wrung them out!

Our two elder children remained at their island home until they reached an age when the thought of separation was less cruel. They then made the voyage around Cape Horn under the kind care of Capt. James Willis and his excellent wife.

Later, our second daughter and son were sent to the United States under favorable circumstances. Our youngest son has returned, and lives near the old homestead.

Once or twice a year the school teachers and leading members of the church were called together in Hilo for the discussion of important questions, and for prayer.

This assembly numbered one hundred, and often more. They came as delegates or representatives from all the villages, either as volunteers or as chosen by the people. When assembled for deliberation a scribe was elected, and a book of records kept, in which minutes of all important acts were entered. The duration of such meetings varied from three days to a week, according to the importance and interest of the discussions.

These representatives we call *Lunas*, overseers. None of them were ordained as deacons or elders, but their office work was much like that of class-leaders in the Methodist church. They reported the state of the schools and of the church members. A list of overtures was prepared, embracing topics for consideration on a great variety of subjects pertaining to "The life that now is and to that which is to come." The meetings were often pervaded with a delightful spirit of tenderness and Christian harmony. Prayers were fervent, and there were exhibitions of native eloquence which were marvelous.

These were excellent occasions for the pastor to instruct the leading minds of his flock, not only in the rules of order pertaining to deliberative bodies, but in the duties of parental, filial, fraternal, matrimonial, social, economical, civil, and spiritual life. The range of subjects was wide, but simple and practical, and the fruits were apparent. Many beside the delegates came in, day after day, to these meetings, both of men and women.

These were sometimes local and sometimes general. When the schools of the two districts assembled at the central station, I think we have had two thousand in the exhibition. Usually the schools would be dressed in uniforms, each choosing for itself the color which their tastes dictated. All floated flags and banners of a tasteful style, and all marched to music, vocal or instrumental, and often prepared by themselves or their teachers. Some made flutes of the bamboo, and some composed sweet songs with simple but pleasing music.

Their marchings and simple evolutions, with songs and fluttering flags, attracted the attention of all, and many came out to witness the gala picture.

The marching over, the children were arranged under a broad canopy of green branches, where hymns were sung, addresses made, prayers offered, and then all partook of an ample feast. Young and old alike were jubilant.

As numbers of our young and active men desired more full and specific instruction in the doctrines of the Bible and the duties of life than they gained in our common exercises, I received about twenty into a class for daily instruction in systematic theology, Scripture exegesis, sermonizing, etc.

This school was kept up in convenient terms for several years. It was not designed to make pastors, but to train a class of more intelligent workers than the common people. Some of these have since become preachers and pastors at home, and some have gone to labor in heathen lands.

The whole number of preachers and missionaries who have gone out from the Hilo church and boarding-school is: on foreign missions twelve, with their wives; in the home field, nineteen, or thirty-one ministers in all.

From the beginning, the Hawaiian churches were taught the duty and the pleasure of giving to the needy. All the missionaries inculcated this doctrine, so that it became one of the essential fruits of their faith. They were not only taught to provide for themselves and their households, but also to "labor with their hand that they might have to give to him that lacketh."

They received these instructions cheerfully, and the stranger, the friendless, the sick, the unfortunate, and all in distress are cared for, and there is less physical suffering from hunger and want in this than in most countries in Christendom.

All this is, of course, favored by the mildness of the climate, but the disposition and the habit of helping those who need are almost universal in these islands.

For long years after the arrival of the pioneer missionaries, the people had no silver and gold, but they had food and kapas and hands and hearts to help. They gave as they could of their substance; a little arrowroot, dried fish or vegetables, a stick of firewood, or a *kapa*. In 1840, the Wilkes Expedition came, and brought silver dollars; for want of small change, Capt. Wilkes ordered a large amount of Mexican dollars to be cut into halves and quarters. The natives have since fully learned the use of coined money.

It has been my habit to preach on some branch of Christian kindness on the first Sabbath in every month, and the monthly concert prayer-meeting has always been kept up in Hilo. The people have been taught that "it is better to give than to receive," and that "the Lord loveth a cheerful giver." They have given freely for the missions in Micronesia, and hundreds of dollars have already come back to our mission treasury from those recently savage islands, so that our natives think they see a literal fulfillment of the blessed promise, "Cast thy bread upon the waters, for thou shalt find it after many days."

They see also that although the Hilo church has given more than one hundred thousand dollars for the kingdom of God, that they have a "hundred-fold" more now than when they began.

Indolent and vicious foreigners have often expressed great pity for our poor natives because they had been trained by "the cruel and covetous missionaries" to give for the objects of benevolence; but it has now and then appeared that some of these tender-hearted strangers would not scruple to eat the natives' fish and fowl and *poi* without pay, or to drive a hard bargain with them in trade, or to refuse to pay an honest debt. Even Catholic priests professed to pity the Hawaiians because of the heavy burdens laid upon them by their teachers! And the Mormon apostles told our people that the Lord "hated and abhorred our New Moons."

As our monthly concerts occurred on the first Sunday of every month, the natives called them "Mahina hou," which literally means new moon, or new month; the word "mahina," moon, being their name for month, or the division of time marked by the moon. This wicked and deceitful catch of the Mormons upon the term for monthly concert so troubled and staggered my people that I went through my whole field, expounding in every village the first chapter of Isaiah, and the troubled minds were relieved and reestablished.

The contributions for benevolence have been given with great apparent cheerfulness, as if in thorough understanding that "the Lord loveth a *cheerful* giver."

Our custom has been to have the donors come forward and deposit their offerings upon the table in front of the pulpit, and there has been an animation and enthusiasm on such occasions most grateful to the pastor's heart to witness. I have seen mothers bringing their babes in their arms, or leading their toddling children, that these little ones might deposit a coin upon the table. If at first the child clung to the shining silver as to a plaything, the mother would shake the baby's hand to make it let go its hold, and earnestly persevere in her efforts to teach the tender ones the *act* of giving before they knew the purpose. There have been instances where the dying have left with wife or husband their contribution to be brought forward at the monthly concert after their death. Such facts make a touching impression.

From our small beginnings of four or five dollars a month, we increased gradually, till the amount has sometimes been two hundred a month. Before our church was divided our collections amounted yearly to several thousands, and in one case were as high as six thousand; and even after we had set off six churches from the mother church, we have collected over five thousand dollars from the remaining church.

Our people are now greatly diminished by death, and by being drawn away to the numerous plantations of the islands, upon ranches, into various industries with foreigners, and by hundreds into Honolulu, and on board vessels, and yet our monthly collections average more than one hundred dollars.

These contributions have been widely distributed in the United States and in other parts; while many thousands of dollars have gone to sustain our missions in the Marquesas Islands and in Micronesia.

We have also given liberally to sustain our home-work —church building, Christian education, relief of the poor, and other objects.

When we arrived in Hilo there was but one framed house. There were no streets, no bridges, no gardens and only a few foreign trees.

Now our town is laid out in streets all named, and with every dwelling-house numbered. The town is adorned with beautiful shade and fruit trees, with gardens and shrubbery, vines, and a great variety of flowers. The scene is like a tropical Paradise. We have read of

"Sweet fields arrayed in living green,"

and here they are spread out before us even on this side of Jordan.

We have foliage of every shade of green, all intermingled; the plumes of the lofty cocoa and royal palms waving, and the leaves of the mango, the breadfruit, the alligator-pear, the rose apple, the tamarind, the loquat, the plum, the pride of India, the eucalyptus, and trailing and climbing vines, with many-tinted flowers, all glistening and fluttering in the bright sun and the soft breezes of our tropical abode.

Formerly all our streams were crossed as best they might be, or suffered to run and roar, to sparkle and foam, to leap their precipices, and to plunge undisturbed into the sea. Over these brooks and rivers, in town, and through the district of Hilo, more than fifty bridges have been built, some of them costing four thousand dollars.

Once our fertile soil produced very little except kalo and the sweet potato, with a few indigenous fruits; now fruits and vegetables have increased ten-fold in variety and value. But the great staple product of the district is sugar.

During our residence here there have been erected seventeen sugar mills with their feeding plantations, whose total value would probably be more than one million of dollars, and whose products might be more than two millions.

If our Government would take hold earnestly of road-making, with the aid of private enterprise, the value of Hilo soil and of our industries might be increased more than four-fold in as many years.

Sailing along the emerald coast of Hilo, one sees the smokestacks of the sugar mills, the fields of waving canes almost touching one another, and the little white villages attached to each plantation, lending the charm of beauty and variety to the scenery.

The mercantile and mechanical business of our town is greatly increased by these plantations. Mechanical shops are abundant; and so are shops of various character, many of which are owned by Chinamen.

But the plantations do not replenish our town with Hawaiians; on the contrary, while foreigners of many nationalities, especially the Chinese, are increasing, our native population is perishing, or mixing its blood with that of foreign races.

Another great change is, that the people are, or may be if they will, all freeholders. The Bill of Rights given by Kamehameha III., followed by a liberal constitution, and by a code of laws, gave to every man the right to himself, to his family, to hold land in fee simple, and to the avails of his own skill and industry. This was what no common Hawaiian had ever enjoyed before; and so great was the change that a large class of the natives could not believe it to be true. Many thought it to be a ruse to tempt them to build better houses, fence the lands, plant trees, and make such improvements in cultivation as should enrich the chiefs, who were the hereditary owners of the soil, while to the old tenants no profit would accrue. The parcels of land on which the people were living were granted to them by a royal commission on certain easy conditions.

Lands were also put into market at nominal prices, so that every man might obtain a piece if he would. I have known thousands of acres sold for twenty-five cents, other thousands for twelve and a half cents, and still others for six and a quarter cents an acre. These lands were, of course, at considerable distances from towns and harbors. But even rich lands near Hilo and other ports sold at one, two, or three dollars per acre.

Thus the people were encouraged to become landowners, to build permanent dwellings, and to improve their homesteads with fences, trees, and a better cultivation. Gradually many came to believe in the new order of things and to improve the golden opportunity, but others doubted and suffered it to pass unimproved. Those who accepted or bought land now find its value increased ten, and, in some cases, a hundred fold.

The organizing of a constitutional government under a limited monarchy with its several departments, legislative, executive, and judicial, and the admission of the common people to take part in the enactment and execution of laws, and the right of trial by jury, produced a vast and sudden change throughout the kingdom; and to this day it is an open question whether there was not too much liberty granted to the people before they had been sufficiently trained to appreciate and to use it. It may be doubted whether universal suffrage and trial by jury has been a benefit to the country.

The old rule of the chiefs was liable to great oppression and abuse, but where the irresponsible chief was thoughtful and righteous, justice was administered promptly and often wisely, without the interference of quibbling pettifoggers and unscrupulous lawyers.

On one occasion when Dr. Judd and his family were our guests, he hired men to take them by land to the western side of the island, where they were to embark for Honolulu. There were about twelve men thus positively engaged, with wages specified and accepted. The hour for departure came; the men were all present; the party, with baggage, all ready; and then the natives struck for double pay!

I said to the Doctor, "Go straight to our chief woman," who, like Deborah of old, was our judge and sole ruler. He went. Her *posse comitatus* were on the ground in twenty minutes, and the strikers were found guilty and put to hard work in one hour without counsel of lawyer or the aid of a jury.

At another time, a rabble becoming angry at some sailors who landed in the boat of a whale-ship, seized the boat and were carrying it inland as an act of reprisal. Old Opiopio called out her posse of strong arms, seized the men with the boat, put them all in prison, and returned the boat to the ship. Such prompt acts of justice struck the people with awe, and led them to reverence "the powers that be."

These are noble exceptions; but we now have a large set of intriguing lawyers who teach their clients to lie and to bribe witnesses, so that often "justice falls in the streets," the most guilty escape unpunished, and the innocent suffer.

Still there is no going back, nor do we wish it; for in spite of all the eddies and swirls, the back-sets and snags, the stream of civilization flows onward, and, with good pilots and skillful navigators, we trust the ship of state will be saved from wreck.

10

Hawaiian Kings – The Kamehamehas – Lunalilo – Kalakaua, the Reigning King – The Foreign Church in Hilo – Organization of Native Churches under Native Pastors.

TRADITION and history alike tell us of Kamehameha I., the Caesar of Hawaii, the iron-framed warrior, the first legislator, and the first law-giver of the Hawaiian race. We are told how he warred and conquered, and how he united all the islands and all the petty principalities under one chief. There are men still living who have seen this stern old king. He died in 1819.

Liholiho, styled Kamehameha II., was the reigning sovereign when the first band of missionaries arrived in 1820. With his queen he visited England, where both died, their remains being returned to Honolulu in the British ship *Blonde*, commanded by Lord Byron, the cousin of the poet. Kamehameha III., son of Kamehameha I., was on the Hawaiian throne when I arrived at the Islands, having been proclaimed not long before.

He was then a young and mild prince, greatly honored and loved by the whole nation. The natives loved to style him "The Good King." Bad men, both foreigners and natives, beguiled him into some unworthy habits; but his disposition was kind and amiable, and he was the king who gave to the people a liberal constitution with all its attendant blessings.

During the great awakening which spread over the Islands in 1837 and onward, he was greatly impressed with the importance of spiritual things. He was not only an attendant on divine service on the Lord's day, but he was often in the prayer-meetings, apparently an earnest seeker after truth. He was also willing to listen to wise counsels; and during his reign his Government enacted a law forbidding the introduction and sale of intoxicating liquors in this kingdom. The nation became a great temperance society, with the king at its head;

and it was reported that he said he would rather die than drink another glass of liquor.

During his year of abstinence he seemed like a new man. He was awake to all the interests of his kingdom, visited the different islands, addressed large assemblies, and greatly increased the love and homage of his people.

His visits to Hilo were like a benediction; the people flocked around him as they would around a father, and he seemed like a father to them. He visited our families, dined and supped with us, and gave us free opportunities to converse with him, not only on the interests of his kingdom, but also on his own spiritual interests and his personal relations to God and to the eternal future. He has gone with me into an upper chamber where we conversed together as brothers and knelt in humble prayer before the mercy-seat of the King Eternal. On one occasion, when he attended our Sabbath service, I preached from Jer. xxiii. 24, "Can any hide himself in secret places that I shall not see him? saith the Lord." The doctrine of God's omnipresence and omniscience was the subject.

The king seemed one of the most earnest hearers in the congregation, often bowing his head in assent to what was said. For months he seemed nearly ready to unite with the visible church, and his true friends rejoiced over him.

But the spoiler came. He that "goeth about as a roaring lion seeking whom he may devour," was lying in wait for him. The French came with their fire and thunder, threatening his crown and kingdom if the prohibition law on intoxicants was not repealed; and the British lion was ready to stand by the French eagle.

The king was called a fool for coming under the influence of Protestant missionaries. He was, as report said, advised to assert his royal prerogative of independence, and urged to drink with his official and distinguished friends. The poor man, through fear and flattery, yielded, and his doom from that hour was sealed. The old thirst was rekindled within him. A despair of reformation seemed to come over him; the fiery dragon held him fast. He continued to yield to his appetite and to the solicitations of his false friends, and died December 15, 1854, in his forty-first year. On the same day Prince Alexander Liholiho, his adopted son, was proclaimed king, under the style of Kamehameha IV.

This young king was the youngest of three sons of Kekuanaoa and the high chiefess of the Kamehameha family. Kekuanaoa was one of nature's noblemen. He was not of the royal family, but he was of kingly bearing; tall, well formed, and courteous in manners. He was Governor of Oahu and Generalissimo of the royal troops. He was also a consistent member of the mission church in Honolulu. For his splendid physique, his noble bearing, and his mental and moral qualities, Kinau, who was daughter of Kamehameha I. and sister of Kamehameha III., chose him for her husband.

Alexander Liholiho in stature and bearing somewhat resembled his noble father. His reign was short but peaceful, and to some extent prosperous. He visited Hilo occasionally, and our social intercourse with him and his intelligent queen, Emma, was pleasant.

Up to this time all the kings were in the habit of inviting the missionaries and their families to an annual reception at the palace during the season of the General Meeting in Honolulu.

Kamehameha IV. was a fair scholar in English literature, and he spoke and wrote the English language with ease and correctness, having enjoyed the advantages of an excellent training in the Royal School and Boarding Seminary under the charge of Mr. and Mrs. Amos Cooke, of the American Mission, and having also had the benefit of foreign travel with his brother Lot, under the care of Dr. Judd.

He was succeeded by this older and only surviving brother, who came to the throne as Kamehameha V.

Lot was a stern man, with an iron will, and a determination to rule his kingdom himself. He at once refused to take oath under the liberal constitution of 1852, that had been drawn up by our excellent Chief-Justice, William L. Lee. He called a convention of delegates from all the islands, and instructed them to frame a new constitution; and while they lingered and debated, and declared that they had no power to annul or amend the former constitution, because it had provided that all changes and amendments should come from a regular legislative body, he dissolved the convention on the 13th August, 1864, and declared that *he* would give them a constitution by his own royal authority. This he did on the 20th August, and the people, though complaining, submitted, as the high officers of the realm had bowed to his behest and took oath under this, as pronounced by high authority, unconstitutional constitution. The king was "master of the situation."

This king, so far as I know, had no concern in matters of religion, and did not attend any church. He spent his Sundays as he pleased, either in business, in sleeping, fishing, or in other recreations.

He visited Hilo occasionally, but never, I think, to call out his people and address them as a father on any subject affecting their present or future interests. I have known him to come to Hilo with his fishing-tackle, spend a season here, and then pass on to Puna, where it was reported he had his nets drawn on Sunday, and, on his return, he entered our town with his animals loaded with nets and other luggage, and his train of attendants, during the time of service on the Lord's day.

At length he died, and was called before the high tribunal of the King of kings. With him ended the famous dynasty of the Kamehamehas.

Our sixth king, Lunalilo, was the son of a high chiefess. His father did not belong to the family of chiefs by blood; but descent by the maternal line ennobles in Hawaii.

On the death of Kamehameha V., without nominating a successor, Lunalilo sent out a proclamation over all the islands offering himself as the rightful heir to the throne, and calling on all the legalized voters to meet in their respective places and ballot for him. This was done promptly; and on the first day of January, 1873, he was elected by 12,000 votes. On the eighth of that month his election was confirmed by the

Legislature then in session, and on the ninth he was proclaimed king.

This popular election introduced a new feature into our government.

Lunalilo was a bright, cheerful, and favorite prince. He had the habit of using liquors freely, but the people loved him for his wit when under the influence of intoxicants, and for his kindness and good sense when he was sober. He appointed good men for his cabinet ministers and for his privy counselors. He was pleased with the upright, and always took their side in argument.

He soon visited Hilo, where he was received with acclamation. He appointed a meeting for all, and men, women, and children came in crowds shouting with joy, "Ko makou alii keia," "This is *our king*," alluding to the fact that the people had elected him, a privilege never before awarded them. After a good speech to old and young, he shook hands with all the hundreds present, stooping down to the little ones and smiling upon them so kindly that he won all hearts. We conversed with him freely, and he took no offense when urged to abstain from all intoxicants. Had he resisted the evil counsels of boon companions and his own appetites, he might still have been our king, to the joy of all. But his reign was shorter than that of any who had gone before him. He died on the 3d of February, 1874, having occupied the throne a little less than thirteen months.

David Kalakaua, our seventh and present king, was born in Honolulu on the 16th of November, 1836, and elected on the 12th of February, 1874. His parents were both chiefs of an ancient line. The family often spent a good deal of time in Hilo, and the mother died here. His queen, Kapiolani, was brought up in Hilo from childhood. Kalakaua is intelligent, having excellent command of the English language, and having also had the advantages of an unusually interesting tour around the world. We believe that he desires to rule well and see his little kingdom prosper and progress.

The reigns of our kings since Kamehameha I. have been short, and the cause is apparent. Little did I think when we came to these islands that I should live to see four kings buried and a fifth upon the throne. How striking the admonition in the 146th Psalm: "Put not your trust in princes, nor in the son of man in whom is no help. His breath goeth forth, he returneth to his earth; in that very day his thoughts perish."

I have said something in regard to evangelical labors for seamen and for our English-speaking residents.

It was resolved at length to organize a church and seek a pastor for this class of our inhabitants; and on the 9th of February, 1868, a church was organized with fourteen foreign members. On the 26th of July the building was dedicated, and on this occasion the Lord's supper was administered, and three candidates were admitted to fellowship. The edifice will seat about one hundred and fifty. It is neat, and well kept within and without. Standing near the larger native church, it shines like a gem amidst our green foliage.

A call was sent to the Rev. Frank Thompson, who, having arrived with his wife early in 1869, was installed on the 15th of May of that year. Upon the resignation of Mr. Thompson, after a pastorate of a little more than five years, the Rev. A. O. Forbes, son of the late missionary, Cochran Forbes, was settled over this church, where he labored faithfully until he resigned to accept the secretaryship of the Hawaiian Evangelical Association.

The foreign church, though small and not wealthy, is active and generous. They pay a salary of $1,200 or $1,400, furnishing a parsonage to the pastor, and they give generous sums for missionary purposes and for other Christian and philanthropic objects.

During the year 1863 the Rev. Dr. Anderson, then corresponding secretary of the A.B.C.F.M., visited the Hawaiian Islands with a view of conferring with the missionaries on the subject of putting most of the churches under the care of native pastors. He urged the plan earnestly, and a full discussion followed. Some of the missionaries favored the new departure at once, others doubted its wisdom, and others still were willing to see the plan commenced on a small scale, and to watch its operations. Each pastor and church determined the time and manner for themselves. And so the experiment began.

At length I began a movement in that direction, and on the 16th of October, 1864, the first church was set off from the mother church, and a native was ordained and installed over it. Not long after, on Oct. 14, 1866, I organized another church in the district of Hilo, and a third in 1868; and pastors were ordained over them.

One was organized in Puna in 1868, and two more in 1869, so that there were now six churches set off from the old one. All these were provided with good and neat houses of worship under my direction, and with church bells. Most of these churches had one, two, or three chapels, or smaller meeting-houses, which served as places of meetings on secular days, and on Sabbaths near evening. For a great many years the natives were accustomed to hold morning prayer-meetings, and they might be seen assembling at early dawn every day in the week.

The original cost of these churches and chapels, with that of keeping them in repair and furnishing them with bells, would amount to about $10,000, and that of the central church and its chapels would be about $20,000.

The number of church members dismissed to organize the six new churches was in all 2,604.

They have had ten pastors. Of these, five are dead, two have been called to other places, one has resigned on account of age and infirmities, and two only remain at their posts. This would be nearly the record of our Hawaiian pastors over the whole group. They waste away rapidly by disease and death, and they change places often. Some wear out; some fall into sin; and some engage in other callings. A goodly number run well, being steadfast in the faith, diligent workers, and patient withal.

We are often asked how our native preachers wear, and whether we were not hasty in making them coordinate pastors with the missionaries. These questions may be answered differently by different observers. Some, perhaps many, of our number think it would have been better to have waited longer before giving them the full power of ordained pastors, that while they should have been trained to work with the missionaries, as they had been, with the most happy results, they should not have been so soon put upon a parity with them.

While subordinate, they are more docile and respectful; when on a parity, they sometimes show a disposition to be assuming and discourteous, an effect occasionally seen elsewhere in men on a sudden elevation.

The native ministers now outnumber us more than five to one, and when we meet in our evangelical associations they know, of course, their numerical power, and it requires great wisdom on the part of the foreign members to secure that influence which is necessary to good order and to harmonious action. In our Association for Eastern Hawaii we have never as yet had any difficulties of a serious kind, and yet we are liable to them, especially when some self-conceited stranger comes in as a disturbing element.

A Democratic or a Republican Government can never be strong, and pure, and permanent unless the people who create it and hold the power are intelligent and moral. And the same law holds true in church polity. From our point of view we think that we see clearly how the Episcopal and the Catholic church governments originated, as a matter of necessity, in the midst of peoples who were ignorant, unstable, and not to be trusted with responsible power. I do not find in the Bible, or in the wisdom of all commentators and expositors of the sacred Scriptures, any definite and fixed rules of church polity, but rather the elements of many.

Congregationalism is excellent where all or most of the members of a church are intelligent and virtuous, or where men know how to govern themselves and their children.

The Presbyterian government is strong, and when exercised wisely and in meekness it is good.

Prelacy might seem necessary in certain states of society, and the right of choice can hardly be disputed by wise, candid, and liberal minds.

Our Hawaiian churches are not called Episcopal, Presbyterian, or Congregational, or by any other name than that of the Great Head, the Shepherd and Bishop of souls. We call them *Christian churches.*

11

Compensations - Social Pleasures - Some of our Guests and Visitors.

FROM the almost entire absence of civilized society, we have now come to enjoy the fellowship of a community of families and individuals equal, on an average, in intelligence, morality, and refinement, to any with which I am acquainted. In addition to the three mission families who have been longest on the ground, there is around us a little community of families of missionary descendants of the first and second generations. The number of cultivated and scientific visitors from other parts of the world is also increasing.

When in 1835 we were stationed at Hilo, a good brother missionary wept and condoled with us because of our banishment from civilized society, our communication with friends so slow and uncertain. But we believed our destination was ordered of the Lord. The feeling of joy with which we first hailed the sight of its beautiful harbor, its fields of living green, its shining hills, has never left us. And while we have tilled our garden, saying, Let its moral beauty outshine its physical, and "its righteousness go forth as brightness, and its salvation as a lamp that burneth," we have found our life full of compensations.

I do not now regret a sojourn in "that great and howling wilderness" of Patagonia, or my perils on the sea and in the rivers; my painful travels on foot over thousands of miles, or my hungerings and thirstings in cold and heat, nor any suffering that the Lord has laid upon me in His service. They all seem light and momentary now, and there is full compensation in the joy the Master has granted me.

I have spoken of the visits of seamen to this port, and of the religious efforts in their behalf. Their coming often added to our social comforts. The very sight of the stars and stripes at their masthead, the snowy canvas, or the weather-beaten and tempest-torn sails, was pleasant. Many of the masters brought cultivated and pious wives, and from time to time they, with their little children, would be left with us for months while the ships were absent on their cruises in the north, the southeast, and west. Not a few sailors' boys and girls have been born in Hilo, and several have been born in our house. We have formed near and lasting friendships with many of these visitors. We have nursed sick sailors under our roof, and sent them home healed, so far as we could judge by their conduct and profession, in soul and body. We have buried the remains of seamen in the soil of Hilo, attended to their secular affairs, and written to parents and friends by their request; we have found out the wandering sons of senators, clergymen, and men of wealth and distinction, as well as of the poor and lowly, and received the tearful thanks of parents, comrades, and friends.

The dust of a wild young English physician lies in our cemetery. He was the son of a clergyman, and his mother, sisters, and brothers were all Christians, while he wandered, like the poor prodigal, into realms unknown to his mourning friends. He was shy of the missionaries, but in his wildness the hand of the Lord arrested him. He fell from a horse and received a mortal injury. In his misery he sent for me; he knew his wound was fatal, and he felt that he must be forever lost. When I pointed him to the Lamb of God and spoke to him of the blood which cleanseth from all sin, he exclaimed, "Can it be possible that is for *me*—that I can be saved?" He came at last to trust, his despair fled, and in three days he died in peace on the very day he had set for his departure from earth. We buried him with tears, and thanksgiving to Him who "giveth us the victory." There was printed on the slab that marks the repose of his mortal part this stanza from one of his own poets:

> "By foreign hands thy dying eyes were closed,
> By foreign hands thy clay-cold limbs composed,
> By foreign hands thy humble grave's adorned;
> By strangers honored and by strangers mourned."

A tender and grateful answer was received to the letter written to his parents.

We had, at different times, not less than five professed physicians who offered their services to our public. But one after another four of them died, and the fifth left the country, and shortly after, he also died. All these were intemperate, and some of them were bitter haters of the missionaries and opposers of the work of the Lord. The career of four of them was very short, and their deaths were sudden and admonitory.

Our great volcano has attracted many hundreds of visitors, and they have come from nearly all the nations under heaven. Many have been distinguished scientists. Statesmen and foreign officials of almost every rank have looked in upon us, and our intercourse has been most precious with the many Christians that we have been permitted to entertain.

Chief-Justice William L. Lee, chancellor of the kingdom, spent many days with us. Coming from the United States in 1846, he was a leader in our government until his death in 1857. His chief labors were the drafting of the Constitution of 1852, the civil and penal codes, and his arduous and gratuitous services as President of the Land Commission, which abolished feudalism, and gave each native his land in fee simple. A man of high ability, integrity, and of charming personal character, his name can never be forgotten in Hawaii.

Prof. C. S. Lyman, of Yale College, was our guest for three months, and his scientific tastes and acquirements, and his mechanical skill, made his visit especially interesting. We used to say that with a jackknife, a file, and a gimlet he could make anything. An excellent sundial, a complicated rain-gauge, with a clock attachment, a self-opening and closing valve, and a scale that marked the day, the hour, and the moment of rainfall, with the exact amount of water, and a bookcase of *koa* wood for my study, were some of the proofs of his skill. He made, also, one of the best surveys of Kilauea crater that I have ever seen.

He once accompanied me along the shores and over the highlands of my missionary field, sharing with me my simple fare and my rocky beds, and cheering me with his delightfully genial companionship.

How vividly I remember one incident in our tour! We were returning from Puna over the highlands where, for fifteen miles, there were no inhabitants. Our trail lay through forest and jungle and open fields of wild grasses and rushes. We heard that about midway between the shore and an inland village there was a small grass hut built by bird-catchers, but now abandoned. We struck for that, and reached it a little before sundown. We entered with our two native burden-bearers, and congratulated ourselves on having found a shelter for the coming cold and rainy night. In less time than I can write the story we began to jump and stamp and dance. What is the matter? we exclaimed, and looking down upon our legs we saw them sprinkled thick with fleas, those terrible back-biters that never talk. We ordered a hasty march and went on at double-quick through bush and brake, scattering our actively bloodthirsty foes by the way. After a mile's walk we skirted a forest, and here, sheltered from the wind, we halted and began our works of defence from the coming rain and cold. Without axe or saw we broke off limbs of trees and made a little booth, which we covered with grass and leaves, and then prepared wood for a fire.

Alas! we had no matches, no lamp, no candle. What next?—One of our natives took his pole, which they call the *auamo* (yoke), on which they carry burdens, and by hard and rapid friction with another dry stick he soon raised smoke, and fire followed. At nine P.M. it was a roaring fire at which we dried ourselves, and when we had eaten our scanty supper, and offered up thanks to the Lord, we lay down to sleep—or not to sleep—as the case might be.

Long after this Mr. Wm. T. Brigham, of Boston, spent a season with us, and went the same rounds with me. On this occasion we visited a pulu station upon the highlands, and in a deep forest. Here were about thirty or forty men and women employed in gathering this soft, silky fern-down for upholstery, and here, ten miles from Kilauea, we saw the natives cook their food over hot steam cracks without fuel. Near the volcano this is frequently done.

The widowed Lady Franklin was our guest for a while. The patient, hopeful, and earnest woman was then (1861) in search of her husband, Sir John Franklin. It was sad to see her hopes blasted.

An honored officer of the British army in India once spent a week with us. He came an entire stranger, but by his great intelligence, his urbanity, his noble figure, and his gentlemanly address, he made an indelible impression upon us. And this impression was deepened by such a frank and affecting tale of his life as filled us with interest in his behalf. His mind was in such a state that his appetite and his sleep often departed from him. He occupied an upper room in our house with a door opening upon a veranda, which afforded a good and quiet promenade. Often during many hours of the night we could hear his foot-falls as he paced to and fro through the still watches. He was always with us at our morning and evening hours of devotion, and he seemed to enter earnestly into these exercises.

At length he could no longer restrain his feelings, and begged that we would hear his tale of sorrow.

He began, saying: "I was once a happy man, but now I am miserable. I had a very dear friend, a fellow officer in the army, and I loved him as my own soul. On a certain occasion, and through a misunderstanding, an altercation took place between us, and he hastily gave me a challenge. I, under a false sense of honor, as hastily accepted. We met, and my bullet pierced his heart. I saw him stagger, and ran to hold him up. His warm blood spurted over me. He said, faintly, 'You have killed me.' He gasped, and was dead. I laid him down; the sight of his pale, ghastly face filled me with horror. That image haunts me everywhere. It comes to me in my dreams. It stares at me in my waking hours; it haunts me like a ghost; it follows me like my shadow; and I am miserable. I have attended church, have read my Bible through and through, to find something on which to hang a hope. I have read sermons and systems of theology; I have wept and prayed, but no comfort comes to me. In spite of all my prayers, and tears, and struggles for pardon and peace, the ghost of my murdered friend haunts me. It wakes me at midnight, it confronts me by day, and what can I do? Is there any hope for such a blood-stained sinner as I am?"

His plaintive story struck us dumb for a while; our hearts were melted with sympathy; but presently we blessed the gracious Lord for this opportunity. We saw his difficulty, that he was filled with "the sorrow of the world which worketh death." He had labored in agony to *save himself*, and the cloud of despair grew thicker and darker over him. I at once pointed him to "The Lamb of God who taketh away the sins of the world." "Yes," said he, "but can Jesus forgive *my* sin? It seems too great to be forgiven." I assured him that "the blood of Jesus Christ cleanses from *all sin*," and that Isaiah had told us long ago, that if we would but listen to our God, "though our sins be as scarlet they should be white as snow, and though red as crimson they should be as wool." And that Jesus "will in no wise cast out" one penitent sinner that comes to Him. It was his duty, and it was an infinite privilege to believe and accept pardon and peace as a free gift of God, while it was an insult to God to doubt His call and His promises; this "treading underfoot the blood of the Son of God" would be a greater and a more fatal sin than to have shed the blood of his friend. He accepted the offer of salvation, and rejoiced in hope. He found, to his joy, that there is "a blood which speaketh better things than the blood of Abel," or the blood of his murdered companion.

After he left us he remained some time in Honolulu, and we there met him again on our annual visit, just before he embarked to return to India.

We have heard from him several times since, and learned that he had been promoted in the army and in civil life, and that he was happy. He was, I think, six feet four inches tall, weighing some 225 pounds, well formed, a man of great physical power, of superior strength of intellect, and excellent executive ability. With a heart and conscience of tender sensibilities, he was "bold as a lion" in all he felt to be right, but he quailed before what he believed to be wrong.

We have not only enjoyed the privilege of entertaining men of rank, but also men of low estate, for poor and friendless strangers came to our distant shores as well as the rich and the noble, and we feel it to be no less, and often a greater, privilege to care for the neglected and needy than for the honorable. The lessons of Christ are plain, practical, and personal. "*I was hungry* and ye gave me meat," "When thou makest a feast—call the poor," "Remember the stranger" and "Be careful to remember the poor." And we have sometimes entertained angels unawares.

I should like to speak of many more of those whose acquaintance we have made, and who have been our guests in our Hilo home; as Admiral S. F. DuPont, the gallant officer, the accomplished gentleman and the sincere Christian, whose dearly-cherished friendship we enjoyed until the day of his death; or of Admiral Pearson, who with his wife and daughter spent a season in our family. On our visit to the United States in 1870 both Mrs. DuPont and Mrs. Pearson spared no pains to see us in their homes.

But time would fail me to speak of the visits of the venerable Dr. Anderson and his wife, of Boston; the gifted Dr. Boyd and his estimable wife, of Geneva, with whom we held sweet converse; the "Friends" Wheeler, of London; Joel and Hannah Bean, of Iowa; President Moore, of Earlham College, through whom we have been brought into Christian fellowship with many of his denomination; of Dr. Thompson, of Detroit, who in his advanced years came to look upon this distant missionary field, and was almost enamored with the beauties of Hilo; of the Rev. Mr. Hallock, who with glowing heart went back to tell his people of what he had seen in these isles of the sea; and of many others whose visits of Christian love and fellowship were cheering and refreshing in this far-off land.

If these brief seasons of communion on earth are so sweet, what will the reunion of kindred spirits be in the eternal world where love forever reigns?

Of one other guest I would speak somewhat more fully, for from our humble abode she went up to the palace of the King in heaven. In the midst of earnest missionary work with her husband, the Rev. J. D. Paris, located on the southern shores of Hawaii, she was stricken down with consumption. They came to our house and were our guests until she died; and here on the borders of the unseen world, while she still lingered, she spoke words of such triumphant faith that I would transcribe them anew.

When told that no one thought it probable that she would recover, she was silent for several minutes; then calling her husband to her bedside, she said: "Do not be anxious about me; I commit all to the Lord, to live or to die. I have had a strong desire to be spared for your sake and that of our little ones. I have hoped that I might live to see the image of Christ impressed upon their hearts. They will need a mother's care, a mother's watchfulness; but let His will, not mine, be done. He has always been good to me, infinitely better than I deserve. Let us leave all with Him; His time is best."

To the question how she felt in regard to her spiritual state, she replied: "I have no distressing fears. I know that I love the Saviour and that He loves me. I sometimes shrink from the thought of death and the cold grave; but when I look beyond all is calm, all is peace."

Hearing one speak of "the dark valley and shadow of death," she asked, "What does that mean? I do not understand it. I look upon death very differently. Jesus will come and take the soul to Himself. It will be released from its house of clay and wafted to immortal glory. The valley does not look dark to me now, perhaps it may; but I think it will not be dark to me anywhere if my Saviour is with me, and He will never, no, never leave me."

One night when her end was near, she urged her husband to seek rest. He objected, as her hands were cold and her pulse feeble and irregular, and he feared she would swoon away and awake no more.

"You ought not to say so," she replied. "It would be a blessed end to swoon away into the arms of my Saviour and awake in His image. Do not be afraid. If Jesus should take me away from your side without a struggle or a groan, would you grieve?"

On another occasion, when Mr. Paris read

"On Jordan's stormy banks I stand,"

and spoke of Bunyan's river of death, remarking that she now stood on the verge of this river, she replied: "I do not like that view of death. Our blessed Saviour has told us that He will come again for His own and receive them to Himself. I love to believe His words and to commit myself to Him. If He takes me to Himself death is swallowed up in victory. What are all the dark valleys and rivers if Jesus is with us?"

I said, "Do you see your way clear?"

"Yes," she answered promptly, "it is all clear; there is no cloud, no darkness; all is light up to the heavenly hills."

Morning was breaking upon the mountains of Hawaii, while a morning of unending brightness was dawning on her soul. Her mortal powers gently gave way; "the silver cord was loosed," and she quietly left us in our tears for the bosom of her Saviour.

12

Seedling Missions – Hawaii sends out Missionaries – Need of a Missionary Packet – The Three "Morning Stars."

IN the prosecution of our work on the Hawaiian Islands, an active missionary spirit was developed in great strength. This was of course one of the legitimate fruits of a faithfully preached and truly accepted Gospel.

We sent a mission to the Marquesas Islands, which for years we conducted under great disadvantages. We had no packet to communicate with that group, but were obliged to charter small and uncomfortable vessels, at high prices, to carry out our missionaries with their supplies and to send out our annual delegates to look after and encourage them.

Then as our funds and men increased we thought that the Marquesan field was too small for our energies, and the idea sprang up in the minds of some of our brethren that we might "lengthen our cords" by exploring among the numerous islands to the west, and establishing a mission in Micronesia in conjunction with the American Board.

This thought ripened into action, and American and Hawaiian missionaries were sent out. Still we had no vessel at command and were obliged to look to others to supply this want. Hence arose the thought of securing the needed packet.

I proposed that we should request the Board to call on the children of the United States to contribute in shares of ten cents for such a vessel, and that her name be *The Day Star*. This was agreed to, and the mission appointed me to write to the Board at Boston on the subject.

The proposal met with favor, with only one amendment, viz., that the name should be *The Morning Star*. The call on the children to take shares in this enterprise was popular, and it spread over many States. The needed sum was raised, and the *Morning Star* (No. 1) was built, manned, and provided. In due time she sailed from Boston with the prayers and benedictions of a multitude and with the old song,

"Waft, waft, ye winds, his story,
And you, ye waters, roll."

On the 24th of April, 1857, having braved the billows of the Atlantic, swept round the stormy Cape Horn, and sped halfway over the Pacific, the beautiful schooner reached Honolulu. Thence she sailed for the Marquesas Islands with supplies; and on her return, early in July, she appeared off the entrance of Hilo harbor, dressed in all her white sails with her flag fluttering in the breeze and with her star shining in the center.

Hilo was jubilant. We had heard of her sailing, had counted on her time, and had been watching for her arrival. Arrangements had been made to give her a hearty welcome. Parents and children came hasting in from all quarters, winding over the hills and along their footpaths and filling our streets.

Captain Moore came on shore with his officers and passengers, and was met by the well-dressed and decorated children in double file, bearing a flag prepared for the occasion. With songs of welcome they were waited upon to the great church, which was soon filled to its entire capacity. Prayers were offered, hymns and an original ode to the *Star* were sung, addresses made, and all went off with a hearty goodwill. We were happy on this occasion to welcome the Rev. Hiram Bingham, Jr., with his young wife, bound to Micronesia, and little knowing what sufferings awaited them in those dark and distant islands.

Afterward the natives were invited on board the vessel, and as our children had given freely for the vessel, they inspected her with many expressions of admiration and delight, feeling their importance as joint owners of the beautiful packet. The people, old and young, brought liberal gifts of fruits and vegetables, fishes and fowls.

The *Star* remained two days and then sailed for Honolulu with the good wishes of all Hilo.

This packet, after years of service in the Pacific, was sold for a merchant vessel, fitted out and left the islands for China, but has never been heard from since her departure.

The *Morning Star No.* 2 was built by the funds received from the sale of the old one, supplemented by further gifts from the children. She was a larger, better built, and more convenient boat than the first and did good service. But her end came all too soon. After a successful cruise among the islands of Micronesia, and on leaving the little islet of Kusaie, or Strong's Island, when all seemed propitious, she drifted upon the rocks and was broken in pieces. All on board escaped to the land to wait an opportunity to return to their homes.

This event seemed sad, and some of us have not ceased to think that we need, and ought to have, steam as an auxiliary motor to help our packet in calms, in adverse currents, and when in danger on entering and leaving dangerous harbors. All the important secular interests of the world employ steam and other discoveries and improvements in all the departments of science, art, and industry. We harness the lightning to our cars; our thoughts flash under deep oceans, over towering mountains, and through mid-air. The business of this world challenges all the forces of nature to its aid, and why should the Gospel move so slowly? Why should the angel that flies through the midst of heaven with the Gospel message move with clipped wings? The artillery of war moves on swift wheels to shake the nations and pour out human blood, while the old sails flap, and the lazy boom squeaks mournfully in the doldrums, as our vessels are driven hither and thither by the squalls and storms of capes that obstruct their way to the lost tribes of men. If the Lord will, I hope to hear the whistle of a missionary steamer in our waters before I go hence.

Two Stars have set in the West, and here comes the *Morning Star No.* 3, fairer and brighter than those which have disappeared, well built, larger and better than the other two.

The insurance money on No. 2, with another lift from the children, had soon brought her keel into the waters, raised her well-shaped spars, set up her standing, and arrayed her running rigging, clothed her with a white cloud of canvas, and run up her beautiful flag to wave in the breezes of heaven. Well furnished, with a well-appointed crew, with an excellent captain and good officers, she is now (1880) on her tenth voyage to Micronesia, taking out supplies to the laborers in that widening field, and a reinforcement, long waited for, for the Gilbert Islands.

13

The Marquesas Islands - Early English and French Missions - The Hawaiians Send a Mission to Them - My Visit in 1860 - The Marquesan Tabu System.

THE Marquesas Archipelago consists of thirteen islands, only six of which are inhabited, viz: Nuuhiva, Uahuna, Uapou, Hivaoa, Tahuata, and Fatuiva. Seven are small islets or rocky piles of little importance.

The group is divided into two chains, trending N. W. and S. E., between the latitudes 7° 50' and 10° 30' south, and longitude 138° 30' and 140° 50' west.

The windward group was discovered in 1595 by Mendaña de Neyra, the commander of a Spanish squadron bound from Peru to colonize the Solomon Islands during the reign of Philip II. of Spain, and was named Las Marquesas de Mendoza in honor of the Viceroy of Peru.

The leeward islands, though but a short distance off, were not discovered until 1791, nearly 200 years later, when they were seen by Capt. Ingraham, of Boston, and named Washington Islands. But the term Marquesas now embraces both groups, as it properly should, the inhabitants being one in language, manners, and race.

The origin of the group, like that of the Hawaiian, is distinctly igneous. All the islands give evidence of having been raised up from the depths of the ocean by volcanic fires. The surface is mountainous and exceedingly broken. The coasts rise from the water like walls. Deep gorges, lofty promontories, bold bluffs, serrated ridges, perpendicular buttresses, sea-walls plunging thousands of feet into the sea, turrets, towers, cones pointed and truncated, rocky minarets, needles, spires, with confused masses of rocks, scoria, tufa, and other volcanic products, testify to the terrific rage of Plutonic agencies in unknown ages past. Many of the ridges are so precipitous and lofty that they can not be crossed by man. And many of the rocky ribs come down laterally from the lofty spine, or dividing ridge, on an angle of 30°, and form submarine and subaerial buttresses, leaving no passage except in canoes. The lowest of these inhabited islands reaches a height of 2,430 feet above the level of the sea, and the highest, of 4,130. Most of them have fertile valleys half a mile to three miles deep, and from one-tenth of a mile to a mile wide, with rills of pure water falling from the high inland cliffs, and rippling along rocky and shaded beds to the ocean.

The valleys are also filled with luxuriant shrubs, vines, and magnificent trees.

The inhabitants are of the Polynesian race, and their language was originally the same as that of the Hawaiian and Society Islands, Cook's Islands, New Zealand, and other islands of the Polynesian archipelagoes.

They are more bold, independent, fierce, and bloodthirsty than most of their neighbors, and they have always been cannibals of the most savage kind. The men are large, well-formed, and powerful, and many of the women do not lack in physical beauty. They dress very little, and mostly in bark tapa, like the ancient Hawaiians. They live in small thatched houses, and feed on cocoanuts, breadfruits, and fish.

They were once numerous, but the introduction of foreigners and foreign diseases have wasted them so that they have been reduced more than two-thirds.

In 1797 the English ship *Duff* took Messrs. Crook and Harris to the Marquesas as missionaries. The natives were fierce-looking and savage, and Mr. Harris preferred to return in the same vessel to Tahiti. Mr. Crook remained alone at the island of Tahuata about six months. He then went to Nuuhiva, where he lived six months more, and then returned in a whale-ship to England, hoping to come back to the Marquesas with a reinforcement of missionaries. Eventually, however, he joined the mission at Tahiti.

In 1821 two natives of the Society Islands were sent as missionaries to the Marquesas, but fearing the savages, they soon returned. In 1825 Mr. Crook revisited the Islands, leaving two Society Island Christians at Tahuata. These also soon returned, and were succeeded by others who remained but a short time.

In 1831 Mr. Darling, an English missionary of Tahiti, visited the group and left native teachers at Fatuiva and Tahuata. These, like their predecessors, had no success and returned.

At length the Hawaiian mission took up the subject of evangelizing the cannibals of Marquesas. The first step was to send a delegation thither to examine the situation; and, in 1833, Messrs. Armstrong, Alexander, and Parker, with their wives, went to Taiohae, Nuuhiva, to labor for the good of the savages. But their situation was so uncomfortable, and the circumstances of the ladies and children so distressing, not to say dangerous, that they all returned after eight months to the Hawaiian Islands, which were even then a paradise compared with the Marquesas.

In 1834 Mr. Stallworthy and Mr. and Mrs. Rodgerson, of the London Missionary Society, arrived from England, and in company with Mr. Darling, of Tahiti, commenced labors at Tahuata. After one year Mr. Darling left, and in 1837 Mr. and Mrs. Rodgerson sailed for Tahiti, Mr. Stallworthy remaining alone until August, 1839, when he was joined by the Rev. R. Thompson. But these two did not continue long, and the London Missionary Society, after repeated and earnest efforts for the occupation of the field, abandoned it without success.

The history of these efforts to tame the Marquesan cannibals is remarkable and the failure sad. For more than forty years company after company of devoted men and heroic women toiled and prayed for that stubborn race, and gave up in despair. And the history of these tribes is unique among the Polynesian family.

And now come the efforts of the Roman Catholics among the Marquesans. In August, 1838, Du Petit Thouars, commander of the French frigate *Venus*, brought two priests and one layman to Tahuata, and in 1839 these were followed by six priests and one layman.

In May, 1842, Admiral Thouars took forcible possession of the Islands, and the priests have occupied them at several stations ever since.

In 1853 the Hawaiian Board of Missions sent out its first band of missionaries to those shores, and these have been reinforced from time to time, and have been visited and encouraged by delegates of our Board.

Our first station was at Omoa, on the island of Fatuiva, the southeast island of the group. Afterward stations were taken on all the inhabited islands except Nuuhiva, where our American missionaries labored in 1833. As a delegate, I have been permitted to visit this Mission twice, and have seen every island and every station of the group.

My first visit was in 1860. We sailed from Hilo, March 17, in the *Morning Star No.* 1, under command of Captain J. Brown, and anchored in Vaitahu, or Resolution Bay, Tahuata, April 11. This bay forms a quiet and safe harbor on the leeward side of the island. It is half a mile wide and half a mile deep, walled on the right and left by lofty and rugged precipices some 2,000 feet high, with a beach of lava, sand, and shingle. From the shore a narrow and rough valley, one-eighth of a mile wide and one mile long, extends inland until it ends in a bold precipice some 2,500 feet high, rising on an angle of 45° to 50°. The island, like the rest of the group, is a great heap of scoria, tufa, cinders, and basaltic lavas, bristling with jagged points, traversed with sharp and angular ridges, and rent with deep and awful chasms. The valley is fertile, and well filled with the breadfruit, cocoa-palm, pandanus, hibiscus, and other trees and shrubbery. The orange, lemon, lime, vi, and guava have been introduced.

The number of inhabitants upon Tahuata at the time of my visit was only 154, though it had once been several hundreds. We had one Hawaiian missionary with his wife in this valley, and they were laboring patiently in a small school, but with little encouragement. The people seemed hardened against Christianity, and no wonder, for in 1842 the French took possession of this bay, after having crushed the natives. They fortified the little rookery at great expense, and only to abandon it after seeing their mistake. They built a strong fortress upon a high bluff commanding the settlement and harbor, and mounted cannon on a high precipice on the right ridge of the valley to enfilade the village. They also built a house for a governor, a chapel, an armory, a bakery, etc.; but when I was there, all was a scene of dilapidation and ruin. The garrison and most of the guns were removed; a priest only remained.

But small and unimportant as this island is, the French did not conquer it without loss of blood and treasure. On one attack, Captain Edouard Michel Halley, commander of a French corvette, was killed, with six of his marines, by the natives. All landed in martial order, formed a line, as reported to me, on the beach, and with drums beating, flags waving, fifes piping, and with bugle blast the line moved forward up the valley in full confidence of subduing the dark savages at a single blow. But as they advanced among the trees and jungle, on the right and on the left, from this bush and that, from behind tree and rock, and from overlooking cliffs came the shots of an ambushed enemy. The deadly missives whizzed and struck. Six of the marines were killed, and also the captain. When the men saw their commander fall, they were struck with consternation and retreated to the ship.

The remains of the fallen sailors were carried up near the head of the valley and buried. With the Hawaiian missionary and Captain Brown, I visited the cemetery. It is an area of about one-quarter of an acre, surrounded by a plastered wall, and full of bushes. Beside the tomb of the captain lie the remains of the marines, covered with slabs of basalt. We found the slabs tilted and sinking into the earth, and the surrounding walls falling. Dilapidation is setting its seal upon all these graves, and after sad reflections on the fate of the gallant heroes, we "left them alone in their glory."

Why should the professed disciples of the "Prince of Peace" endeavor to propagate the Christian religion by the use of fire and sword? And why do men who call themselves "priests of the Most High God" call in the aid of weapons, and go and come and live under the cover of cannon?

Did the Captain of our salvation teach His disciples such doctrines?

From Vaitahu we went to Hivaoa or La Dominica. The missionary at this station was the Rev. Samuel Kauwealoha, a native of Hilo, and a member of the Hilo church. He came out in his boat, boarding us five or six miles from the shore, and gave us a most hearty welcome. We landed on a beautiful beach of white sand, and walked half a mile through a charming grove of tropical trees, along the margin of a crystal brook. This runs through the whole length of the valley, which is one mile in length and one-fourth of a mile wide, enclosed on three sides with lofty and steep hills, and opening to the sea in front. It is a paradise of natural loveliness, charmed forever with the music of its rippling stream.

We found Mr. Kauwealoha living in a substantial stone house, 25 by 44 feet, with walls ten feet high, a cellar, floor, glazed windows, and thatched roof, and all built by himself. He dived for the coral, burnt it into lime, hewed the blocks of basalt, made the mortar, and did all the work of the carpenter and mason. Here, amidst the shade of lofty trees, he was living with his devoted wife, teaching the children to read and write, and preaching "Christ our Life" to 149 savages; and here, under the shadow of a towering tree, I spent one of the happiest Sabbaths of my life. The almost naked and tattooed savages came out and sat quietly in semicircles under the tree, with the bright-eyed little children in front, all seeming to love their teacher, and to welcome the stranger, to whom they listened, Kauwealoha interpreting. When service was over, they came forward with outstretched hands and glistening eyes and gave me their *Kaoha*, the same as the Hawaiian *Aloha*, "love and greeting."

One service was held at sunrise in the house; the next service under the tree, at 10 A.M., when sixty were present. We had also a Sunday-school, where the pupils recited the Lord's prayer and the ten commandments, with some other lessons, in tones and inflections of voice which were soft and melodious.

At 11 A.M. Captain Brown and his mate, Captain Golett, a good Christian man, who had commanded many a ship, came on shore with the crew of the *Morning Star*, and we had service in English. At 4 P.M. another service was held with the natives, making four for the day, beside much time spent in conversation with those of the islanders who lingered around and seemed tame and docile.

The wilder savages would come up now and then to the outer side of our circle, half concealed among the trees, gaze at us with their keen black eyes, talk and laugh among themselves, strike fire and smoke their pipes, and then retreat a little into the bushes and lie down to sleep. Some were armed with muskets and spears, or bayonets fastened to poles. The men were naked, except the maro. The women wore a light drapery made from the paper-mulberry.

Wars had raged in this valley, but after the arrival of the missionary, there had been quiet for a longer time than usual. It had been nearly a universal fact that the inhabitants of no two valleys had lived in harmony. Every valley had its chief who was constantly watching the people of the valleys on either side of him. These were separated only by narrow and high ridges, upon the jagged crest of which enemies would lie in ambush in the night. As soon as the morning dawned they watched the huts below and fired upon the first one who came out of doors.

Even in this little Eden-like valley there were two hostile clans, one at the head of it and the other near the shore. These watched each other, as the tiger of the jungle watches his prey, and when opportunity offered they killed and ate one another. It was hoped that the presence of our missionary would prevent all further hostilities. Our hopes were vain. Before my second visit to the Marquesas, a fiendish quarrel arose among the cannibals; Kauwealoha's fine house was plundered and torn down, and he with his heroic wife fled the valley never to return. Thus the savages extinguished the rays of light which had begun to dawn upon them.

On Monday, April 16th, we took our energetic friend, Kauwealoha, on board the *Star*, as my companion, guide, and interpreter, and sailed for the island of Fatuiva. At Omoa, its largest and most populous valley, was the resident missionary, J. W. Kaivi. It was at this station that our pioneer missionaries were first landed, and here they labored together for a long time before they separated to occupy other islands. The fruits of these concentrated labors are seen in the greater tameness of the people, especially of the children.

On landing, I found myself surrounded with merry and bright-eyed boys and girls, all shouting in glee, "Kaoha, kaoha, ka mikiona"—Love, love, to the missionary. Many struggled to get hold of my hands to lead me to the house, and to please as many as possible, I offered a finger to one and another. Thus I was led by ten laughing children, while others caught hold of my arms, and elbows, and of the skirts of my coat, shouting *kaoha*, until we entered the house of Kaivi. Surely, thought I, here is material for a Christian civilization, and with wise and faithful training, these boys and girls may become kind and good men and women, and never kill and eat one another. I have not seen brighter or sweeter looking children than these on the Hawaiian Islands.

Not the children only, but many of the adults rallied around and filled the house, while scores remained outside for want of room within. My heart was touched by the scene, it was so different from that on Vaitahu, when powder and iron hail had driven the people of the valley to madness.

The valley of Omoa is three miles deep and, in some places, one mile wide, with five lateral branches half a mile or more deep, and like Hanatetuua, it is walled with towering precipices on both sides and in the rear, filled with magnificent trees, breadfruit, cocoanut, palm, candlenut, hibiscus, pandanus, banana, South Sea Island chestnut, orange, and others. The soil is of great richness. A fine stream of water, which runs the whole length of the valley, furnishes an excellent place for watering ships.

The day after our arrival, Kaivi, Kauwealoha, Timothy, one of my Hilo church members who accompanied me, and myself, took a stroll of four hours up the valley, and we were more and more delighted with its beauty and fertility. But we were everywhere pained with the marks of savage idolatry and cannibalism. The number and nature of the tabus were shocking. We saw tabu houses, tabu trees, tabu hogs, tabu tombs, tabu places for offering human sacrifices, and tabu theaters or places for lascivious dances, where with midnight drums and infernal howlings the most obscene orgies were performed. These theaters are oblong spaces of 100 or 200 feet in length, and fifty feet in breadth, cleared, leveled, and sometimes paved with slabs of basalt, and enclosed with a wall four to eight feet high and as many wide. On this broad parapet, or wall, the men are crowded to witness the lascivious dances in the space below, while the masses of women are kept outside of the enclosure.

Kauwealoha told me that he had sometimes stolen visits to these places of lust and blood and human sacrifices, and found them strewed with human bones, the remains of men who had been slaughtered, roasted, and eaten in part, and in part offered to the gods. These and scores of other tabus have their histories of cruelty and horror which I can not here find time and space to explain. But what was uttered by a prophet of old is still true: "The dark places of the earth are full of the habitations of cruelty."

At an examination of the school of Omoa which we attended, forty boys and girls were present, and were examined in reading, writing, geography, arithmetic, and Scripture recitations. Some of the pupils read and wrote well, and many gave evidence of bright and active minds. I spoke to parents and children on the salvation through Christ and on the value of education. In the evening the little church of six members, together with the missionary Kaivi and his wife, and three from the *Morning Star*, partook of the Lord's supper. Here were some of the first-fruits of the Gospel among the Marquesans. There sat the tall and dignified Natua, now baptized Abraham, with his quiet wife Rebecca. Abraham was a chief and a man of influence, and we hoped he might be the leader of many faithful disciples. The other members were Eve, a very aged woman, Joseph, Solomon and his wife Elizabeth.

All these had eaten human flesh, and drank the blood of their enemies. They were now sitting at the feet of Jesus, and in their right minds, eating and drinking the emblems of that body which was broken, and that blood which was shed for man. It was a precious season, and one which may be remembered with joy during eternal ages.

But notwithstanding the success which has attended the Gospel and the school at Omoa, the large heathen party are still bloodthirsty cannibals, and always at war with the people in Hanavave, a valley five miles distant. The watchful belligerents kill and cook one another, whenever they can do it secretly. Only a short time before our visit a robber came within ten yards of the missionary's house to kill a woman who was alone in her hut. Kaivi and his wife heard the rustle of the dry fallen leaves and went out softly under cover of shrubs and descried the assassin, and began to throw stones, when he ran, and the woman was taken into Kaivi's house for protection. On another dark night a blind woman was sleeping alone, her husband having gone on board of a vessel, when a cannibal with a long knife entered the house to dispatch her; but before the bloody deed was done, a large dog seized the monster, and in the struggle the neighbors were aroused, and the invader fled up a steep precipice and escaped to his own place on the other side of the ridge.

A spy also came to Omoa professing great love for the people and hatred for those of his own valley. So insinuating was he, that the Omoans were deceived, and adopted him as a friend. He became a favorite with parents and children, and after some days he invited two boys to go with him upon the ridge dividing them from Hanavave, where they would find ripe berries. The boys went cheerfully, and when they had ascended high and were out of sight of the people below, he drew a large knife, seized one of the lads, and severed his head from his body. The other boy fled for his life down the hill and gave the alarm, but the assassin went on and down to his valley with the bloody trophy in his hand.

We visited the hostile Hanavave in two of the ship's boats, as the distance is only five miles, and the sea smooth. The natives of Omoa were afraid to go with us, lest they should be killed, but our Hawaiian missionaries are safe and free to travel where they please, so Kaivi went with us.

The sail along the lofty sea-wall was delightful, and the white foaming streamlets rushing down deep and precipitous gorges, or leaping from a height of 1,500 feet, presented a scene of exquisite beauty.

Our missionaries in this valley are the Rev. Lot Kuaihelani and his wife. We examined a school of twelve boys and girls under the care of Mrs. K., who taught them to read, write, and sing. Then after a season of prayer and exhortation with the people who came together, we took a stroll through the valley. It was a scene of charming loveliness, but most of the people looked wild and savage.

Bare-legged soldiers were strutting about with old muskets, rusty swords, and bayonets fastened on poles, and all seemed to feel as important as imperial guards. Near the center of the valley we found a military captain with a squad of soldiers engaged on a zigzag fortification of stone six feet high, four feet thick, and nearly half a mile long, pierced with loopholes for muskets. I asked the stern man in command, why they fortified with so much labor and zeal. He replied, "To protect my people." "But suppose you make peace with your enemies and live quietly?" "I can't; they come in the night, and lie in their canoes behind the rocks, and when we rise in the morning they fire at us, and their bullets whiz and strike our trees and houses, and kill our men and women." "Yes, and you try to kill them." "That's right; we good, they bad. You go talk with our enemies in Omoa." "I have been there and told them to love their enemies and stop fighting, and they say yes if you will stop." He replied, "They are *bloody liars*; they will come to kill us, and I must defend my people." And then lifting up his foot, he showed me a scar where a bullet had gone through his leg. Another came and turned his naked body to me, asking me to look at his shoulder-blade which had been pierced by a bullet, and then feel the ball lodged just within the skin of his breast. I examined and found it so. I said to him, "Let me cut that bullet out, it can easily be done."

"No, no," said he, "I will always carry that bullet in my breast. It makes me strong to fight!"

Only three weeks before our arrival, there was a sea-fight between three double canoes of Hanavave valley and three whale-boats of Omoa. One man of the canoe party was shot through the body, and the canoes made a hasty retreat.

We returned to the *Star*, and the next day sailed for Puamau, on the northern side of Hivaoa. This is the station of Rev. James Kekela and his good wife Naomi.

Puamau is a large valley, with 500 inhabitants. With Kekela and Kauwealoha, I went all over it to its head, two miles inland, where it terminates in an abrupt precipice 2,000 feet high. We passed over hill and vale, and through forest and open spaces, and saw the houses and large numbers of people and many bright-eyed children.

We visited the tabu houses and grounds, and in a forest of lofty trees we saw their great *Heiau*, or place of feasting, dancing, and of offering human sacrifices. Walled terraces were built up of large stones, and with great labor, and a paved floor was prepared for dancers, who with naked, oiled bodies, adorned with feathers and fantastic ornaments, keep up the most obscene orgies all night till daybreak.

On these terraces stood several stone images of enormous size, in the form of men and women. Some had fallen, some were mutilated, but one stood perfect in gigantic proportions. This figure was nine feet high and three feet six inches in diameter, with head, eyes, mouth, neck, breast, trunk, and upper and lower limbs. The base of the stone was planted deep in the ground. It was made in ancient times, and brought half a mile from the quarry to this place. Probably it would weigh ten tons. The natives have been offered one hundred dollars to remove it to a ship, but the present generation know of no mechanical power to do it.

It was to this place of infernal rites that Mr. Whalon, first officer of the American whale-ship *Congress*, was brought in 1864, bound hand and foot for slaughter, and to be devoured by savages.

A Peruvian vessel had stolen men from Hivaoa, and the people were waiting for an opportunity to revenge the deed. Mr. Whalon went on shore to trade for pigs, fowls, etc., and the natives, under the pretence of hunting pigs, decoyed him into the woods, where, at a concerted signal, large numbers of men had been collected. Mr. Whalon was seized, bound, stripped of his clothing, and taken to this *heiau* to be cooked and eaten. This was in the afternoon. The savages then began to torment him, bending his thumbs and fingers backward, pulling his nose and ears, and brandishing their hatchets and knives close to his head. Kekela, our missionary, was then absent, but a German, hearing of the affair, went to the place and begged the savages to release their victim. This, with ferocious grins, they refused to do, saying that they relished human flesh, and they were now to feast on a white man. On the return of Kekela the following morning, he hastened to the scene of action, and begged for the life of the poor man. But the savages were inexorable, unless for a ransom. They demanded Kekela's boat and all his oars. It is said that a chief of another clan objected to the boat being taken from him, as they were often accommodated with it on going on board ships.

Finally an exchange was effected among the contending cannibals, and for a gun and various other articles Mr. Whalon was released. The missionary took him to his house, and with his intelligent wife showed him the greatest kindness and attention.

The ship, on account of this tragic event, had gone out to sea, keeping at a safe distance from land until the mate was brought on board with great rejoicing.

Mr. Lincoln was then President of the United States. Hearing of this deed of Mr. Kekela and his helpers, he sent out the value of five hundred dollars, with a letter of congratulation, as a reward for the prompt and successful action which saved an American citizen from death at the hands of Marquesan cannibals.

Kekela had only twenty-six pupils in all, and those were very irregular in their attendance. We spent a Sabbath at

Puamau, and I preached to fifty people inside of the house, while numbers were standing or walking outside, some looking in at the windows, some pacing to and fro, talking, laughing, or lying down, getting up, lighting pipes and smoking. Old warriors, fantastically decorated with feathers and sharks' teeth, and carrying axes, hatchets, spears, old muskets and rusty swords, and whalers' harpoons, scouted around us among the trees, with their sharp, black eyes glaring upon us, and anon disappearing in the thicket.

In the afternoon I preached to an assembly of one hundred, who sat quietly before me under a large tree. Boys meanwhile were climbing trees around us, swinging upon the branches and chattering like monkeys, and noisy children were gamboling upon the ground. Guns were often fired during the day; the ring of the tapa-beater was heard from the huts; fishing canoes were scattered over the bay, and the multitudes went on with their work or sport as on other days. There was no Sunday.

Near Kekela's house there is a Catholic station; but it was painful to hear that the priests do little to create respect for the Lord's day in the minds of the people.

Several individuals appeared interested in religious instructions, and we believe that faith and love and patient labor will not be lost upon this benighted people. But they are a hard race, bold, independent, and defiant. The longer I remained, the more deeply I was impressed with the depravity into which they are sunk. In theft, in licentiousness, in guile, they are unrivaled; in revenge they are implacable. They know no mercy, and their selfishness is unmixed.

Their government, so far as they have any, is feudal. Every valley has its chief; some have twenty or thirty chiefs; and feuds, robberies, wars, and bloodshed are the normal condition of the people. Scarcely a clan can live in peace with its neighbors. There are no laws to forbid or to punish crime. Every man must be his own protector and avenger. If his wife is ravished, his house burned, his property stolen, he has no appeal but to his own arm, his own weapon, and the red vengeance which boils in his heart. If he is a weak man, he keeps a close mouth, lest a lance or a bullet pierce his heart. His only redress is to watch his opportunity and do as he has been done by.

Among the men, tattooing, which is a long and painful process, is nearly universal. Their faces and bodies are so nearly covered with grotesque figures that they appear almost as black as Africans.

The shaving of their heads is equally grotesque and fantastic. Some shave only the crown, or one side; some leave a small tuft of hair on the apex only; others shave a zone quite around the center of the head, and others still shave several such belts.

Were it not for these artificial disfigurations, the Marquesan physique would be fine. The males are tall and well formed, and dwarfishness and obesity are very uncommon with them. But at Puamau we saw one monstrous exception, a man with a full-sized head and body, with legs only one foot four inches long, and arms but one foot long. The limbs were of ordinary thickness.

In the valley of Hanahi, Mr. James Bicknell, son of one of the English missionaries of the Society Islands, was stationed by his own request. Capt. Brown hearing that there was no safe harbor here, sent Mr. Bicknell's supplies in a boat, in which I took passage. This is a new station, with a population of only ninety souls, but there is a populous valley on each side of it. There was no school here, but Mr. Bicknell has one convert, whom he has baptized. The valley is small, rocky, not well watered, and less inviting than the others that I visited.

In 1859 a little boy was roasted alive in Hanahi as a sacrifice to the gods, and I was shown the place where this horrid deed was done.

The romantic little valley of Hanatita, on the north side of Hivaoa, is occupied by the Rev. A. Kaukau and wife, Hawaiian missionaries.

All the missionaries of the three islands met in this place to hold a convention. There were eight in all, with most of their wives and several delegates, representing 3,000 Marquesans and reporting 34 church members, 221 pupils, 76 readers, 40 writers, 67 in the outlines of geography, and 104 in arithmetic. The chief woman of Kauwealoha's station labored over the lofty ridges on foot with her 24 girls to attend this convention and examination. As all canoes and boats are rigidly taboo to the women, they have no other way to leave their valley except to climb the rugged steeps, or swim around the cliffs and headlands, resting now and then by clinging to some jutting crag or rock along the sea-walls.

These twenty-four bright-eyed girls were neatly robed in a profusion of thin white tapa, worn loosely and tied in a large knot on the shoulder. Their hair was gathered into a crown on the top of the head, and confined by bands and nets of tapa so thin and delicate as to resemble gauze. Many of them wore delicate ear and wrist ornaments made by the natives. This picture looked like the dawn of civilization, and was in delightful contrast with most of the scenes I had witnessed in the group. After the examination of Kaukau's school of nine girls, we went on with the business of the convention, spending five days in deliberations and discussions on a great variety of practical questions, interspersed with frequent prayers. The meetings grew in interest from day to day, and the parting scene was touching. Every member of the convention offered prayer, and there was not a dry eye in the company.

Learning that a landing could be effected at Heteani, on the south side of the island, where Paul Kapohaku, "Paul the Rock," had been stationed, our captain agreed to return the missionaries to Fatuhiva, and then sail round the eastern end of Hivaoa, and lie off and on opposite Heteani, while I with Mr. Bicknell, Kapohaku, and his wife, should climb the heights of the mountain, some 3,500 feet, to visit that lone station where he would send in his boat to receive me on board.

Early the next morning, May 1st, taking one of the ridges which led to the summit of the mountain, we commenced our toilsome ascent, sometimes on an angle of 10°, and at other places of 30° to 40°. Our path led up steep and sharp ridges, down which on either hand we looked into depths of 500 or 1,000 feet below. I measured the breadth of the spur or rib on which we ascended; it was two feet and four inches wide in one part of the way; in another it was only one foot in width, with awful gorges on either side. Mr. Darwin, describing a similar climb which he took in the island of Tahiti, says: "I did not cease to wonder at these ravines and precipices; when viewing the country from one of the knife-edged ridges, the point of support was so small that the effect was nearly the same as it must be from a balloon." The extraordinary sharpness of these ridges and abruptness of these mountain slopes may be accounted for by the absence of violent storms in these groups, and more especially by the fact that there is never any frost to disintegrate these sharp ridges and fine-drawn peaks.

After two hours of exhausting toil and heat we stood on the dividing ridge of the island. The summit was a level plateau about half a mile broad, and covered in most part with a dense jungle of ferns, hibiscus and other trees and shrubs. Here we were shown the fighting grounds of the clans from the north, where they met those of the southern valleys, and engaged in deadly conflict with spears, clubs, and stones. Many of the abraded stones brought up from the shore were still seen scattered over the battlefield.

The scene from this height was grand in the extreme. At our feet lay the broad Pacific, shining like molten silver, and from this elevation showing no ripple. Around us was a vast panorama of cones, ridges, spurs, and valleys. Hills heaped on hills, and spires bristling among spires, the whole appeared as if a sea of molten rocks, while raging, tossing, and spouting in angry billows, had been suddenly solidified by an omnipotent power. It was a wild assemblage of hills and ridges, of gulfs and chasms, of towers and precipices.

Our descent on the south side of the island occupied three and a half hours, and was even more difficult than the ascent, on account of the roughness of the trail. Over many steep declivities we had to let ourselves down over the rocks with the utmost caution; one false step would have plunged us into certain destruction. But we arrived at the shore safe and weary at 4 P.M.

We found the people of Heteani cordial, and our labors there were as at other places. Nowhere did we meet a more enthusiastic "*kaoha!*" But in all the valleys on this side of the island cannibalism is fearful. Paul showed me the place where he had witnessed the cooking and eating of human flesh by the heathen party, and he had no power to prevent it. He also told me shuddering stories of the fightings, the murders, and the fearful cannibalism which prevailed all around him.

On the morning of the 3d of May, the good *Morning Star* came into the offing, and the boat landed and took me on board.

Sailing down the smooth channel, three miles wide, which separates Hivaoa from Tahuata, we looked into all the valleys as we opened them, until we rounded the bluffs of Tahuata. On the 4th we were off the mouth of the spacious harbor Taiohai, the principal harbor of Nuuhiva. This bay is about two miles deep, half a mile wide at the entrance, between two grand headlands, and expanding to a mile in breadth as we came to the center. Its shore is a beautiful crescent of sand, interrupted here and there with shingle and boulders.

The French, on seizing this island, fortified the harbor at great expense, and for many years kept up a strong garrison on the land with ships in the harbor. They built a large arsenal, a house for a governor, a cathedral for a bishop. We looked into the fort, and upon the shore battery cut into the rock, called on the bishop and the governor, saw all the public buildings, and rambled over the town. We also found the house where our missionary brethren, Armstrong, Alexander, and Parker, with their families, sojourned for eight months in 1833. But we found no war-vessels and no garrison except half a dozen gensd'armes. The shore battery was dismantled, the fort and other public works in a state of dilapidation, and the folly of making war on savages as a means of civilizing and Christianizing them was apparent.

We also visited the grounds where the gallant Captain Porter of the United States ship *Essex* pitched his tents in

1813, indulging his crew in those pleasures which were but the prelude to the day of slaughter which soon fell upon them in Valparaiso. The steep and lofty precipice was also shown us up which his marines were made to drag his cannon to thunder terror and death upon the poor Marquesans in an adjoining valley.

The tabu system, in the Marquesas Islands as in other parts of Polynesia, is ancient, complex, and deeply rooted in the social and religious polity of the people. A few notes upon it may interest the student of the subject. The following are forms of the tabu:

Toua, war.—When the men go to war it is tabu for the women to go out of doors to bathe, to attend to their toilet, or to eat more than is necessary to sustain life. The god of this tabu is *Fu*.

Fae Pue, house of prayer.—This house is built and dedicated to the god *Hiniti* by a feast, at which swine's flesh and other food are offered to the god. No woman can ever enter this house, and no man except those who are invited to the dedication feast. After the dedication the *fae pue* is closed, signals are placed upon it, and it is never again entered. I saw many of these houses.

Tehe, circumcision.—This must be done in a new or sacred house, dedicated to the god *Nukukoko*.

Wauupoo, shaving the head.—This must be done in the sacred house, and no one must ever step on a lock of the hair.

Utatapu, the *hula* or dance.—The actresses undergo long previous training, during which time their persons are sacred to the gods.

Tahu, tattooing.—During this long and painful process the subject is shut up in a house with the operator, and may not be seen by his friends until he is healed. This often requires months.

Boring the Ears.—The subject and the operator are closely confined in a sacred house, where offerings of food, fish, hogs, etc., are made to the gods.

Tabu Food.—*Poi* pounded by a man is strictly *tabu* to women; not so *vice versa*. Bananas, cocoanuts, squid, skipjack, and many other articles, must not be eaten by men and women together, though each may eat cocoanuts from separate trees. Food planted, cooked, or pounded by a child may not be eaten by the mother.

Tabu Places.—Houses standing on posts, and all raised structures, as platforms and seats around *hula* or other public places, and stone structures for the pounding of *poi*, are *tabu* to women.

All roads and paths made by men are *tabu* to women.

Places of human sacrifice are *tabu* to all but priests. We could not get consent to visit one.

Charnel houses are *tabu* to all but friends.

Miscellaneous *tabus*.—Mats may never be carried or handled by men, though they sleep on them.

When a man is in the cabin or hold of a vessel, it is *tabu* for a woman to be on deck. So of all other superposition. On board the *Morning Star* we had some droll scenes resulting from this *tabu*.

The heads of all males are *tabu*. One day I ignorantly laid my hand on the head of a man who sat on the ground beside me. He instantly started, shook his head, brushed off my hand, looked wild, and ran off as if his hair had been lighted with a lucifer match. I saw him no more. Seeing us laugh with incredulity at their faces, another man crawled up to my feet, took my hand and laid it on his head. Most of the Marquesans observe this tabu, though some are brave enough to despise it.

Canoes are strictly *tabu* to women. They never sail in them, nor dare they touch them. This is a cruel tabu. If a woman wishes to visit a ship, she must swim to it. If she have wares to sell, as pigs, bananas, fowls, etc., she must swim them off to the vessel. All the women that came on board the *Morning Star* swam from the shore. If she wishes to visit friends on another island, she can never do it; if to go to another valley, she must climb rugged mountains and struggle over ridges where her life is in danger; or if the way by land be quite impassable, as is often the case, she must swim around bluffs and along the rugged shores until she reaches some point or crag where she can hold on and rest; pursuing her way, endangered by sharks and by the surf, until she makes her port, or perishes in the attempt.

It will be seen from the above, that the subjection and servitude of women are a principal feature of the tabu.

Returning on board the *Star*, we bore away around the western side of Nuuhiva, looking into all the valleys and dells as they opened one after another to our view. Among others, we passed the famed valley of Taipi (Typee), the scene of Herman Melville's narrative drawn from the life. Bearing away for Hawaii, we dropped anchor in Hilo on the 16th of May, having been absent just two months.

On this visit to the Marquesas I gathered, from the reports of the missionaries at their general convention, the following statistics:

The whole number of pupils, more or less, under their instruction, ...	221
Whole number of readers, ...	76
" " of writers, ...	40
" " in rudiments of geography, ...	68
" " in mental arithmetic, ...	125
Whole number of church members, ...	34
Whole number of the population to whom they had access, ...	2,800

These results, though on a small scale, seemed encouraging, compared with the long, repeated, and unfruitful efforts which had been made before, and there seemed hope that, by patience and perseverance, many of these savages might be tamed, and the diabolical and bloody rites which had been practiced from time immemorial be utterly abolished.

The laws enacted and enforced by the French governors in the Marquesas have checked murders and cannibalism wherever they could be brought to bear upon the guilty. And some of the governors have been liberal in their sentiments, and willing that the savages should be tamed and Christianized by any who would undertake the self-denying task.

14

Second Visit to the Marquesas – The Paumotu Archipelago – Arrival at Uapou – An Escape by Two Fathoms – Nuuhiva – Hivaoa – Kekela's Trials – Savage Seducers – A Wild Audience.

ON the 3d of April, 1867, I embarked again, on board the *Morning Star No.* 2, to revisit our Marquesan mission. The *Star* was commanded by the Rev. Hiram Bingham, Jr., who had brought her out from Boston, and who was still her captain. My associate delegate was Rev. B. W. Parker, and we had for fellow-passengers Mrs. Bingham and Mr. Parker's daughter, and a daughter of our missionary Kekela.

We also had on board the body of Joseph Tiietai, one of the first converts of Omoa, who had died at Honolulu while on a visit there.

In 1865 Mr. Bicknell left the Marquesas and returned to Oahu, bringing with him seventeen Marquesans, male and female, in order to train them on the Hawaiian Islands, and then return them to teach their people. Of these seventeen, nine died within two years, and the eight who survived were anxious to return to their old homes. We therefore took them on board. They were all baptized before they left Oahu, Mr. Bicknell recommending them as converts to Christianity. On our eighth day from Hilo, Meto, the wife of one of the returning Marquesans, died after a sickness of several weeks, professing her faith in Jesus. At four P.M. the corpse, having been prepared for burial, the *Morning Star,* as she was rushing along at the rate of nine knots an hour, was hove to, and lay quietly on the bosom of the deep, as if conscious of the power, and listening to the voice of Him who "rules the raging of the sea." All hands were assembled in the cabin, and appropriate services were held, when the remains of the poor woman were committed to the deep, to be seen no more until "the sea shall give up her dead."

It was a solemn scene, and the first of the kind I had ever witnessed. All the attendant circumstances of committing a fellow-being to a lone grave in the deep and dark waters of a vast ocean combined to impress us with the worth of man. The winds, the waves, the inanimate ship, and all surrounding objects, seemed to pause, and, with rational beings, to bow in silent reverence before Him whose high behest remands our bodies to the grave and calls our spirits before His bar.

Sleep, Meto, in thy cold and silent tomb, and let the waves of mid-ocean roll over thee! They shall not disturb thy quiet slumbers until the voice of the archangel calls thee from thy long repose. Thou wast once blind, and a savage, but "the day-spring from on high" dawned upon thee ere thou wast called away, and we have hope for thee that thou wilt appear a shining angel among the joyous throng who have been redeemed from among all nations and kindreds and peoples and tongues.

On the 21st of April we made the Paumotu Archipelago, a group of about one hundred atolls, or coral reefs, enclosing lagoons. This group lies between the Marquesas and the Society Islands. Their name, Paumotu, signifies "all islands." Those that we sighted were Taroa and Taputa, in lat. 14° 22' south, and lon. 144° 58' west. We sailed within two miles of the shore, and saw the beautiful islets resting like swans upon the smooth water, while the rippling wavelets lapped the white beach, and the palm and emerald shrubbery adorned the coral ring.

Different islands of this archipelago were discovered by different navigators and at various times: by Quinos, in 1606; Maire and Schouter, in 1616; Roggewein, in 1722; Byron, in 1765; Wallis and Carteret, in 1767; Cook, in 1769, 1773, and 1774; Bougainville, in 1763; Boenecheo, in 1772 and 1774; Edwards, in 1791; Bligh, in 1792; Wilson, in 1797; Turnbull, in 1803. Later and more careful observations have been made on this beautiful group by Kotzebue, in 1816; Bellingshausen, in 1819; Duperry, in 1823; Beechey, in 1826; Fitzroy, in 1835; and Wilkes, in 1841. Wilkes estimated the population at 10,000. The people were represented as in a semi-savage state. The islands are all of coral formation, and were built up by that silent and wonder-working architect, the so-called coral insect.

Our view of these islands, garlanded with green, and shining under a tropical sky, was enchanting, but the moral picture was dark. Why are these thousands of immortal beings left to perish in ignorance, poverty, and paganism?

The *Star* went about and stood off from the shore, and in a short time these beautiful gems of the Pacific, with their white beaches, their silvery lagoons, and their emerald chaplets sunk below the horizon and disappeared, and we bade adieu to the charming sight with a sigh.

Our first anchorage at the Marquesas Islands was on the 28th of April, in the bay of Hakahekau, island of Uapou. The Rev. Samuel Kauwealoha, whom we left in 1860 in his beautiful valley and nice stone house at Hivaoa, and who, as before reported, was driven out by savage war, had come with his wife and a few Marquesan friends to this island, which had not been occupied before by our missionaries.

Before we had anchored he came on board the *Star*, and in an ecstasy of delight, welcomed us to his simple home. He piloted our vessel into the harbor, where she was anchored. We sat down to dinner after prayers and thanksgiving, supposing that all was well. On rising and going on deck, Capt. Bingham perceived that the *Star* had dragged her anchor. The current was strong, and the wind was blowing in squalls from one side of the bay to the other. Every strong gust caused the anchor to drag, and we were going slowly but surely toward a jagged and rockbound shore. All hands were called, a kedge was carried out from the bows and planted in the bay, to check the drag; but anchor, kedge, and schooner were all moving at every gust toward the shore, on which the vessel must, if not arrested, be smashed like a cockle-shell.

A line was coiled into the boat, with one end fastened to the capstan, and with this the men in the boat struggled for an hour or more against the wind and current, before they could reach the opposite shore. At last they gained it when the stern of the vessel was only about two fathoms from the frowning rocks, on which the surf dashed high and fearfully. They made the line fast to the rocks on shore, and men at the capstan began to turn, slowly and carefully at first, fearing that the line would part, which would have resulted in sure and swift destruction to our beautiful *Morning Star*. But she began to move slowly to the windward, and our hearts beat with hope and joy at every foot gained. At length she was moored by a hawser to the rocks on the windward shore of the harbor and our agony was over. It was near night, and the natives on shore had waited in vain to welcome us, and to attend divine service, it being Sunday; several, however, came off in their light canoes to help us. The tact and great strength of Kauwealoha, and the help of his boat and crew, were of great service to us; indeed without this help our escape might have been impossible.

At evening we went on shore and held service in the missionary's house. On the next day we explored and admired the beautiful valley of Hakahekau. It is three miles long and one-fourth of a mile wide, with a limpid brook babbling through its whole length. The whole valley is crowded with magnificent trees, evergreen vines, and shrubbery.

The mountains, hills, ridges, spurs, domes, and lofty cones of this island are very grand. Within a vast amphitheatre of rugged hills which send down their spurs to the shore, buttressed by lofty precipices, are eight remarkable columns, two hundred to three hundred feet high, and fifty to one hundred feet in diameter, rising in solitary grandeur, and standing against the sky. They give the island the appearance of a castellated fortress, and are landmarks which may be seen far at sea, marking the bay. The fantastic mountain forms in the Marquesas Islands are amazing.

The population in 1853 was supposed to be 1,000 but ten years later the small-pox carried off most of the people, so that only 300 remain, and this luxuriant valley is nearly depopulated. Not a house remains in the upper part, and only five or six are clustered along the shore. Thousands of ripe cocoanuts and breadfruits fall to the ground and rot, for want of hands to gather and mouths to eat them. Solitude and silence reign in the old heiaus, and on the grounds where midnight fires once burned, where human sacrifices were offered, where the lascivious dance and the wild orgies of heathen souls made the groves resound, where the shouts of the warrior were heard, where the *hulahula* drum beat during the livelong night, and where dark savage forms move like ghosts amidst the spectral gloom. Those baleful fires are extinguished, and the voice of revelry is hushed in death. But, alas! darkness still broods over the few who remain on this island. We will, however, hope and pray for brighter days.

Leaving Uapou, we crossed the channel twenty-two miles and anchored in Taiohai, Nuuhiva. We had heard that the French government in Tahiti was displeased because Mr. Bicknell had taken a number of Marquesans to Oahu, without first asking leave. Our mission at this time was to explain to the governor that the Marquesans had been taken to Honolulu only to be instructed, and the explanation satisfied his excellency.

On the 30th of April we sailed from Uapou to Nuuhiva, twenty-two miles due north. At Taiohai, or Port Anna Maria, the principal harbor of the island, we took a French pilot, Mr. Bruno, who brought us to anchor at 5 P.M. Taiohai is a noble bay and safe harbor, some two miles deep and one mile wide, but narrower at the entrance. The views in this bay are enchanting. The peaks of the island rise to the height of 3,860 feet. Almost every pinnacle is carpeted with grass and mosses, or festooned with vines; even on the perpendicular walls of the precipices a tapestry of shrubs and verdure hangs. This is the harbor where Capt. Porter, of the *Essex*, reveled in 1813. From this bay, in 1842, the gifted Herman Melville, with his friend Toby, absconded to the hills, and made his devious and toilsome way to the Taipi valley, from which, in spite of its paradise-like beauty and its bewitching enchantments, he was but too glad to escape. I saw the valley he threaded, the cane-brake through which he struggled, the ridge he bestrode, the jungle where he concealed himself, and the towering summit over which he passed. Melville lost his reckoning of distances as well as his track. The enchanted valley of Taipi, Melville's "Typee," is only four hours' climb by the trail from Taiohai; and from ancient times there has been a well-known trail from the head of one valley to the other. This of course the young fugitive did not find. The distance is not over five miles, and the Marquesans walk it, or rather climb it, in three or four hours. The valley of Hapa, (Mr. Melville's Happar) lies between Taipi and Taiohae, and is only two or three hours' walk from the latter. These three valleys are all on the south side of the island, and adjoin each other. During all his four months of romantic captivity, the gifted author of "Typee" and "Omoo" was only four or five miles distant from the harbor whence he had fled.

We called on the bishop, who received us politely, and entered into free conversation with us, and with two English gentlemen, residents, we visited the French nunnery. The Lady Superior received us with great urbanity, and introduced us to the two Sisters. The Superior was a large woman, of fair complexion and dignified bearing. All of the ladies were ideals of scrupulous neatness in their attire. Their institution was inclosed with a high wall of basalt, in which two buildings of thatch, some sixty feet each, were erected, with school-rooms, dormitories, kitchen, and chapel. The grounds were ample and well kept, and there was an air of neatness about the whole establishment. The number of girls was reported to us as sixty, ranging in ages from four to fifteen years. They are taught to read and write, to sew and embroider, and to gather breadfruits, cocoanuts, etc., and to cook their own food. The expenses of this institution are borne by the French Government, and the annual estimate is $120 for each girl.

The island of Uahuna is thirty miles east of Nuuhiva. Here, on the 3d of May, our missionaries, Laioha and his wife, welcomed us to their thatched cottage, and the people were called together by the sound of the horn. Donning their light tapas, they came streaming in from all the jungle trails of the valley, bringing their children for examination. Boys, girls, and adults gathered around us with beaming faces, grasping our hands and saluting us with their melodious "Kaoha." Thirty-two pupils were examined, after which we held religious services, and celebrated the Lord's supper as was our habit at the various stations. We then returned to the *Star*, taking with us Laioha, and José, a Peruvian whom I had baptized at Puamau in 1860, when he took the name of David.

The history of this David José after his baptism was interesting. Desiring to labor for Christ, he went of his own accord in 1863 to Hooumi, a valley adjoining Taipi, on Nuuhiva, where he labored earnestly and without pay to convert the people to Christ, working with his own hands to supply his bodily wants. He collected thirty pupils, who were greatly attached to him, and for whom he had high hopes.

Soon the small-pox struck the people with the blast of death. Consternation seized the multitude, and leaving friends and relatives to their fate, many fled to the mountains or wherever else they might hope for shelter. And faithful David had forty cases under his care with no one to help him. Of these, twenty died, and he buried them all with his own hands. He labored on until 1866, when the French sold the valleys of Hooumi, Taipi, and Hapa, adjoining one another, to a company who ordered David to leave.

Again we crossed the channel to the valley of Hanamenu, on the island of Hivaoa. Here we landed the six surviving Marquesans, brought from Honolulu, who belonged to this place. On landing, there was a rush to the shore and a great wailing. Fathers, mothers, brothers, and sisters wailed fearfully for their kindred who had died on Oahu. Soon, however, were heard the thuds of the falling breadfruits, and the squealing of pigs, and a great feast was prepared in a short time.

Mr. Bicknell had made Hanamenu one of his stations, and had labored earnestly with the people. Kekela also, and Kauwealoha had visited this beautiful valley, and many of the people seemed tamed. A Marquesan catechist was stationed here, and taking the old hopeful converts, and those just returned from Oahu, we were requested to organize a church at this station. This was done, and Kekela was chosen pastor for this church of ten members, seven men and three women.

On our way from Taiohai to Puamau we had heard of savage war in this valley, and had been warned to approach it carefully. Kauwealoha and others advised us not to land until Kekela came on board to report, as the only safe landing-place had been in the hands of savages hostile to the friends of Kekela. So we kept off and on, outside. At length two boats came out of the harbor; one steering westward soon disappeared, and Kekela came alongside in the other, informing us that the westward-bound boat was the last of a large fleet of war canoes returning to their own valleys. Kekela leaped on board with tears, and was surprised to find his daughter, who came passenger with us, weeping on his neck.

He told us that the war had just ended, that the last fighting had been three days before, that the people who for months had been hidden in caves and in fastnesses, were now crawling out, and that the cannibal chief who had been so eager to eat Mr. Whalon was shot dead on the previous Sunday. So the door was opened to us, and just in time for our entrance.

Kekela seemed discouraged. The war had demoralized his people. He had no church, his school was broken up, his congregation dispersed, his pigs and potatoes were stolen, his mules and donkey killed and eaten, and one of his out-houses burned; bullets had struck his house, and several nocturnal attempts had been made to burn his large stone dwelling, and this had been saved only by vigilant night-watching. After doing what we could to calm and encourage the peace party, we took Kekela and wife with four children and sailed for Atuona, a station on the south side of Hivaoa, and occupied by Mr. Hopuku and wife.

We examined a school, organized a church of five members, found an interesting people and good working missionary and his wife, and left the valley, impressed with the great romantic beauty of its natural scenery and its luxuriant growth of tropic trees, and with a hope in its moral advancement. We sailed the same evening for Omoa, Fatuiva, where we were to carry the remains of Joseph Tiietai, one of their chiefs and an early convert to Christianity. Here again we had been warned to approach the bay with caution, because it had been reported that the people were greatly exasperated at the death of this chief, and of a number of others of the valley, in Oahu. The *Star* was kept out at a good distance from land to watch the movements on shore, for it was said that armed boats and canoes would come out to take her. Soon, however, Kaivi's boat was alongside, bringing good old Abraham, a brother of Joseph, and several others. By them we were assured that it was safe to land, as they had succeeded in quieting and reassuring the people, who had been very angry and threatening.

The remains of the chief were taken on shore and received by his friends with loud wailings. All the night after the funeral exercises were held, the most fearful wailings were kept up, especially by his sister. Men and women tore their hair, and cut themselves with sharp bamboos till they were smeared with blood.

The next day, May 12, being Sunday, we sat up until midnight to converse with the people who came in, to examine candidates for the church, and Mr. Hopuku for ordination. On the morrow the ordination took place; seventeen candidates were baptized and received to the church on profession of faith, and one by letter. Ten had been received before, making the whole number gathered into this church twenty-eight. Of these four had died. The Lord's supper was then administered to about forty communicants, representing seven nationalities.

The decrepit Eve Hipahipa of fourscore years was brought in the arms of friends. She clasped our hands in both of hers, and with tears and a fervent *kaoha* laid them on the top of her head as if to ask a benediction.

At the general meeting held in this place, where the *Star* remained five days, it was resolved that Mr. Kekela endeavor at once to establish a boarding-school for boys, and Mr. Kauwealoha one for girls, at their respective stations. The

Omoa school was examined. It had gained since our former visit fifteen pupils and sixteen readers.

On Friday, May 17th, there was a rush and roar of the savages, and we were startled by loud shouts coming down the valley. On looking out I saw a large company of tattooed savages carrying a canoe to the sea. It was covered with a broad platform of bamboo, on which was erected a small round house covered with mats. In the canoe were a live pig, a dog, and a cock, and breadfruit, cocoanuts, *poi*, etc. The canoe was ornamented with trappings, and rigged with a mast, a sprit, and a sail of *kapa*. Naked swimmers, with much noisy demonstration, launched this singularly equipped craft, and pushed it out, through a roaring surf, into the open sea. There the swimmers left it, and returned to the shore. The canoe, left to the tide, drifted slowly out of the bay. But the wind not being favorable, it struck on the northern headland of the harbor, advancing upon the rocks and then receding; borne, like a ram, by the rush and the retreat of the surf. Seeing the danger it was in, a native ran to the point and shoved off the struggling craft, when, the wind filling its sail, it headed out seaward, moved off, and disappeared.

I had a long talk with Teiiheitofe', a high chief, about the ceremonial of this canoe. He said that it was a last offering to their god, Kauakamikihei, on the death of the prophetess or sorceress, and that this sacrifice propitiated the god, expiated their sins, and closed the *koina*, or tabu, which had then lasted six weeks. During this *koina* "all servile work and vain recreations are by law forbidden."

While the *Star* was at Omoa, I revisited Hanavave on a sad and fruitless errand. The wife of one of our missionaries had been enticed by two young savages, brothers, and she was living with them among the trees up the valley. Although warned of danger, as these seducers were desperate, I was determined to seek for her, and beg her to go with me to the *Star* and to her husband and children. I found her forlorn and desiring to return; but she said she feared her seducers, as they would surely kill her before they would let her go. While we talked, the young savages came in, armed with sheath-knives, and took seats so as to look her full in the face, keeping their keen eyes fixed on her. She dared not speak again. Through an interpreter I labored with them, but they were relentless, and their prey was fast. I left them with a heavy heart, wishing that some power might release her from their grasp. Poor woman! she died in misery not long after.

It is sad to relate that the wife of Kaivi of Tahuata came to a similar end.

The *Star* returned to the stations of Hapuku and Kekela to land these brethren, and at Puamau, it being Sabbath morning, Mr. Parker and I went on shore to attend service, while the *Star* remained outside. We were happily surprised to find more than a hundred collected under some large trees to hear the Gospel. It was a wild group. Just from the war, many of the men were still armed with their formidable weapons. Before service, Kekela's house was jammed full of men, women, and children, filling every room with their grotesque figures and the odors of their pipes. They were like the frogs of Egypt; no place was sacred.

We had much talk with groups and individuals. One old warrior, Meakaiahu, heavily tattooed, held quite an earnest debate with me. When I spoke to him on the beauty of peace, and said that we should love our enemies, he answered, "No, no; we should hate our enemies and kill them." When I urged the example and teachings of Christ, he shook his head, and said, "What if I love my enemy and he *shoot me?*"

I urged and illustrated the reciprocal law of love, and how it begets love. He seemed to feel the truth, and began to yield. He said, "I have killed five men; I have a bullet in my body, but I will listen to you and fight no more."

He then requested me to talk with his chief and persuade him to give up fighting. He took my hand, pressed it hard, looked up into my face from under a great leaf which screened his eyes, and said with emphasis, "*Kaoha oe*" "love to thee." Holding on to my hand, he led me through a crowd of steaming natives to his chief, a tall, old man named Moahau, introduced me to him, and watched our conversation with eager interest. The old chief was friendly, but witty and skeptical. When urged to abandon his former habits and become a Christian, he replied: "I am too old to change my life; let the children go with the missionaries; it is too late for us old folks."

When told that Jesus loved all; that He died for the old and the young; that He would take all who obeyed Him to heaven, where there is no hunger, no sickness, no war, no bullets or barbed spears, or death, he replied, with a twinkle of the eye: "That will be a good place for cowards and lazy folks who are afraid to fight and too lazy to climb breadfruit and cocoanut trees." This shrewd wit excited a laugh in the listening crowd. But order was soon restored, and taking the old man's hand in one of mine, and the warrior's in the other, I begged them to unite on the side of the Prince of Peace, and to use their influence to prevent wars, cannibalism, and idolatry, and to cheer and help their good teachers, Kekela and Naomi. The old man yielded and said: "I will stand by my friend, the warrior, and by Kekela; and now let us go out and hear you talk to us under the trees."

The horn sounded and the people flocked together, and for an hour, while Mr. Parker and myself addressed them, the attention was unusually marked. When we pronounced the services ended, the old chieftains shouted out: "No! no! We are not weary. We want to stay and talk with you." To this call there was a hearty response from all, and we remained until near sundown, while hands were raised from all parts of the group, and voices called out, "Come *here*, come to *me*, come and talk to *us*." The scene was marvelous, and we felt that the Lord was there.

Kekela, who had been greatly depressed and had well-nigh given up all hope, was wonderfully encouraged. He proposed a meeting in the evening and the communion of the Lord's supper, saying: "I have seven candidates for the church of long standing, but the war and the confusion had so disheartened me, that I was on the point of giving all up as lost."

The seven were examined, approved, and baptized, and with those who had been baptized five to seven years before, making ten in all, we commemorated the death of our Lord. It was a precious season, "a night long to be remembered."

The French have made several wholesome laws for the islands, forbidding wars, murder, cannibalism, sorcery, etc., on the leeward, or northwest islands, including Nuuhiva, Uapou, and Uahuna. These laws were beginning to take effect.

We had to carry back Laioha and Kauwealoha, who had been with us all the time among the islands as guide, interpreter, and companion, to their stations. When this was done, we offered thanksgivings to God for our safe and prosperous voyage; and then, with all sails set, the prow of our good vessel was turned to the northwest, and we left the Marquesas, where we had spent twenty-three days. We anchored at Hilo on June 6, 1867.

The number added to the Marquesan churches during this visit of the *Star* was forty-eight. The whole number from the beginning was sixty-two.

In closing the history of my visits to this group, I can not forbear expressing regrets that the mission has been so depleted. In September, 1880, we had only three laborers with their wives in that field. The broad opening to the west, the call for laborers, for funds, and for the services of our missionary packet, have led many of the friends of missions on our islands to feel that we can not afford to send out reinforcements to the Marquesas, or to spare the *Morning Star* to make an annual or biennial trip with a delegate to that group, and so out of ten stations which we once occupied, only three remain with teachers.

The commencement of our work there was auspicious, and its progress and fruits were encouraging, more so than of the mission to the Society Islands, or to China, or to many other parts of the world.

But as it is said in Scripture, "The destruction of the poor is his poverty," so we must say of our work. And this is the wail over all the earth,—want of laborers to gather the harvest, and want of material means to give strength, courage, and due success to the weary toilers in the field. Our three missionaries in the Marquesas are doing what they can, and there is still encouragement that war, idolatry, and cannibalism would soon cease, could we but continue the Gospel work among that people.

15

Visit to the United States - Salt Lake - Chicago - Washington City - Brooklyn - Old Killingworth - Changes in the Homestead - Passing Away - Return to Hilo - Death of Mrs. Coan.

AFTER an absence of more than thirty-five years from the United States, we were persuaded by the kind solicitations of friends, and by a repeated invitation from the American Board, to return for a visit. The health of Mrs. Coan being precarious, and no medical skill at the Islands affording relief, it seemed the more desirable to go.

We arrived at San Francisco May 5, 1870. Spending fourteen days in California, we took an Eastern train, spent a Sabbath at Salt Lake City, saw the Prophet and several of his apostles, met several of the Mormon missionaries whom we had seen in Hilo, attended service in the great tabernacle, heard much bold assertion without proof, and witnessed a singular observance of the Lord's supper, the elements being distributed by laughing boys, while a speaker was haranguing the audience without making a single allusion to the death of Christ, or to the ordinance which commemorated that event. We also saw the foundation of the great temple, which a bold declaimer said was a literal fulfillment of the prophecy of Isaiah ii. 2: that "the mountain of the Lord's house shall be established in the top of the mountains, and shall be exalted above the hills; and all nations shall flow unto it."

The speaker affirmed that this prediction was now fulfilled before the eyes of the Mormons, and all the people shouted *Amen*.

We spent a little time in Iowa, and arrived in Chicago June 1st. Here I was called to labor more abundantly, and here we met many warm friends, and two sons of our esteemed associates Mr. and Mrs. D. B. Lyman; one of them a physician of prominence, the other a lawyer. In this marvelous city we spent two weeks, and then came eastward. In all, we visited more than twenty States and Territories, everywhere finding multitudes of Christian friends; many of whom we had seen before, and many more whom we had not seen in the flesh, but who were fathers and mothers, brothers and sisters and friends in Christ Jesus.

We found our country broad, fertile, populous, and wealthy. It had extended from ocean to ocean; its villages, towns, and cities had multiplied, and its population increased beyond a parallel in history. Its schools, its colleges, its churches, and its humane and benevolent institutions had multiplied marvelously. Its railroads formed a web-work over all the land, and its telegraphic wires were quivering through the atmosphere. Its progress in science, in art, in discovery, in intelligence, in invention, in wealth, and in Christianity, seemed to make it the pride of all lands.

And yet the scars of war were everywhere. The empty sleeves, the crutches, the trunks without a leg, the sightless eyes, the disfigured faces, were marks of the ghastly wounds of war. And then the dead of Gettysburg, Arlington Heights, and other silent hecatombs, the youth, the strength of the country; the millions that sleep in dust to be numbered no more among the sons, the fathers, the husbands, the citizens of our beloved land!

But our country needed this fiery chastisement, and it will be better in the end if so be that the North and South understand and profit by the lesson.

Our social intercourse, not only with personal friends and old acquaintances, but with a multitude of new-formed friends, was precious and endearing. It would be a great gratification to mention names, were it possible, and to record our tribute of gratitude and thanks to God for the many kind and Christian attentions shown us everywhere—attentions that left impressions on our hearts which time and space can not eradicate.

My opportunities to meet Christian conventions and associations, Sabbath-schools, Monday meetings of clergymen, meetings of benevolent societies, of working-women, etc., were numerous and exhilarating; and one thing which charmed me, if possible, more than any other, was the fact that partition-walls were gradually giving way between different evangelical denominations.

I was glad to be invited by brethren of various denominations to speak in their assemblies of the love of God and of His wonderful work among the heathen tribes of the Pacific. More than once I was in the pulpit and on the platform with beloved ministers of the Episcopal Church. In Monday morning meetings of pastors for prayers and consultation, I met Presbyterians, Baptists, Methodists, Congregationalists, and many others, and my tongue longed to sing with David: "Behold how good and how pleasant it is for brethren to dwell together in unity."

My talks in large and smaller assemblies during the eleven months we were in the States numbered two hundred and thirty-nine.

Assuredly the Lord has commanded the blessing to rest on all such unions of heart among His people. There need be no harm in the varied organization of Christian workers. There may be a beauty and an increased efficiency in it, as there is in the organization of armies, or other corps of officers or laborers, if only there be harmony of heart, "the unity of spirit in the bonds of peace."

One of our happiest weeks was spent in the city of Washington. Every day was full of interest. We looked in upon our institutions, legislative, civil, literary, benevolent, and religious, and were cheered to see so much of good sense, philanthropy, and earnest piety modifying and refining life in the metropolis of the Union.

We visited the Howard University, in company with its President, and attended one of its commencements in a crowded church in the city. The exercises did honor to the faculty and the speakers, and the large and cultivated assembly, in which were seen many if not most of the clergy of the city, with numbers of the Senators and Representatives of the nation, manifested a lively interest in all the ceremonies of the occasion. Several of the students were graduated with honors. The speeches of the colored students were good, and that of one of the darkest in his class was not only sensible, but brilliant.

I need not speak of our visits by invitation to theological and female seminaries—Andover, Bradford, Vassar, Union, Auburn, and Princeton, and of our great enjoyment on these occasions.

The meeting of the American Board for 1870 was held in Brooklyn, and for the first time we had the privilege of attending this annual gathering.

Here we met missionaries and men of distinction from the Orient and the Occident, from every continent, and from many an island of the globe. Never shall I forget that great congregation of glowing faces and earnest listeners. I have seen larger and more compact assemblies on Hawaii, but they were less responsive. This was like a sea of shining silver. It was mind and soul looking out of its windows; it was intelligence, culture, piety, beaming like sunlight from human faces.

I have seen Mauna Kea veiled with the mantle of night, and casting its gigantic shadow of darkness upon us. Again I have seen it when the first rays of the rising sun began to gild its summit. Watching it for a little while, the light poured down its rocky sides, chasing the night before it, until the mighty pile stood out clothed in burnished gold, and shining like a monarch arrayed in robes of glory.

And when I gazed upon that platform in Brooklyn, and cast my eyes upon the great assembly which filled the house, I said in my heart, "When will Polynesia and Micronesia display such a gathering of wisdom, piety, and moral power? A brighter than a natural sun begins to illume the darkness of those lands, chasing away the night of ages; but when will the full-orbed Sun of Righteousness ascend to the zenith and pour a flood of light and glory over all our benighted islands?" And then I reflected that even these lights of the Christian churches were yet to flicker as distant tapers before the coming glories of Zion, as predicted in the sixtieth chapter of Isaiah.

Our visit to Killingworth, my native town, was full of interest. Tender memories of childhood and youth often drew tears. Sixty-nine years had swept along the flood of time since my eyes first saw the light of day, and forty-four since I had left the home where I was born and nourished. The homestead where my father taught his boys to plow and harrow, to plant and hoe, to sow and reap, to cradle and bind, to mow and rake, and pitch and gather into the barn the winter's feed for cattle, was there. The orchard, where we children gathered apples and other fruits, was there; but many of the choice trees were gone, and the great sugar-maple and the nut-bearing trees where we had contested with the squirrel for our winter stores had disappeared. The cottage, where eight children had been reared, and where, as years passed on, we gathered at our annual thanksgivings, was desolate and silent, and no living voice came up from lawn and meadow and field which once echoed with the shout and merry laughter of childhood. The cool waters of the well were unruffled, and the sweep and "the old oaken bucket " were no more. The "Cranberry Brook" sung and babbled amidst the alders and witch-hazels, but with no response from eager, gleesome anglers and bathers. Birds built their nests and sang and reared their broods without disturbance.

The old schoolhouse, with its broad fireplace, and its benches of slabs; the round side-down, with rough wooden legs and lacking supports for the children's backs, were replaced by a convenient room, with stove, and easy seats, and other improvements. The barn-like meeting-house, with its high galleries and lofty sounding-board, and the little foot-stoves which comforted the mothers, while the fathers sat chilled on bleak, wintry Sundays, had disappeared, and a new building was in its stead. I went to it; there was a new pastor, and the congregation was mostly new. Here and there a white-crowned head in the assembly revealed a schoolmate or a friend and companion of my youthful days. Ah, memories how tender, how dear, how deathless! I went to the cemetery, where friends once near to me had been gathered one by one, and where each of the departed ones slept alone unconscious of his proximity to the dust of his dearest earthly friend. On the marble I read the sober epitaph of father, mother, sister, neighbor, and friend. Stones in other graveyards already marked the resting-places of all my brothers save one, and he has since that time departed.

Thankful for one more view of my boyhood's home, with chastened reflections I turned from it for the last time.

On our return to Hilo we met a cordial welcome from all, and the church and people were in a prosperous state. But a heavy shadow darkened over our home. The dear one who had been its light and joy for thirty-six years was growing feebler day by day, and the signs of her departure could not be mistaken.

Calmly she began to set her house in order, to be ready to welcome the coming messenger. She assured us of her unshaken faith in Christ, and prepared farewell suggestions for the dear ones she was soon to leave.

On Sunday, Sept. 29, 1872, the faithful spirit took its flight upward. Her sojourn on the earth was three-score and two years; her life above is "where eternal ages roll."

There were tender and solemn funeral services in our church on Monday, but the day was stormy, and it was not till the following morning that the dust of our beloved one was laid to rest in the cemetery on Prospect Hill, where hers was the first grave. On the marble that marks the spot, these words are inscribed:

"'Faithful unto death,'
Crowned with life."

The cemetery is in a beautiful place; the towering mountains are upon the west and south. East and north stretches the ocean, and a glorious emerald landscape is on every side. The soft breezes that rustle the leaves, and the murmurs of the distant surf, do not wake the sleeping form that awaits the behest of Him who is "the Resurrection and the Life." The soul unfettered, unchained, has drawn nearer than they to the throne.

The dear one was an extensive and eclectic reader, a clear and logical thinker. Her mind and heart were well prepared to take an active part in the literary and religious discussions and activities of the age, but she freely chose the life of a missionary to the heathen. To me she was a peerless helper. Her self-denial was marvelous. The same self-abnegation which led her to say to me, in answer to the question, "Shall I go to Patagonia?" "My dear, you must go!" controlled her whole life. She never objected to my going on my most severe or perilous expeditions along the shores or on the mountains of Hawaii; or held me back when duty called me to the Marquesas Islands. When I expostulated with her against remaining alone in the house, as she sometimes did, she would answer, "I am not afraid."

To her tender love, her faithful care, her wise counsels, her efficient help, and her blameless life, I owe under God the chief part of my happiness, and of my usefulness if I have had any, as a laborer in the Master's vineyard.

16

Notes on the Stations - Hawaii - Governor Kuakini - Maui - Crater of Hale-a-ka-la - Molokai - The Leper Settlement - Oahu - Kauai - The State of the Church.

A FEW notes on other parts of the Hawaiian Islands may not be irrelevant in this narrative.

The great awakening of which I have written so fully was felt in a greater or less degree over all the islands of the group, and the ingatherings into all the churches, from the beginning to the present day, have been more than 70,000. My visits to the different islands and stations, my fraternal communion with the faithful laborers, and the cordial interest I have found among many thousands of Hawaiians in the things pertaining to the kingdom of God, have been "as the dew of Hermon, and as the dew that descended upon the mountains of Zion" to my soul.

On the north of Hawaii I have met my earnest brother Lyons, full of poetic fire; have passed several times through Hamakua, once a populous district of his field, and have seen the gathering thousands in their places of worship. I have visited at his cool and elevated station in Waimea, surrounded like Jerusalem by mountains, having Mauna Kea on the east, Mauna Loa on the southeast, Hualalai on the south, and the mountains of Kohala on the north, and all these towering heights in full view. In the midst of this amphitheater of hills stood his great stone church, where 1,000 or 2,000 natives would assemble on special occasions to hear the Gospel, to worship the Lord, and to unite in happy festivals.

During one of my visits at Waimea I was prostrated by fever, and for two Sundays was unable to occupy the pulpit; the only time, according to my recollection, that I have been prevented by sickness from going to the sanctuary of the Lord since I came to these islands.

On one occasion I went with Mr. Lyons over the northern hills to Kohala, the most northerly district of our Islands, once a part of his parish, where we spent a week in religious services, and where we saw many penitents asking the way to Zion. And I have visited this field again, since the arrival of its present faithful and successful occupant, the Rev. Elias Bond, and rejoiced in all its fruit-bearing prosperity.

I have descended into the deep and grand valley of Waipio, filled like a bee-hive with human beings, garmented in the living green of its vegetation, shining with its running streams, with its silvery cascade leaping from a precipice 1,500 feet in height, and thundering forever in the deep basin below.

I have stood on the very summit of Mauna Kea, 14,000 feet above my Hilo home, and looked down upon the three neighboring mountains, over the great valley of Waimea, upon the green fields and shining bay of Hilo, and right opposite upon the calm waters of Kawaihae, and over and beyond the thirty miles' channel upon the sleeping mountain of Maui, and the quiet heights of Lanai and Kahoolawe.

On the coast at Kawaihae I have seen and measured the last great *heiau*, or heathen temple, of the renowned Kamehameha I., where human sacrifices were offered to the gods that can not save or destroy. I have also visited other heathen temples in Kona, Puna, Hilo, on Molokai and in other places. In the forest under the shadow of Mauna Kea, I have seen the bullock-pit where the dead body of the distinguished Scotch naturalist, Douglass, was found under painfully suspicious circumstances, that led many to believe that he had been murdered for his money. A mystery hangs over the event which we are unable to explain.

Leaving Northern Hawaii, let us glance at the western coast. Here lies the extended and once populous district of Kona, sheltered from the trade winds by the great mountains, with a smooth and glassy sea lapping its shores, with many a quiet boat-landing in little bays and coves along its coast; and with the deep and safe harbor Kaawaloa, near the center of the coast-line. On the Kaawaloa side of this bay is the place where Capt. Cook fell under the blows of the enraged Hawaiians. On the south, or Kealakeakua side of the bay, we see the little *heiau* built for Opukahaia, or Obookaia, and the cocoa-palm which his young hands planted, before he was taken to the United States.

A few miles south of this bay we find, perhaps, the largest and most renowned idol temple in this group, with a house and yard attached called "Hale a Keawe"—House of Keawe. This house was once filled with grim idols, and in this heiau the most obscene and bloody rites were observed. It was also called *Puuhonua*, meaning place of refuge, and resembled, in some of its features and uses, the old Hebrew cities of refuge. No place on the Islands was considered more sacred and awful than this. Life and death hung on the wills of the kings and priests who worshiped in this temple. When I first visited the place, many of the old idols remained, some standing within, others on the outside, in front of the house, as guardians and to blast the lawless wight whose temerity led him to approach the habitation of the gods. These idols were blackened and blear, and ready to depart like frightened ghosts, and I understand that they have all disappeared, as was long ago predicted by Isaiah, "The idols He shall utterly abolish."

At Kailua, with my now sainted companion, I visited the venerable father and mother Thurston in the days of their strength, and also the good and kind-hearted Artemas Bishop, and our hearts burned with love and veneration for those devoted servants of the Lord Jesus. Mr. Thurston was a man of great power, both physical and spiritual. He wielded a battle-axe, and yet he was meek and modest to a fault. He was often invited and advised to visit the United States before his earthly course was finished, and we have heard that he replied, "No, I had rather die than to return to the father-land." His good wife was a "mother in Israel," full of wisdom and grace.

In Kailua one would see the gigantic chief Kuakini, or John Adams. His weight was near four hundred pounds. He was governor and lord of all Hawaii, with an iron will, fearing neither man nor monarch, proud to call out a thousand men to build a causeway, or a dam for enclosing fish, to cut sandal-wood in the mountains, or to build a large church edifice. A member of the Kailua church, he often visited Hilo, and he sat in his arm-chair, under shelter, to superintend the building of the vast native church in the days of Mr. Goodrich. He loved power and flattery, and, like Jehu, "he took no heed to walk in the law of the Lord with all his heart." He sometimes refused to obey his king, saying that on Hawaii his power was supreme. He was somewhat oppressive of the people. For example; he would occasionally make the tour of the whole island, sending messengers before to command the natives to build him large houses at all places where he would spend a night or a day or two, and also to prepare large quantities of fish, fowls, pigs, eggs, poi, potatoes, etc., against his arrival. When he swept around the island his attendants would number two or three score of men, women, and children, all to be fed by the people where he lodged. In some favorable place he would sometimes encamp for a month, consuming almost all the eatables within a radius of two or three miles. He loved money; and when his pastor advised his people not to plant tobacco and *awa*, he would say to those on his own lands: "Listen to your teacher; do what I tell you. I tell you to plant tobacco."

I had testimony that he would sometimes purchase a barrel of rum or whisky, put it in a secret place, and order appointed agents to sell it out for two dollars a bottle secretly. Some of these acts came to the knowledge of his pastor, Mr. Thurston, at whose kind and faithful efforts to reform him the Governor took offense, and retorted with abusive language. Finally, he was suspended from the church, and in this state he remained for a long time, when he fell ill and died.

I was in Kailua, and visited him on his death-bed, conversing and praying with him, with his consent. His mind was dark and gloomy, and he said: "I am a great sinner, and I do not think the Lord will care for me or save me." There we leave him, thankful for all the good he did, and sorrowful that his light did not shine brighter.

At Kealakeakua we visited our good friends, the Rev. C. Forbes and his wife, and here we rejoiced in the good work of the Lord. As in Kailua, the people were numerous, and the

Sabbath congregations large. All things looked promising at this station, and our fellowship with the teachers and the people was of the most happy character. Mr. and Mrs. Van Duzee were assistants in missionary work. And after all had left, the Rev. J. D. Paris, whose first station was in Kau, was located there, and labored in that field for many years.

Kau was only seventy miles from Hilo, and he was our nearest neighbor. Here I have visited frequently, meeting at different times the various mission families who succeeded one another as vacancies in the field occurred through removal or death. The Rev. Messrs. Paris, Hunt, Kinney, Gulick, Shipman, and Pogue, with their wives, have all been laborers in this district.

In the six districts or counties of Hawaii the native population has greatly decreased, and of the numerous missionaries of the American Board who have occupied the several stations, none remain except at Kohala, Waimea, and Hilo. We who still hold on are soon to pass away, leaving the churches in the hands of Hawaiian pastors.

As I have visited the churches and missionaries on the other islands of the group, and felt a deep interest in the pastors and the people, I will give a brief sketch of most of them.

Lahaina, the capital of Maui, was once full of natives. The large stone church, with galleries, was full on every Lord's day, morning and afternoon, and the things of the kingdom of God seemed prominent in the minds of the people. The beloved Mr. and Mrs. Richards were highly esteemed, and their doors and hearts were ever open to their missionary brethren and sisters who landed feeble and faint from the sluggish Hawaiian craft on their way down from Hawaii to attend the annual meeting in Honolulu or on their return voyage. What relief, what comfort, what cheer we all found in the hospitality of this halfway station! It was like an oasis in the desert, and a fountain of cold water amidst burning sands. Here our children gamboled under the waving palms and the spreading hau-trees, eating delicious grapes and cocoanuts, while the parents conversed on themes of paramount interest.

We have met here not only the patriarch Richards, but the active seaman's chaplain, Spaulding, the faithful Dr. Alonzo Chapin, and the hospitable brother and sister Baldwin, he being the last missionary pastor of that church. There were several distinguished native Christians in this place with whom we held pleasant intercourse. Well do we remember the good and noble Governor Hoopili and his wife. They were the soul of kindness and Christian friendship. Whenever we approached their neatly-kept dwelling, their doors were opened at once with a warm welcome, and with outstretched hands and benignant smiles they would call out, "Aloha! komo mai"—love to you! come in!

But most of those with whom we took sweet counsel in Lahaina, have long since gone the way of all the earth; the population of the town has decreased, and the place has become a cane-field, with a crushing-mill and boiling-house in the center of the village, a large amount of sugar being made there. A native pastor has charge of the church.

Lahainaluna, or Upper Lahaina, is about two miles back of Lahaina, and elevated several hundred feet above it. This is the seat of our Hawaiian College, established, and for many years sustained, by the American Board. It was designed as a training-school of high grade for preparing young men for teachers, preachers, and for the occupation of the more important stations in the nation. This school was in operation when we arrived at the Islands, under the care and instruction of the Revs. Lorrin Andrews, E. W. Clark, and Sheldon Dibble. All these brethren and their wives are dead. The institution has been transferred to the Hawaiian Government, and a large number of teachers have been employed there since the first corps removed.

In early years we usually paid an annual visit to this seminary, on our way to or from Honolulu. These visits were always refreshing, on account of the height, coolness, and grand scenery of the station, the cordial welcome of the teachers, and the profound interest we felt in the prosperity of the school.

The views from Lahainaluna are beautiful and sublime. Inland rise the serrated mountains, and the deep valleys of West Maui; in front are the placid roadstead and shining channel separating Maui from Lanai; the latter name signifying veranda or porch, and so called because it stands like a portico directly in front of Maui. To the right we look across a channel some twelve miles wide, separating Maui from Molokai. This channel is often disturbed by strong trade winds which lash the waters into white foam, rendering the passage for boats difficult and sometimes dangerous.

We have been several times at Hana, a station on the eastern shore of East Maui, and looking directly across the wide Hawaiian channel upon Kohala. It is a beautiful and romantic little place, but very difficult of access. On one side are numerous and deep gulches, with rapid streams of water, often dangerous to cross. On the other side there are extended fields of sun-heated lavas, without water or human habitations.

This station was once occupied by the Revs. D. T. Conde and Eliphalet Whittlesey. On our way to Honolulu our vessel has stopped at this place to take the missionaries there to the General Meeting, giving us an opportunity to spend a Sunday and to meet the natives.

Once we found these isolated laborers destitute of almost all edibles except arrowroot and milk. In spite of their regrets, we spent a very happy day notwithstanding this lack of provisions. We ate and were satisfied, and we rejoiced in the privilege of Christian fellowship with these self-denying teachers. It is now a long time since these families returned to the United States.

The Rev. Sereno Bishop, only son of the missionary Artemas Bishop, labored there for a while with his devoted Christian wife, but subsequently assumed the charge of the institution at Lahainaluna. Hana is now occupied by a native pastor, and is greatly reduced in population.

Wailuku on Maui is an important missionary station. This field, like many others, was once teeming with thousands of natives. Its romantic valleys, its lofty precipices, its sparkling rills, and its perennial verdure on the one side, and, on the other, its broad plains, its sand dunes, its emerald foothills, and the towering mountain, Haleakala, with the blue ocean on the left, make it a spectacle of beauty, of variety, and of grandeur not often surpassed.

This station was once occupied by the devoted Miss Ogden and the Rev. J. S. Green, who conducted a large and flourishing boarding-school for Hawaiian girls. This was afterward sorrowfully abandoned for lack of funds.

We have visited Wailuku when the beloved brother and sister Clark, and the energetic Armstrong and his wife, were toiling here with success; and we have been the guests of our honored brother and sister Alexander, still living and laboring for the Master in this important field. The Greens, the Clarks, Miss Ogden, and Dr. Armstrong have all gone, and those who remain will only "a little longer wait." Two native pastors are settled here over small congregations, and there is also an English-speaking church for the foreign residents.

This district is now full of agricultural energy. Vast fields of sugarcane wave where weeds grew before; crushing-mills groan, boiling-trains steam, smoke-stacks puff, centrifugals buzz, and shiploads of sugar are produced in and around Wailuku. Extended and expensive ditches bring water from the mountains of East Maui, converting vast fields of dry and hot sand into rich and productive soil; the telephone, the telegraph, and the railroad are there, and the material improvements multiply. All would be matters of rejoicing and congratulation could we but report equal progress in moral and spiritual power.

On the highlands of East Maui stands the Makawao Female Seminary, an important institution, conducted by Miss Helen Carpenter, a lady of great skill and devotion in this necessary work. A few years ago I attended the annual examination of this seminary, and spent a week as a guest of the principal. I was exceedingly interested in the appearance of the pupils, and in the remarkable skill and tact of the teacher. All the instruction is in the English language, and it was delightful to see the acquisitions of the scholars in the various studies they had pursued.

During this visit at Makawao we made up a party to ascend to the summit crater of Haleakala—"House of the Sun," the distance from this point being about thirteen miles, with a bridle-path for horses all the way. Notwithstanding many previous visits to Maui, I had never before indulged myself with a trip to this monster of craters. We had a delightful ride over hills and swales, and through fields of strawberries and ohelos. About midway of the distance we rested for a short time under shade trees near a lovely rill of cool limpid water, a beautiful spot which has since been selected by the Alexanders, as an invigorating retreat from the heat and dust of Wailuku and Haiku, and which they have named Olinda.

We arrived at the summit about 3 P.M. We were now 10,217 feet above sea-level, and yet the sun was hot and the mercury high. In eight hours the thermometer had fallen forty degrees, and the cold was intense. Our guide and some of the party had collected such scanty fuel as could be found, and we made ourselves as comfortable as was possible for the night, around the fire that was kindled, and under shelter of an overhanging rock. In the morning the ground was whitened with frost, and water was frozen.

The view of this vast cauldron needs to be repeated and continued for a long time, in order to get a full and clear impression of its magnitude. It has been estimated that the circumference on the outer rim is thirty miles, and the depth 1,800 feet. The floor of this amphitheater is studded with sixteen cones, four to six hundred feet high, composed of scoria and cinders, appearing from the upper rim like small sand dunes dropped from a dumping-car.

The eastern rim of the crater is broken down as low as its floor, furnishing a broad passage for the molten flood to the sea. This river of fire, some three miles wide, must have been a terrific spectacle, as it rushed in raging billows from the mouth of the crater and hurried down the mountainside and into the ocean.

It is supposed that this crater is the largest and deepest on our planet, and more nearly resembles some of the yawning craters of the moon. Time was when the raging fires on this mountain must have surpassed in grandeur and brilliancy any that have been anywhere seen by later generations. For ages these lurid fires have been extinct, and from time immemorial silence has reigned over the sleeping hill. Can geology, can all human science tell us when these fires were kindled? how long they raged and roared? and when they were extinguished? Was it before or after the Prophet Isaiah uttered, in sublime language, a description of the Tophet near Jerusalem? "For Tophet is ordained of old. . . . . He hath made it deep and large: the pile thereof is fire and much wood; the breath of the Lord like a stream of brimstone doth kindle it."

But another scene, if less grand, yet more beautiful, awaited us. As the sun descended lower and lower in the west, the fleecy clouds came drifting in from the sea, and, massing around the bases of East and West Maui, covered all the seas, and bays, and channels in every direction, leaving only the tops of Hawaii, Maui, and Lanai visible. The upper surface of these clouds was fleecy white, and appeared like a vast sea of eider-down. We stood above the clouds in bright sunshine, but we saw no water and no land in any direction, except the summits of the mountains gilded in the setting sun. We gazed upon the scene below us with intense interest. As the sun went lower and lower, his rays began to dance, and play, and sparkle upon this vast sea of snowy whiteness, in lambent beauty, and as he dipped into the fleecy bed a flood of glowing scintillations flashed over the whole surface, the prismatic tints twinkling, dancing, gleaming, and quivering in inimitable beauty. A scene unique indeed, and unexcelled by anything of the kind I had seen from the heights of Chili or of Hawaii.

Then the night came on, and the clouds rested like a pall over land and sea, while in the clear heavens above us the bright constellations sparkled as on a winter's night in the far-away home-land.

In 1836 I visited the island of Molokai, which at that time was occupied by the earnest and laborious missionaries, the Rev. H. R. Hitchcock and his wife. Congregations and schools were large, and the people seemed to come readily under the influence and leading of their teachers. The Revs. Lowell Smith, Samuel G. Dwight, A. O. Forbes, and Mr. Bethuel Munn have all labored on this island, but now for years past no American missionary has resided there.

Molokai is strongly marked with *palis*, or precipices, and at the base of one 3,000 feet high, lie the Kalaupapa plains, stretching seaward, and having no other communication than by sea with the outside world. Thither more than a thousand of our poor suffering people have been carried during the last decade and a half, to linger through a living death until the fearful leprosy brings them to the grave. Our sanitary laws are relentless, and in the case of this disease they doom husbands and wives, parents and children, brothers and sisters to lifelong separation.

The scenes upon our wharves when a company of lepers is being embarked for transportation to their settlement are often agonizing.

The present number in the settlement is about 700, among whom are many of our well-educated Christians and some of the native pastors. A physician and medicines, a church edifice and chaplain are provided by a kindly Government; friends are allowed to communicate with their banished kindred, and all that thoughtful kindness can do to ameliorate the miseries of those forlorn beings is done.

Oahu is better known to the reading world than any of the other Hawaiian Islands. Thousands of strangers have visited Honolulu; it is the capital of the kingdom, and has a population of about 15,000. When I first saw it, on the 6th of June, 1835, it was anything but an inviting place. The streets were narrow, irregular, and dirty, the houses mostly small and thatched with grass, some being built of adobes, or sun-dried mud-bricks, and others on posts set in the ground. Only a few stone or framed houses were then seen, and these were mostly owned by foreign residents and native chiefs. Hardly a green tree or shrub was seen within the limits of the town. On its western flank, a small creek came down the valley called Nuuanu, furnishing muddy water for the taro ponds, and bathing and washing places for a multitude of natives with their pigs, ducks, and dogs. At several points removed from the stream, shallow wells had been dug six to ten feet deep, where hard and brackish water was found, but this water satisfied none but Hawaiians.

Along the shore in sandy and marshy places the cocoa-palm flourished with rushes, hibiscus, and pandanus growths; but over the extended plain, some three miles in length and about one mile in breadth, there was little but an arid desert of burning coral sand and detritus from the rocky hills, the reflection from which was scorching.

But times, and scenes, and scenery are changed. Industry, civilization, and science have made this scorched desert blossom as the rose. The organization of a good government, the increase of revenues, the introduction of capital, with brain power and muscular energy, have made Honolulu a place of remarkable beauty. Large reservoirs have been constructed high up the valleys, pipes have been laid all over the city, and spouting hydrants cool the air and refresh the trees, plants, and flowers of a thousand yards and gardens. Viewed from the sea as one enters the harbor, or from one of the hills that guard it in the rear, the town is a picture of enchanting loveliness. It is a tropical paradise, glowing in perennial beauty.

And, to add to the richness of the soil, the value of products and the charm of the scenery, artesian wells are beginning to throw up their pure jets and to pour out their limpid streams to cheer the plains around.

Honolulu also has an improved and excellent harbor, in which are often seen the waving flags of nearly all civilized nations, with five or six home steamers, and an inter-island fleet of which so young and so small a nation need not be ashamed. Its wharves, its esplanade, its custom-house, its palace, its fine Government house and other public buildings, offer a surprising contrast to what we saw forty years ago. It has two large Hawaiian churches, a seamen's bethel where many thousands of the sons of the deep have heard the sound of the Gospel, first from the lips of the Rev. Mr. Diell, and now for some forty years from Dr. Damon. There is also the flourishing Fort Street church, under the care of the Rev. Walter Frear, where the Gospel is preached faithfully to an intelligent audience. Just across the street is the Catholic cathedral with its bishop, and not far from this an English Reformed Catholic church with its bishop and priests.

The city is provided with schools of various grades, and its literary, social, and benevolent associations are numerous and active.

The Hawaiian Board of Home and Foreign Missions has its seat in Honolulu, with a yearly income of more than $30,000 to be appropriated to the several branches of Christian work under its care.

It may be doubted whether any city in Christendom of equal size has a larger proportion of intelligent Christian workers, who give more of their substance in the cause of beneficence, than the foreign residents of Honolulu.

The first native church in this city was organized under the pastoral care of the Rev. Hiram Bingham, who came to the Islands in 1820. In 1836 his congregation, which sometimes numbered 4,000, were worshiping in a thatched house that covered an area of 12,348 square feet; this afterward gave place to the stone church, which stands as one of the landmarks of the city. The plan of the building was made by Mr. Bingham, and most of the materials for it were collected under his supervision. The massive walls were raised to a considerable height, when he was called to return to the fatherland on account of the failing health of his beloved wife. Both husband and wife died in the United States, leaving behind them examples of rare devotion and blessed memories.

The Rev. R. Armstrong became the successor of Mr. Bingham, until called to be Minister of Education for the Hawaiian kingdom, when the Rev. E. W. Clark assumed the pastorate until he left for the United States. In 1863, the present incumbent, Rev. H. H. Parker, was ordained and installed the fourth pastor of this church.

The second Hawaiian church in Honolulu was organized many years ago under the pastoral charge of the Rev. Lowell Smith, and since his resignation, it has been successively under the care of the Rev. A. O. Forbes, and of two native pastors.

Near the large stone church is the flourishing Kawaiahao Female Seminary. Its germ was a small family school, under the care of the Rev. L. H. Gulick and wife. Miss Lydia Bingham, principal of the Ohio Female College near Cincinnati, was called to take the charge of this school. Under her patient energy and tact, with the help of her assistants, it prospered greatly, and became a success. When Miss Bingham came to Hilo, the seminary was committed to the charge of her sister, whose earnest labors for seven years in a task that is heavy and exhausting so reduced her strength, that in June, 1880, she was obliged to resign her post. It is now occupied by Miss Helen Norton, a graduate of South Hadley.

At Punahou, about two miles east of Honolulu, stands a quiet little institution called Oahu College. The location is beautiful, healthy, and convenient. The buildings stand just at the opening of an enchanting valley, and near a spring of cool crystal water; there are lofty and verdant hills in the background, and the broad waters of the Pacific in front. The land was once owned by the Rev. H. Bingham, and was given by him to this institution.

The foundations of the Punahou school were laid with the prayers and benedictions of all the fathers and mothers of the mission, and of its friends and patrons. For years it was devoted exclusively to the children of the missionaries; but as foreign residents and their children increased, the accommodations were enlarged and the doors opened to others. The college has grown and been greatly prospered. It has had many graduates, who have done honor to their professors, to themselves, and to the cause of science and Christianity. It needs and deserves endowments. We doubt not it would receive generous and efficient aid from American benefactors, could they come near enough to feel its wants and appreciate its merits.

The missionary out-stations on Oahu were but three, viz: Ewa, Waialua, and Kaneohe. I used to visit these places when large congregations assembled to be instructed by their pastors; but the population has decreased, the churches are diminished, and the remnants of these once prosperous flocks, now under the care of native pastors, show but little of their former life.

At Waialua there was established, by the Rev. O. H. Gulick, a boarding-school for Hawaiian girls. On his removal as a missionary to Japan, the institution obtained as an efficient principal the daughter of the Rev. J. S. Green (Miss Mary Green), under whose care the school still flourishes.

Mr. Parker and I once went as delegates of our mission around Oahu, visiting every station, going much from house to house, teaching, exhorting, and praying in families, in fields, and by the wayside, and holding meetings in schoolhouses, churches, and private dwellings, and endeavoring to reach all with the life-giving Word. It was a laborious but interesting tour. In some villages we found many ignorant, stupid, and misled people. Some were Romanists, some Mormons, and others without any creed, or faith, or hope. Like brutes they were living, and like brutes dying.

We met many confident Romanists, some with their catechism and rosary, and with full assurance that they were on the direct road to Paradise, and that all who differed from them were bound to perdition. I asked some of them if they read the Bible, and they answered "Yes," showing me their little catechism, with more prayers to Mary than to God. I asked one who claimed to be a teacher how many commandments there were in the Decalogue. He answered "Ten"; but on going through with them in order, I found that he omitted the second, and divided the tenth into two parts to make good the number.

The island of Kauai is separated from Oahu by a channel some seventy-five miles wide. It is 8,000 feet high and nearly circular, being thirty miles long and twenty-eight wide. It is a lovely and fertile island, and some of its mountain and valley scenery is exquisitely beautiful. Although of igneous origin, yet the degradation caused by time, by winds and water, gives the island the appearance of a more ancient formation than that of the other islands of the group. Its cones and hills are rounded by attrition, and its pit craters are so nearly filled by alluvial deposits that they are far less distinctly marked than those of Maui and Hawaii.

Historic geology tells us that the Islands were probably formed in a successive order, commencing with Kauai in the northwest and continuing in a southeast direction to Hawaii, which is still in the hands of the Founder, and unfinished.

Kauai was very early occupied as a mission field, and the Whitneys, Gulicks, Lafons, Doles, Wilcoxes, Johnsons, and Rices have been faithful laborers there; but all have left the scenes of time or engaged in other pursuits; and the good Dr. and Mrs. J. W. Smith and Mrs. Rice alone remain of the mission band.

As this island was somewhat remote and out of the track of my annual voyagings to Honolulu, and in former years could be reached only by schooners that were liable to make slow passages, I never felt that I had the time to visit it until in 1874. An opportunity then offering to make the circuit-trip in a steamer, I enjoyed the privilege of spending one night with the hospitable family of Dr. Smith, and of touching at a few points, where I found the beauty and luxuriance of the island equal to their fame.

Much capital has been invested there in sugar plantations, and the skill and industry of those who have enlisted in this enterprise have produced crops worth millions of dollars. The island has a considerable proportion of arable land, its flora is luxuriant, and its vegetation covers the island even to the highest hilltops.

This rapid glance at the different islands is mainly to mention a few facts respecting the transformations in this so recently heathen archipelago. Over all the group the changes, physical and moral, are wonderful. Everywhere schools and churches abound; knowledge and wealth increase; commerce is active; more than a hundred thousand acres of our soil wave with crops; the noise of artisans is heard; our smelting-furnaces glow at midnight; and day and night the steam-whistle echoes among our hills. Our climate, our scenery, our peace and security, are privileges that are hardly rivaled in any land, and all that we need to secure permanent peace and prosperity, with ever advancing progress, is thankfulness to the Giver, and a faith devoted to all that is pure.

The amount given by the churches of the United States for evangelic work here must have been, from the beginning, about one million and a half dollars, and the number of laborers sustained, in whole or in part, by appropriations of the American Board, has been one hundred and seventy.

At the present time there are only four foreign pastors for the twenty native churches of Hawaii; on Maui, Molokai, and Lanai there are nineteen native churches with no foreign pastors; on Oahu there are eleven native churches and but one foreign pastor; on Kauai six native churches and no foreign pastor, making in all, fifty-six Hawaiian churches with only five foreign pastors.

Many of the fathers and mothers of the mission have finished their course and gone home; their dust sleeps in this land of their adoption, or in the land of their birth. Some were recalled, some entered the Government service, and some of those who were still at their posts, earnest and active, were advised to resign. Then the Board, feeling that its work as a Board was virtually accomplished here, ceased to consider this a mission field, and, entering upon a new policy, sent out no more reinforcements, and urged the installation of native pastors over churches that had been gathered and fed with tender care by the faithful shepherds of the flock.

Some of our thoughtful brethren feared that a retrograde movement would come with such a change; others reasoned that where the Word and the Spirit converted the heathen, the same regenerating power would provide among those converts, suitable men to act as pastors and teachers. But our native converts were as children, and up to this day many of them need milk rather than strong meat. They are weak, fickle, and easily turned from the way. Intelligent and patient adherence to a work which calls for watchfulness and continuous care, and a deep and conscientious feeling of responsibility, can not be found or soon developed among a primitive race like the Polynesians. China, Japan, and India have their old civilization with its literature, their men of keen intellect, capable of heading and guiding enterprises of importance; men of reasoning and thinking minds, who when convinced of the truth and importance of the Christian religion, and persuaded to receive it as a rule of life, are soon prepared to become leaders and teachers of others.

It is not so with the Polynesians. Prematurely to leave them to teach, guide, and govern themselves in the concerns of the soul, may be more disastrous and more fatal than to leave babes to take care of themselves while the parents withdraw. The Word and Spirit of the Lord have, in the missionaries, provided agents for the conversion of the savages, and in these missionaries God has provided "nursing fathers and nursing mothers" for these infant churches. To my mind the only practical question in regard to our Pacific Islands churches is, *when* may they be wisely and safely left to the care of pastors from among themselves, or in other words, when does this child come to his majority?

Nearly all of our native pastors have been slack in church discipline, indiscriminate in receiving to church communion, and remiss in looking after wandering members, so that our church statistics are in so confused a state as to be past remedy. Out of more than 70,000 who have been received to the churches, our last report returns only 7,459, or about one in ten of those received. Is our case so much like the ten lepers healed by Christ, of whom only one "returned to give glory to God"? Or are the shepherds in fault? Do we come under the searching rebuke of the prophet: "My sheep wandered through all the mountains, and upon every high hill: yea my flock was scattered upon all the face of the earth and none did seek after them"?

But it is right to add that the present low state of the Hawaiian churches must not all be laid at the door of the pastors. These are times of trial on account of material prosperity. There is an opportunity to gain money and luxuries, and the world seems to be in most men's hearts, so that we are all passing through a struggle and a strait.

We hope for a brighter day. There has been a renewed effort to train up a class of young men for the ministry, who will, we trust, be better qualified for the office than many of their predecessors have been. To accomplish this, and at the earnest request of our Evangelical Association, the American Board has selected and sent to our aid the Rev. C. M. Hyde, D.D., a minister and pastor of ripe experience, to become president of our North Pacific Missionary Institute in Honolulu.

In this institute he has been laboring, with several assistants, with a wise and earnest zeal, for about three years, during which time the school has been gaining steadily in reputation.

17

The Hawaiian Character – Its Amiability – Island Hospitality – Patience, Docility – Indolence, Lack of Economy, Fickleness – Want of Independence – Untruthfulness – Decrease of the Population.

THAT the Hawaiians are amiable and gentle in disposition is, I think, admitted by all candid observers who are well acquainted with them. They are not excessively vindictive, but easily pacified when offended. In this trait they excel most of the other Polynesian tribes, especially the Marquesans and the New Zealanders.

They are naturally generous and hospitable. Of old, they welcomed the weary and hungry traveler to their huts, sheltered and fed him to the best of their ability, and without charge. And this generous hospitality was extended to all without respect to nationality, color, wealth, or rank. Wherever night fell upon the traveler, he found shelter and welcome in the nearest cabin. I speak of them as they were. Our civilization has greatly, if not happily, modified their natural habits in this respect.

They are docile. Few, if any, of the races of men would believe with such simple faith, or, if I may so call it, credulity. This trait, though it exposes them to deceitful wiles, also disposes them to listen to correct and useful teachings. Until wicked and infidel foreigners came among them, a Hawaiian could hardly be found who would deny the existence and character of the true God, or the truth of the Bible revelation. But they are too ready to receive false teachings as well as true, to be beguiled by fallacious arguments, and attracted by false leaders. This is why so many accept the old or the modern error.

As a rule they are patient under sufferings, losses, and poverty. Sometimes we look upon them as stolid and without brain or heart. I have seen many lingering and wasting away under a painful disease, and die with little or no emotion or regret. It would seem as if their indifference to life were a reason why they succumb so easily to disease.

They are superstitious, of course. What savage or barbarous race is not? And we might be amazed, were the facts published, at the amount of foolish and false signs, relics of heathenish superstitions, which still exist among enlightened nations. Many natives believe in ghosts, incantations, demons, and the power to take the life of one's enemy by prayer *(pule anaana)*; but I think that these superstitions are yielding faster than in most other countries.

They are naturally indolent. This has been fostered into a national trait by circumstances. A warm climate does not require energy in labor. A perpetual summer gives no occasion to lay up stores for a fruitless winter. A native's wants are few. These satisfied, why labor? To him it would be like beating the air or felling the forest without motive. When a want is felt, he will work for it as earnestly as other men. Civilization has increased their wants, and their houses and horses and clothing, their boats and carriages and money have come of labor.

But they lack economy. This is true, personally, socially, and politically. They lack the gift of order and frugality; and this applies to time, to talent, to industry, and to the use of property of every kind. As a rule, they know not how to "gather up the fragments, that nothing be lost." It is now easy for natives to get money; even the children, if they will work, can earn from twenty-five cents to fifty cents a day, while the wages of laboring men are from one dollar to three dollars a day, according to their skill and fidelity; but few of them know how to keep or use money wisely. And so it is of houses, furniture, tools, clothing, horses, lands, etc. Such things are lost or ruined by neglect, or slip out of their hands to pay unwise debts. They gather and scatter; few accumulate for permanent use. We teach them industry, economy, frugality, and generosity; but their progress in these virtues is slow. They are like children, needing wise parents or guardians.

They are changeable, or, it may be said, fickle. They love variety; they often take new names. In cases where divorce is pending, the lawyer sometimes sends to the pastor who married the couple for a certificate of marriage, that given at the time of the ceremony having been lost, and perhaps the long search for their names in the marriage records is all in vain, when, at last, it is ascertained that they are now known by different names. Some build comfortable houses at the cost of all they have, and in a little while leave them desolate, and remove to other districts or islands. To seek after and to find them in their frequent removals is often like searching for lost sheep upon the mountains. Some take letters of dismission to another church, and return without delivering them. Some go without letters, not intending to stay away, but never return; and when the name is changed, as well as the place of residence, it adds a heavy burden to the pastor's care in looking after his church members. About five hundred of the members of the Hilo church are now absent in different places.

They are amorous. Climate, lack of education, want of full employment of mind and body on matters of superior importance, and the seductions of vile men from foreign lands, endanger the morality, the piety, and the life of this infant race. With the examples of the rich, and of men of office and rank, the temptations of gold acting upon yielding natures, how can a pure morality and virtue be preserved among a people like the Hawaiians? Some of our laws are so framed by unprincipled men as to offer a premium to licentiousness, and even wholesome laws are so nearly a dead-letter for want of execution, that the villain is oftener protected in sin than punished. What can be done when vice is bold and shameless, and only virtue blushes?

They are followers, not leaders. Few, if any, of them are able to head any important secular enterprise. In agriculture, commerce, the mechanic arts, education, traffic, and in all things which require clear thought, sound judgment, tact, patience, and a deep sense of responsibility, they are deficient. Hence they are mostly servants or subordinates. The Chinaman goes ahead of them in all business matters. If a

Hawaiian holds office, the office is a sinecure, and its duties are usually committed to foreign clerks.

Naturally they are untruthful. They go astray as soon as they are born, speaking lies. This is a severe charge, but it is a trait probably in all savage races. To lie under slight provocation is to a native as natural and as easy as to breathe. The fact is patent, and it is one of the traits in the Hawaiian character which costs us the greatest pain, and the most earnest and persistent labor, to eradicate. The sin seems like an instinct; but by "eternal vigilance" it gradually gives way, and is succeeded by better habits. The Hawaiian begins to build a house which should be done in two weeks, and it may not be completed in six or twelve months; it will then be years before it is supplied with doorsteps. The servant tells you the flour or the potatoes are all gone, and you find several pounds remaining. Or he pronounces the work assigned him as "all done," when it is only two-thirds done. One informs you that all the people in a given village are drunk. You make farther inquiries and find only two out of fifty who have fallen. The washerwoman must have the same wages when she washes for the family that is reduced to half its numbers, as when it was full. Their character is not rounded and fully developed in anything. The Hawaiian is an unfinished man.

Their piety is of course imperfect. Their easy and susceptible natures, their impulsive and fickle traits, need great care and faithful watching. But we have seen many cases that have become steadfast in faith and fidelity—broken out of the "Rock" by the hammer, and formed into symmetry and beauty by the chisel of the Almighty. I believe that thousands have been converted, and that many thousands are in heaven. And if bad men would let the Hawaiians alone for one or two generations, the land would be filled with an enlightened and godly nation.

What is the cause of the decrease in the population? This is an old question, and its answers have been various, sometimes vague, and seldom satisfactory. This is not surprising, as some of the causes are occult and complex. Tradition informs us that long before the arrival of the missionaries, a pestilence like a plague swept off multitudes. Foreigners introduced a vile disease, of which many died, and the blood of many was poisoned. Inherited diseases weakened many others. The too rapid change of national habits especially produced barrenness. Unguarded and early habits of children were highly injurious. There were many Magdalens who came to the Saviour after the introduction of the Gospel, and were made whole in spirit, and prepared for a higher and purer life, while their bodies were deeply marked with the scars of sin. But to this day the artful wiles of a certain class of foreign visitors and residents have not ceased to ensnare and ruin many.

Ignorance of the laws of physical life was universal among the natives, and the missionaries have labored hard and continuously from the beginning to enlighten the people on this subject. In my ministry among the thousands of Hilo and Puna, I have witnessed not only scores who have died in early life from the effects of bad habits, but also hundreds whose days have been shortened from sheer ignorance of physiological law.

It may be surprising to some to be told, that the sudden and great changes brought on by civilization check the population. The changes in dress, in food, in dwellings, and in the occupations of life, often bring on consumption, fevers, and other diseases which almost decimate a community. Natives that once lived almost as nude as the brutes, and were yet hardy, because adapted to their surroundings, often succumb to new habits of life. Instead of wearing the *maro* and the loose bark tapa, they often put on two pairs of pantaloons over a thick woolen shirt, with tight boots, and a thick coat or heavy overall, and thus appear in church or in a public gathering, panting with heat and wet with perspiration. On returning to their homes they doff all but a shirt or maro, and sit or lie down and fall asleep in the coolest place to be found, rising with a cold and a cough which may end in disease and the grave. Even the civilized houses of some prove charnel houses, for instead of ventilating them wisely, they often close every door and window of a small and close room, lie down, cover their head with a woolen blanket, and thus sleep all night, the air growing more and more impure.

In 1848 a fearful epidemic of the measles carried off 10,000 of our people, a tenth of the whole population. Five years later, the small-pox took 3,000 more. These were days of darkness and sorrow. The natives were strangers to these diseases; physicians were few, and lived mostly in Honolulu. The natives had no remedies for these burning plagues, no wise and faithful nurses, and no food suited to their condition. Tormented with heat and thirst, they plunged by scores and hundreds into the nearest water, salt or fresh, they could find, and the eruption being suppressed, they died in a few hours. The scene was awful. The Government did what it could in its inexperience, and missionaries and all benevolent foreigners lent a helping hand to those in distress around them. But the masses of the people were beyond their reach; and the angel of death moved on by night and by day, amidst the groans and dying agonies of households and villages. The fiery darts of the destroyer flew thick over all the land, and there was no effective shield to protect the multitudes from their poisoned barbs.

And now, for many years, that persistent, unrelenting plague, the leprosy, has been poisoning the blood and lowering the vitality of thousands of our people. We have a humane government, a competent board of health, and wholesome sanitary regulations, and yet the plague is not stayed. Notwithstanding a crowded leper settlement on Molokai, there are hundreds dying inch by inch, scattered all over the Islands, some of them hiding from the public eye, some concealed by friends, and some not yet pronounced upon by physicians. The leper question is one of the gravest before the nation.

Thus the decrease of the Hawaiians goes on slowly, surely, irresistibly. They are not an exceptional case; many other races originally savage have melted away and disappeared before the unrelenting march of civilization.

18

Kilauea – Changes in the Crater – Attempt to Measure the Heat of its Lavas – Phenomena in Times of Great Activity – Visitors in the Domains of Pele.

THE volcano of Kilauea is always in action. Its lake of lava and brimstone rolls and surges from age to age.

Sometimes these fires are sluggish, and one might feel safe in pitching his tent upon the floor of the crater. Again the ponderous masses of hardened lava, in appearance like vast coal-beds, are broken up by the surging floods below, and tossed hither and thither, while the great bellows of Jehovah blows upon these hills and cones and ridges of solidified rocks, and melts them down into seas and lakes and streams of liquid fire.

As the great volcano is within the limits of my parish, and as my missionary trail flanks it on three sides, I may have observed it a hundred times; but never twice in the same state.

Its outer wall remains nearly the same from age to age, but all within the vast cauldron undergoes changes. I have visited it when there was but one small pool of fusion visible, and at another time I have counted eighty fires in the bottom of the crater. Sometimes I have seen what is called Halemaumau, or South Lake, enlarged to a circuit of three miles, and raging as if filled with infernal demons, and again domed over with a solid roof, excepting a single aperture of about twenty feet in diameter at the apex, which served as a vent to the steam and gases. On my next visit I would find this dome broken in, and the great sea of fiery billows, of near a mile in diameter, rolling below.

On one occasion, when there with a party of friends, we found the door of entrance to the floor of the crater closed against us. A flood of burning fusion, covering some fifty acres, had burst out at the lower end of the path, shutting out all visitors, so that we spent the day and night upon the upper rim of the abyss.

On another occasion I found the great South Lake filled to the brim, and pouring out in two deep and broad canals at nearly opposite points of the lake. The lava followed these crescent fissures of fifty or more feet deep and wide until they came within half a mile of meeting under the northern wall of the crater, thus nearly enclosing an area of about two miles in length and a mile and a half in breadth.

A pyrometer, sent out by Professor J. D. Dana, was put into my hands to measure the heat of melted lava. I had taken it with me twice to the crater unsuccessfully, the fusion being too deep in the lake to be reached. I had also sent it up by others, with instructions, hoping to get it inserted; but failing, I went up again with my friend, Dr. Lafon. We descended the crater and traveled south about two miles, when a vast mound like a truncated cone rose before us. Not recognizing this elevation, I said to my companion, "This is a new feature in the crater; I have not seen it before. It is about where the lake used to be; but let us pass over it, and we shall probably find the lake on the other side." With the instrument in hand, we began to ascend the elevation on an angle of about twenty degrees. When halfway up, there came over a splash of burning fusion, which fell near our feet. Our hair was electrified, and we retreated in haste. Going to a little distance, we mounted an extinct cone which overlooked the eminence we had left, when, lo! to our amazement, it was the great South Lake of fire, no longer, as often, one to two hundred feet below us, but risen to a level of about twenty-five feet above the surrounding plain, and contained by a circular dam of cooled lava some three miles in circumference. The scene was awful. Over all that high and extended surface the fiery billows were surging and dashing with infernal seething and mutterings and hissings. The whole surface was in ebullition, and now and then large blisters, many feet in length, viscous films, of the consistency of glutinous matter, would rise in gigantic bubbles created by the lifting gases, and then burst and disappear.

We were struck with amazement; and the question was, Shall we again venture near that awful furnace? We could frequently see the lava flood spilling over the rim like a boiling cauldron, and what if the encircling dam should burst and pour its deluge of fiery ruin over all the surrounding area! But unwilling to fail in our experiment we came down from the cone, and carefully, and with eyes agaze, began to ascend the wall; again and again we were driven back by the splashes of red-hot lava. We persevered, and watching and dodging the spittings, I was at last able to reach so near the top of the dam as to thrust the pyrometer through the thin part of the upper rim, when out burst a gory stream of lava, and we ran down to wait the time for withdrawing the instrument. The shaft of the pyrometer was about four feet long, with a socket into which I had firmly fastened a ten-foot pole. When at last we grasped the pole and pulled, the strength of four strong arms could not dislodge the pyrometer. We pulled and pulled until the pole was wrenched from the socket. The instrument was fast beyond recovery, and with keen regret we left it in the hardened lava.

We turned to retreat from the crater, and before we had reached the upper rim, we looked back and saw that awful lake emptying itself at two points, one of which appeared to be in the very place where we had stood only half an hour before. The whole southern portion of the crater was a sea of liquid fire, covering, as I estimated, about two square miles, with a probable depth of three feet.

This circular dam which enclosed the elevated lava-lake was formed gradually by successive overflowings upon the rim, depositing stratum upon stratum, until the solidified layers had raised the dam some twenty-five feet; when the lateral pressure became so great as to burst the barrier and give vent to this terrific flood.

I have heard great avalanches of rocks fall from the outer walls of the crater some eight hundred feet into the dread abyss below with thundering uproar. At the distance of two miles I have heard the soughing and sighing of the lava waves, and upon the surface of that awful lake I have seen as it were gory forms leaping up with shrieks, as if struggling to escape their doom, and again plunging and disappearing beneath the burning billows. To stand upon the margin of this lake of fire and brimstone, to listen to its infernal sounds, the rolling, surging, tossing, dashing, and spouting of its furious waves; to witness its restless throbbings, its gyrations, its fierce ebullitions, its writhing, and its fearful throes as if in anguish, and to feel the hot flushes of its sulphurous breath, is to give one sensations which no human language can express.

Sometimes an indurated film, two to four inches thick, will form over all the central part of the lake, while its periphery is a circle of boiling lava, spouting, leaping, and dancing as if in merry gambols. All at once the scene changes, the central portion begins to swell and rise into a grayish dome, until it bursts like a gigantic bubble, and out rushes a sea of crimson fusion, which pours down to the surrounding wall with an awful seething and roaring, striking this mural barrier with fury, and with such force that its sanguinary jets are thrown back like a repulsed charge upon a battlefield, or tossed into the air fifty to a hundred feet high, to fall upon the upper rim of the pit in a hailstorm of fire.

This makes the filamentous vitrifaction called "Pele's hair." The sudden sundering of the fusion into thousands of particles, by the force that thus ejects the igneous masses upward, and their separation when in this fused state, spins out vitreous threads like spun glass. These threads are light, and when taken up by brisk winds, are often kept floating and gyrating in the atmosphere, until they come into a calmer stratum of air; when they fall over the surrounding regions, sometimes in masses in quiet and sheltered places. They are sometimes carried a hundred miles, as is proved by their dropping on ships at sea. This "hair" takes the color of the lava of which it is formed. Some of it is a dark gray, some auburn, or it may be yellow, or red, or of a brick color.

Another mode of action in this lake is to encrust nearly all the surface with the hardened covering, while active boiling is kept up at the margin on one side only. When this ebullition becomes intense, the fusion rises on that side, while the other side is quiet. After a little, this agitated lava will rise and fall over upon the crust, pressing or breaking it down, and rolling in a fiery wave across the lake, and thus covering its whole surface with an intense boiling and surging, so fierce and so hot that the spectator withdraws from the insufferable heat to a cooler and safer position.

To be struck with this heat in its intensity, is to be death-struck, and to inhale a full draught of this sulphurous acid gas in its strength would be to extinguish life. All visitors must keep on the windward side of the lake and avoid all currents of hot steam and gases.

Some visitors are too daring. Others are too timid. I have known several gentlemen who have ventured into places of peril, and escaped death as by a miracle; and I have known one at least so timid as to turn back to Hilo as soon as he saw smoke and steam, and smelt sulphur, though he was still more than a mile distant from the volcano.

And I have seen ladies tremble and almost faint on going down into the crater while yet a full mile from any visible fire. One who was in my charge was so terrified that no assurance of safety and no effort to persuade could move her. She sat down upon a rock a mile from Halemaumau, and would not move until we led her out of the crater. Others, though transfixed and awestruck at first, become so fearless that they play with the pools and little rills of lava, dipping up specimens of it to take away. In order to carry it conveniently, one lady put a specimen which had hardened, but not yet cooled, into her handkerchief, when, instead of remaining, it burnt through and fell at her feet.

19

Eruptions from Mauna Loa – The Eruption of 1843 – A Visit to it – Danger on the Mountain – A Perilous Journey and a Narrow Escape.

DURING the night of January 10, 1843, a brilliant light was seen near the summit of Mauna Loa. In a short time a fiery stream was rushing rapidly down the mountain in a northerly direction toward Mauna Kea.

On the 11th, vast columns of steam and smoke arose from the crater. After a few days the orifice on the top of the mountain ceased to eject its burning masses, and the action appeared more vivid upon the slope of the mountain, until the lava reached the valley below, and struck the foothills of Mauna Kea.

The Rev. J. D. Paris and his family were our guests at the time, and, our good wives consenting, we prepared to go up to the flow, which shone with a strong glare in the valley between the mountains, and had the appearance of turning toward Hilo. Neither of us had ascended Mauna Loa before, and we started with great enthusiasm. Taking a guide and men to carry our food and sleeping-cloaks, we followed the bed of a mountain stream which empties into the bay of Hilo. The pathway was rocky and full of cascades from ten to 150 feet in height; but the water was low at this time, and by wading, leaping from rock to rock, and crossing and re-crossing the stream from ten to twenty times in a mile, and taking advantage of parts of its margins which were dry, we made good progress, sleeping two nights in the forests on its banks, and coming out of the woods into an open, rolling country on the third day. This is a region where thousands of wild cattle roam.

A little before night of this day, we came directly abreast of a stream of liquid fire half a mile wide, and bending its course toward Hilo. Passing along the front of this slowly-moving flood, we flanked another of about the same width, flowing quietly to the west toward Waimea; while far up on the side of the mountain we saw another stream moving toward Kona. This higher stream was a lateral branch of the main trunk, and this trunk was again divided at the base of Mauna Kea. As these lower branches were pushing slowly along upon level ground, and as the feeding flood had ceased to come down upon the surface from the terminal vent, but flowed in a subterranean duct or ducts, most of the flow was solidified above, and we could see the flowing lava only in a belt of a few rods wide across the ends of the streams, and at several points upon the side of the mountain.

Having satisfied ourselves with the day's labors, we set about preparing our camp for the night. Besides our guide and burden-bearers, a number of natives had begged the privilege of going with us. Selecting an old wooded crater, about two hundred yards from the lava stream, and elevated some sixty feet above it, we prepared a booth of shrubs and leaves, collected fuel, made a rousing fire, ate our supper, made arrangements for the morrow, and lay down for the night.

But before our eyes were closed by sleep, a dense cloud settled down upon us, covering all the wide uplands between Mauna Kea and Mauna Loa. We were now at an elevation of about 8,000 feet above the ocean level, and the air was cold. Soon the vivid lightning began to flash from the clouds that covered us, instantly followed by crashing peals of rattling thunder. We found that we were in a sea of electricity, and that the full-charged clouds rested on the ground. It was a flash and a crash simultaneously; the blaze and the roar were nearly coincident. The very heavens seemed ablaze; the hills and trees dropping their veil of darkness as if engaged in a fairy dance, while the thunder roared and reverberated among the mountains.

I had never before seen a tempest of equal grandeur. But the danger was imminent. The storm continued without intermission until near morning, and a great rain fell. The sun rose, and the mountains on both sides of us were crowned with glory. A heavy fall of pure snow covered their summits.

Looking down from our lofty watchtower toward Hilo, we saw the clouds that had blazed around us during the night rolled down and massed along the shore, hiding the sea from our sight, the upper surface shining with light, and alive with dancing and quivering rays. We could also see the flashes of lightning dart among the clouds, followed in measured time by the booming thunder. The scene was of equal grandeur with that of the past night, but without its danger. We were in bright sunshine, thousands of feet above the clouds, while the coast and bay of Hilo were shrouded; and, for the first time in years, a great storm of hail fell upon the northern part of the district.

But to the hills! to the hills! was the summons of the morning. Onward and upward was our motto. We each selected a man who volunteered to go with us to the summit. From our point of view we could trace the stream in all its windings from its source to its fiery terminus before us. The surface was all hardened except the fused belt of some 200 feet wide at the lower end of the flow, pushing slowly out from under its indurated cover. Above this the whole flow was a shining *pahoehoe*, or field lava, steaming in light puffs from a thousand cracks and holes.

We set out at sunrise with our two native guides, carrying a little food, a small supply of water in a gourd, and our camp-cloaks. We flanked the fresh lava stream some part of the way; crossed it occasionally, and walked directly upon it for many miles, making as straight a course as possible. Much of the way we were obliged to walk over fields and ridges, and down into gorges of *aa*, or clinker lava, as sharp and jagged as slag around an iron furnace.

The work was so severe that our men fell behind, and we were forced to halt often and encourage them to hasten up. At length, weary of this lingering pace, we hurried on, leaving them to follow as well as they could, but before noon we lost sight of them, and saw them no more until our return to camp. Taking with them all our supplies, they had turned back to enjoy rest and shelter with their companions who remained behind.

We passed over hills and through valleys; saw steaming cones and heard their hissings. We came to openings through the crust of twenty to fifty feet in diameter, out of which issued scalding gases, and in looking down these steaming vents, we saw the stream of incandescent lava rushing along a vitrified duct with awful speed, some fifty feet below us. Still pressing up the mountain, we saw through other openings this rushing stream as it hurried down its covered channel to spread itself out on the plains below. We threw large stones into these openings, and saw them strike the lava river, on whose burning bosom they passed out of sight instantly, before sinking into the flood. Far off to the right we heard the crashing and roaring of the lava-roof as it fell into the channel below made by the draining of the stream.

Noon passed, and the summit was not reached. "Hills peeped o'er hills," and we were weary. We came to the snow. One, two, and three P.M. made us anxious. We counted the hours, half hours, and minutes, while we plodded some five miles in the snow. We had no food, no wrappers for the night, and no shelter. Our condition was now not only one of suffering, but one of peril. Our strength began to fail. But to fail of the object before us when just within our grasp! Could we bear the disappointment?

We fixed 3:30 P.M. as the latest moment before we must turn our faces down the mountain. To remain later where we were was death. At the last moment we came to the yawning fissures where the crimson flood had first poured out. The rents were terribly jagged, showing the fearful rage of the fires as they burst forth from their caverns into the midnight darkness.

We had seen the object of our quest, and now life depended on our speedy return.

Full twenty-five miles of rugged lava, without guide or trail, lay before us. We had tasted no food nor a drop of water since daylight.

We knelt a moment, and "looked to the hills whence cometh help," and then began the descent. We ran, we stumbled and fell; we rose and ran again amidst scoria and rocks, up and down, until at sunset we reached the point where we had stood at noon. Far off among the foothills of Mauna Kea, in the north, we could descry the green cone where our camp was pitched.

Night came on apace. The moon was a little past her first quarter, and her mild light never appeared so precious to us as now. Down, down, we ran, falling amidst the scoriaceous masses, scaling ridges and plunging into rugged ravines, tearing our shoes and garments, and drawing blood from our hands, faces, and feet. Once in about a mile we allowed ourselves a few seconds only to rest. To sit down fifteen minutes would stiffen us with cold, and to fall asleep in our exhausted condition would be to wake no more on earth.

As we grew weaker and weaker, our falls were more frequent, until we could hardly rise or lift a foot from the ground. More than once, when one of us fell, he would say to his companion, "I can not rise again, but must give up." The other would reply, "Brother, you *must* get up," and extending his weary hand, and with encouraging voice he would aid the fallen one to rise. Thus we alternated in falling and rising; while our progress became slower and slower. When about halfway down the descent, we saw clouds rolling up from the sea, and our anxiety was intense lest such a storm as we had felt the preceding night should fall upon us. The clouds covered the moon and stars, and darkened all the volcanic lights of those breathing-holes, which by night shone like lamps on a hillside. Our camp-hill, and the flood of lava near it, were covered with the cloud, and "darkness which was felt" came over us. It now seemed as if all was over. But thanks to God the veil was removed, the stars reappeared, and we ceased to wander as we had done under the shadow of the cloud. We had left the snow and the colder heights far behind, and now we felt that we were saved. When within half a mile of camp our natives heard our call, and two came out with torches to meet us. We came in like wounded soldiers who had been battling above the clouds, limping and bleeding. We threw ourselves prostrate upon the ground, and called for water and food, and did not rise until near noon of the next day.

Our providential escape filled us with too much gratitude to allow us to chide severely the guides who had deserted us, and whom we found with the rest of the party, full-fed and happy.

This expedition taught us useful lessons. One of them was never to attempt another enterprise of this kind without completer arrangements for its success. We learned practically the truth, that "Two are better than one, for if they fall, the one will lift up his fellow, but woe to him who is alone when he falleth."

When about to leave our mountain camp, our chief guide, a wild-bird catcher and bullock hunter of the highlands, came to me with a sober and thoughtful countenance, and after a little hesitation said: "Mr. Coan, we have guided you up the mountain for so much, and now how much will you give us to guide you back?" Looking him square in the face, I replied, "You need not go down, you can stay up here if you like." The fellow was dumfounded and stood speechless. His companions, who had gathered around him hoping to share in the double price for services, burst out into a laugh, and called him an ass. He submitted, took up his burden, and gave me no more trouble. But all the way down his comrades kept up the joke until he accepted the title and said: "Yes, I am a jackass."

We reached home after three days of hobbling on lame feet, but thankful to Him who guides the wanderer.

20

Eruptions of Mauna Loa - The Eruption of 1852 - The Fire-Fountain - A Visit to it - Alone on the Mountain - Sights on Mauna Loa.

MY account of the eruption of Mauna Loa in February, 1852, was originally published in *The American Journal of Science and Arts* (September, 1852). It is here reproduced with slight corrections from later observations. I visited the locality three times; first while the lava fountain was playing a thousand feet high, and twice since the crater had cooled.

It was a little before daybreak on the 17th of February, 1852, that we saw through our window a beacon light resting on the apex of Mauna Loa. At first we supposed it to be a planet just setting. In a few minutes we were undeceived by the increasing brilliancy of the light, and by a grand outburst of a fiery column which shot high into the air, sending down a wonderful sheen of light, which illuminated our fields and flashed through our windows. Immediately a burning river came rushing down the side of the mountain at the apparent rate of fifteen to twenty miles an hour. This summit eruption was vivid and vigorous for forty hours, and I was preparing to visit the scene, when all at once the valves closed, and all signs of the eruption disappeared; accordingly I ceased my preparations to ascend the mountain.

On the 20th, the eruption broke out laterally, about 4,000 feet below the summit, and at a point facing Hilo; from this aperture a brilliant column of fire shot up to a height of 700 feet, by angular measurement, with a diameter of from 100 to 300 feet. This lava fountain was sustained without intermission for twenty days and nights, during which time it built up a crater one mile in circumference, lacking one chain, and 400 feet high. It also sent down a river of liquid fire more than forty miles long, which came within ten miles of Hilo.

The roar of this great furnace was heard along the shores of Hilo, and the earth quivered with its rage, while all the district was so lighted up that we could see to read at any hour of the night when the sky was not clouded. The smoke and steam rose in a vast column like a pillar of cloud by day, and at night it was illuminated with glowing brilliants, raising the pillar of fire thousands of feet in appearance. When it reached a stratum of atmosphere of its own specific gravity, it moved off like the tail of a comet, or spread out laterally, a vast canopy of illuminated gases. The winds from the mountain brought down smoke, cinders, "Pele's hair," and gases, scattering the light products over houses and gardens, streets and fields, or bearing them far out to sea, dropped them upon the decks of vessels approaching our coast.

The light of the eruption was seen more than one hundred miles at sea, and sailors told us that when they first saw the light flaming on the mountain they exclaimed, "Look there, the moon is rising in the west!" Much of the time our atmosphere was murky, and the veiled sun looked as if in an eclipse.

On Monday, the 23d of February, Dr. Wetmore and myself, taking with us four natives as assistants, set out for the mountain. One of these natives was familiar with the woods and wilds, having been a bird-catcher, a canoe-digger, and a wild-cattle hunter in those high regions. His name was Kekai, "Salt Sea."

We passed our first night in the skirt of the forest, having taken with us long knives, an old sword, clubs, and hatchets, purposing to cut and beat our way through the jungle in as straight a line as possible toward the fiery pillar. On Tuesday we rose fresh and earnest, and pressed through the ferns and vines, and through the tangled thicket, and over, under, and around gigantic trees, which lay thick in some places, cutting and beating as we went, our progress being sometimes half a mile, sometimes one, and again two miles an hour. At night we bivouacked in the ancient forest, hearing the distant roar of the volcano and seeing the glare of the igneous river, which had already passed us, cutting its way through the wood a few miles distant on our left.

On Wednesday Dr. Wetmore decided to return to Hilo, apprehensive that the stream might reach the sea before we could return from the crater, and that our families might need his presence. Taking one of the men, he hastened back to the village, while I pressed on.

Sleeping once more in the forest, we emerged on Thursday upon the high, open lava fields, but plunged into a dense fog darker and more dreary than the thicket itself. We were admonished not to journey far, as more than one man had been lost in these bewildering fogs, and wandering farther and farther from the way had left his bones to bleach in the desert; we therefore encamped for the fourth time. A little before sunset the fog rolled off, and Mauna Kea and Mauna Loa both stood out in grand relief; the former robed in a fleecy mantle almost to its base, and the latter belching out floods of fire. All night long we could see the glowing fires and listen to the awful roar twenty miles away.

We left our mountain eyrie on the 27th, determined, if possible, to reach the seat of action that day. The scoriaceous hills and ridges, the plains and gorges bristled with the sharp and jagged *aa*, and our ascent was rough and difficult. We mounted ridges where the pillar of fire shone strongly upon us, and we plunged down deep dells and steep ravines where our horizon was only a few feet distant, the attraction increasing as the square of the distance decreased.

At noon we came upon the confines of a tract of naked scoriae so intolerably sharp and jagged that our baggage-men could not pass it. Here I ordered a halt; stationed the two carriers, gave an extra pair of strong shoes to the guide, gave him my wrapper and blanket, put a few crackers and boiled eggs into my pocket, took my compass and staff, and said to Mr. Salt Sea, "Now go ahead, and let us warm ourselves tonight by that fire yonder." But I soon found that my guide needed a leader; he lagged behind, and I waited for him to come up, but fearing we should not reach the point before night I pressed forward alone, with an interest that mocked all obstacles.

At half-past three P.M. I reached the awful crater, and stood alone in the light of its fires. It was a moment of unutterable interest. I was 10,000 feet above the sea, in a vast solitude untrodden by the foot of man or beast, amidst a silence unbroken by any living voice. The Eternal God alone spoke. His presence was attested as in the "devouring fire on the top of Sinai." I was blinded by the insufferable brightness, almost petrified by the sublimity of the scene.

The heat was so intense that I could not approach the pillar within forty or fifty yards, even on the windward side, and in the snowy breezes coming down from the mountain near four thousand feet above. On the leeward side the steam, the hot cinders, ashes, and burning pumice forbade approach within a mile or more.

I stood amazed before this roaring furnace. I felt the flashing heat and the jar of the earth; I heard the subterranean thunders, and the poetry of the sacred Word came into my thoughts: "He looketh on the earth, and it trembleth; He toucheth the hills, and they smoke; the mountains quake at Him, and the hills melt; He uttered His voice, the earth melted; the hills melted like wax at the presence of the Lord."

Here indeed the hills smoked and the earth melted, and I saw its gushings from the awful throat of the crater burning with intense white heat. I saw the vast column of melted rocks mounting higher and still higher, while dazzling volleys and coruscations shot out like flaming meteors in every direction, exploding all the way up the ascending column of 1,000 feet with the sharp rattle of infantry fire in battle. There were unutterable sounds as the fierce fountain sent up the seething fusion to its utmost height; it came down in parabolic curves, crashing like a storm of fiery hail in conflict with the continuous ascending volume, a thousand tons of the descending mass falling back into the burning throat of the crater, where another thousand were struggling for vent.

For an hour I stood entranced; then there came to me the startling thought that I was *alone*. Where was my companion? I looked down the mountain, but there was no motion and no voice. The vast fields and valleys of dreary scoria lay slumbering before me; the sun was about to disappear behind the lofty snow-robed mountain in the rear. What if my guide had gone back! Remembering my former experience in 1843, only about five miles from this place, I could not be otherwise than anxious. Minutes seemed as hours while I watched for his coming, when lo! there is motion upon the rough *aa* about a mile below me: a straw hat peers up on a ridge and again disappears in a gorge, like a boat in the trough of the sea. Then at length "Salt Sea" stood forth a life-sized figure in full view. Weary but faithful he was toiling upward. If ever my heart leaped for joy, it was then. As he came within speaking distance, he raised both his hands high above his head and shouted: "Kupaianaha! kupaianaha i keia hana mana a ke Akua mana loa!"—Wonderful, wonderful is this mighty work of Almighty God.

Could I help embracing the old man and praising the Lord?

We chose our station for the night within about two hundred feet of the crater and watched its pyrotechnics, and heard its mutterings, its detonations, and its crashing thunder until morning. Occasionally our eyelids became heavy, but before we were fairly asleep some new and rousing demonstration would bring us to our feet and excite the most intense interest. In addition to the marvelous sounds, the kaleidoscopic views of the playing column were so rapid and so brilliant that we could hardly turn our eyes for a moment from it. The fusion when issuing from the mouth of the crater was white-hot, but as it rose through the air its tints underwent continuous changes: it became a light red, then a deeper shade, then a glossy gray, and in patches a shining black, but these tints and shades with many others were intermingled, and as every particle was in motion the picture was splendid beyond the power of description. Thousands and millions of tons of sparkling lava were pouring from the rim of the crater, while the cone was rising rapidly, and spreading out at the base. From the lower side of this cone a large fissure opened, through which the molten flood was issuing and rushing down the mountain, burning its way through the forest. No tongue, no pen, no pencil can portray the beauty, the grandeur, the terrible sublimity of the scenes of this memorable night.

Morning came, we offered our prayers, ate our breakfast, and descended the mountain with regrets. Rejoining the men whom we had left the preceding day, we retraced our steps to Hilo, and reached home in health and safety, though not without an experience it may be interesting to relate. In the upper skirts of the forest in a narrow pass we were confronted by a magnificent wild bull. Coming suddenly upon a small herd in this defile, the cows and smaller cattle fled and were soon out of sight; not so the bull; he wheeled and faced us boldly, covering the retreat of the cows and calves, and bidding us defiance. As he stood with head proudly erect, we estimated the tips of his splendid horns to be eight feet from the ground.

We were challenged by this mountain sentinel to stand, and stand we did. We were unwilling to retreat; to deploy to the right or left seemed impossible. We held a council, feeling that "discretion was the better part of valor." The bull was armed with ugly horns; we were unarmed. He stood and we stood. Our guide, an old mountaineer, advised us to arm ourselves with stones, and directed that when he hurled his missile and shouted, we should do the same. We all hurled and yelled at once. The proud monarch snorted, shook his head, turned slowly on his heels, retreated a few paces, and then suddenly wheeled right-about and again held the passage. We hurled another volley and shouted. The Bashan bull wheeled slowly round, walked about a rod, and a second time turned and faced us, bidding defiance. We feared a charge, but as we had pushed our Goliath back some feet, we let go a third volley, and this decided the conflict. He turned, but he neither ran nor trotted; he maintained his dignity and retreated deliberately, while we waited for his highness to disappear, without attempting to disarm him or make him a prisoner. It was a compromise which we accepted thankfully. We breathed easier and moved on with lighter steps.

This splendid eruption of 1852 was in blast only twenty days.

21

The Eruption of 1855 - A Climb to the Source - Mountain Hardships - Visits to Lower Parts of the Lava Stream - Hilo threatened with Destruction - Liquidity of the Hawaiian Lavas - Are the Lava streams fed from their Sources only?

THE great eruption of 1855-56 continued fifteen months and the disgorgement of lava exceeded by millions of tons that of any other eruption we have seen.

It was first observed on the evening of the 11th of August, 1855, shining like Sirius at a small point near the summit of Mauna Loa. This radiant point expanded rapidly, and in a short time the glow was like that of the rising sun. Soon a deluge of liquid fire rushed down the mountainside in the direction of our town.

Day after day, and night after night, we could trace this stream until it entered the deep forest, when the scene by day would often be made beautiful by the vast clouds of white vapor rolling up in wreaths from the boiling streams and water-basins below. In the nighttime the spectacle was one of unrivaled sublimity. The broad and deep river of lava, moving resistlessly on through the festooned forest trees, would first scorch the low plants and fallen timber of the jungle, until they took fire, when suddenly a roaring flame would burst forth, covering perhaps a square mile, and rushing up the hanging vines to the tree tops, leaping in lambent flashes from tree to tree, would make the light so gorgeous that for the time being night was turned into day.

These brilliant scenes were long continued, and all Hilo watched the progress of the stream with increasing interest.

On the 2d of October, in company with a friend and several natives, I set off to visit this approaching torrent of lava. As the jungle through which it was burning its pathway was too dense to be penetrated, we chose for our track the bed of the Wailuku river, the channel in which Mr. Paris and I went up to the eruption of 1843. We slept three nights in the great forest on the banks of the river, and the fourth night in a cave on the outskirts of the forest. Early in the morning of October 6th we emerged and came to the margin of the lava stream in the open plain. We had flanked it at the distance of some two miles on our left, and its terminus was about ten miles below us on its way to Hilo. Where we first struck it, we estimated the breadth to be about three miles, but twice that width in places where the country was level, and where it could easily expand. The surface was solidified, and so nearly cool that we took it for our highway. And highway indeed it was, for it was raised in some places twenty, fifty, and a hundred feet above the old floor on which it came down. In some places the walking was comfortable, and in others all was confusion thrice confounded. Ridges, cones, bluffs, hills, crevasses, *aa*, swirls, twistings, precipices, and all shapes congealed, were there. No fire yet. Little puffs of white steam were coming up from unknown depths below. Far down the mountain terrible fires were gleaming, cutting down a mighty forest and licking up rivers of water. High above us raged a glowing furnace, and under our very feet a burning flood was rushing with an unknown commission, perhaps to consume all Hilo, to choke our beautiful harbor, to drive out our people, and leave this gem of the Pacific a heap of ruin. Thoughts of what might be could not be silenced; like ghosts from the buried cities of Pompeii and Herculaneum, they haunted our path.

Onward we went; the ascent grew steeper. We were startled; a yawning fissure was before us—hot, sulphurous gases were rushing up—the sullen swash of liquid lava was heard. We took the windward side of the opening, approached carefully, and with awe we saw the swift river of fire some fifty feet below us, rushing at white heat, and with such fearful speed that we stood amazed. The great tunnel in which this fiery flow swept down was a vitrified duct apparently as smooth as glass, and the speed, though it could not be measured, I estimated to be forty miles an hour. Leaving this opening, we pressed forward, and once in about one or two miles we found other rents from thirty to two hundred feet in length, down which we looked, and saw the lava-torrent hurrying toward the sea.

These openings in the mountain were vents, or breathing holes for the discharge of the burning gases, and thus perhaps prevented earthquakes and terrific explosions. They were longitudinal, revealing the fiery channel at the depth of fifty to a hundred feet below, and exposing a sight to appall the stoutest heart. To fall into one of these orifices would be instant death. From 10 A.M. we were walking in the midst of steam and smoke and heat which were almost stifling. Valve after valve opened as we ascended, out of which issued fire, smoke, and brimstone, and to avoid suffocation, we were obliged to keep on the windward side, watching every change of the wind. Sometimes hot whirlwinds would sweep along loaded with deadly gases, and threatening the unwary traveler.

In one place we saw the burning river uncovered for nearly 500 feet, and dashing down a declivity of about twenty degrees, leaping precipices in a mad rage which was indescribable. Standing at the lower end of this opening we could look up, not only along the line of fire, but also thirty feet or more into the mouth of the tunnel out of which it issued, and see the fiery cataract leaping over a cliff some fifteen feet high, with a sullen roar which was terrific, while the arched roof of this tunnel, some forty feet above the stream, and the walls on each side of the open space were hung with glowing stalactites, tinged with fiery sulphates and festooned with immense quantities of filamentous glass. At the upper end of this opening we cast in stones of considerable size, and when they struck the surface of the rushing current, they were swept from our sight with a speed that blurred their form, and with a force that was amazing.

Amidst clouds of steam and the smell of gases, jagged fissures opening all along the track and wonders of force arresting our attention, we still ascended, until at 1 P.M., October 6th, we reached the terminal crater. This was Saturday and the fifth day of our journey, and we were a little weary, but we set ourselves at once to examine this point where the first red light of August 11th had been seen, and whence the amazing flood of melted minerals had been poured out to startle all eastern Hawaii. From this summit elevation, for six miles down the side of the mountain we found a series of crevasses of a similar character, but no rounded or well-defined crater. This upper cleft was wide, some 500 feet long, and indescribably jagged. It had vomited out floods of lava which now lay in bristling heaps forming a scoriaceous wall 100 feet high on each side of the opening. These walls were so rough, so steep, and in such a shattered state, that it was very difficult to surmount them, but by care and effort we gained the giddy crest of the one on the windward side and gazed down into the Plutonic throat of the mountain. No fire could be seen. Blue and white steam with the smell of sulphur came curling up from unknown depths below, while the fearful throat that had so lately belched out such floods of fiery ruin was nearly choked with its own *debris*. The action had ceased; the fountain, no longer able to throw out its burning stream from this high orifice, had subsided, probably a thousand feet, and found vent at the lower point where we had seen the flow in our ascent.

We were now more than 12,000 feet above our home, and sitting on the lip of this mountain mortar, we could meditate on its recent thunder, and seem to see the belching of its fire and smoke and brimstone, while its stony hail lay heaped around us. What a battlefield of infinite forces in these realms of thunder and lightning, of stormy winds and hail and snow, of rending earthquakes and devouring fires!

The source of this eruption is about midway between those of 1843 and 1852, and these three igneous rivers ran in parallel lines about five miles apart. This eruption was also only a few miles north of Moku'aweoweo, the great summit crater, whose deep cauldron has so often boiled with intense heat, and whose brilliant fires have thrown a sheen of glory over the firmament and lighted all eastern Hawaii. Moku'-aweoweo is probably the great chimney or shaft which reaches the abyss of liquid lava below, and which furnishes the materials for all the lateral outbursts of Mauna Loa, except for those of Kilauea, which are independent eruptions.

It was evening before our explorations of the surrounding scenery closed, and the next day was Sunday. Unfortunately our guides had failed to supply our gourds with water. We had passed pool after pool, and had charged our natives to be sure and fill the gourds in time, but they as often answered that there was plenty of water further on. In this they were mistaken, and we reached our destination with only one quart of water for four persons. But we agreed to spend the Lord's day and offer our sacrifices of prayer and praise on this high altar.

It was cold and dreary, and our bed was hard and rough lava, but raising a low wall of lava blocks, as protection against the piercing night winds, we endured cold and thirst until Monday morning, having no fuel—we were above vegetation—and only one half-pint of water each from Saturday until the afternoon of Monday.

In itself we would not have deemed it wrong to go down the mountain on the Sabbath, but as our natives are slow to discriminate and reason on points of religion, and as multitudes in all parts of the islands would be sure to hear that the teacher who had so often dissuaded them from unnecessary labor on the Lord's day had himself been traveling on that day, it was prudent to give them no occasion to stumble on this point. I have never regretted the self-denial.

October 8th we marched rapidly down to find water. On our way we passed the famous cone of one mile in circumference formed in 1852, and around the base of this cone we found patches of white frost. So painful was our thirst that we lay down and lapped the frozen vapor. A little before noon we came to a spring of pure, cold water, and here we sat and drank abundantly. At evening we reached Kilauea, a distance of thirty-five miles from our morning position. Here we rested, explored, etc., and on Thursday we reached Hilo, well rewarded for the journey. It was all the way on foot, the whole distance being over 100 miles.

On our return we found all Hilo in a state of anxious suspense, and eager to hear what we had seen and what were the probabilities that the eruption would reach the town. The light of the blazing forest was evidently drawing nearer and nearer daily, but no one had as yet penetrated the dense thicket of ferns and bramble and of tangled vines and fallen trees. A few native bird-hunters had gone up some distance into the forest, and climbed lofty trees to prospect, and had reported the locality of the lower end of the stream. I resolved to pierce the jungle if possible, and on the 22d set off early in the morning with an English gentleman who had offered to accompany me, and with one of the natives who had seen the fire from the treetop. Upon entering the woods we soon took the channel of a watercourse south of the Wailuku, and wading, leaping from rock to rock, and crossing and recrossing a hundred times to work our way along the margin, we advanced at the rate of about two miles an hour.

Early in the day a cold and dreary rain set in, and continued all that day and night. What with wading and the falling rain, we were thoroughly soaked. But action kept up our warmth, and we pressed on that we might reach the fire before dark. Several times in the afternoon our faithful guide climbed trees in order to descry the fire, and to determine its course and distance. The day declined, and we began to fear that we should be left to spend a dark and cheerless night in the forest without light or fire. At length, however, there was a welcome shout from the last tree climbed: "I see the fire! it is on our right, two miles distant." We turned at right angles to our previous course, left the water-channel, and began to cut and beat our way through the thicket under a fresh inspiration. At a little before sundown we reached the lava river, two miles, perhaps, above its terminus. When within a few rods of it, and we saw its glaring light flashing upon us through the jungle, my companion, who had never seen such a sight, was startled, and inquired earnestly if we were not in danger, and if the forest would not soon all be on fire and consume us.

The place where we stood commanded a scene of surpassing interest. We estimated the flow to be two miles wide, and our view of it to extend about ten miles, giving it some twenty square miles of area. Perhaps three-fourths of the surface was solidified, but hundreds or thousands of pools, and active fountains and streams of lava boiled and glittered and spouted, presenting a scene of marvelous brilliancy and beauty.

The margin where we stood was hardened, but red-hot; open pools were within a few rods of us, and cracks revealed the moving fusion below. In order to warm ourselves, and partially to dry our soaked garments, we stood as near the fire as we could bear it, on a little knoll under a large tree about six feet from the margin and as many feet above the stream.

Here we prepared our supper, hanging a small teakettle over the red-hot lava on a pole, and toasting our ham and bread on a spit. Rain fell during most of the night, and we could not lie down; so, supporting our backs against the trunk of a tree, we watched the marvelous scene until morning. The river of devouring fire was moving slowly on toward Hilo, partly under cover of its own hardened crust, and partly open to our sight. Near the center of the flow was an open river, some half a mile wide, forming a central channel of lava, deeper and more active than the rest, while lateral branches gushed out on both sides, and boiling lakes and spouting jets abounded.

Two miles below us, along the whole front of the stream, a fiery edge, like the front of a war-column, was consuming the jungle, and leaving the giant trees standing in the burning flood to be brought down and consumed in their turn. All night long we watched this process. Trees of seventy feet in height and three or four feet in diameter were not felled in an hour, but were gradually gnawed off by the continuous action of the igneous stream. A large number of these trees fell, and we were often startled by their crashing thunder, and amazed at their heavy fall and plunge into the destroying current. Here they would lie until they took fire, and then startling explosions would sometimes occur, and the livid flames would rush and roar while these Titans of the forest were consumed.

The more rapidly-flowing lava often submerged the trunks and branches of trees, and during the consuming process the surface of the flood would be covered with thousands of little points of purple and blue flame of the burning gases coming up from below.

Great changes took place during the night. The mountain furnace was in full blast, and millions of cubic feet of lava were rushing down in the pyroducts to replenish this river and to push it onward to the sea. The surface of the stream before us was constantly heaving and changing under the force of these fiery dynamics. Large fields of the solidified crust would break up like ice on a great river in springtime, and melt. There were detonations at various points, and the uplifting and cracking of the crust would call our attention from one point to another, while we noted that the whole surface of the flow seemed to be rising like a river in a freshet. The hot and hardened lava near us, where we had warmed our feet, dried our clothes, and cooked our supper, had been melted, and a superincumbent stratum of liquid fire had raised it nearly six feet, so that its surface was nearly on a level with our hillock. Lateral streams, like skirmishers, were being pushed out, new fountains were opening, and vertical jets were leaping and dancing before us like ghosts in flame. A tree fell within a few yards of us; and finally we heard the crackling of the brambles just on our left—a small stream of lava, like a fiery serpent, was creeping along behind us, while the rising stream on our right was about to go over the bank, and thus we were threatened to be surrounded by a ring of fire.

It was nearly daylight, and the rain and cold continued, but the call to retreat was imperative. We withdrew to the rear. In about ten minutes more our nest was covered with a fiery flood, our sheltering tree stood in the midst of it, and the flames were running up its clinging vines and leaping among its branches.

I had determined to find, if possible, some place where we could cross over the lava stream and go down to Hilo on the other, or north side. Working our way along the southern margin, and searching for some point where it should be so nearly crusted over that by zigzagging we might reach the opposite side, we at length ventured, my companion and our guide following me closely. We made a serpentine track, winding up and down, and often diverging from our course to avoid open pools and streams. But the hardened surface was swelling and heaving around us by the upheaving pressure of the lava below, and valves were continually opening, out of which the molten flood gushed and flowed on every side. Not a square rod could be found on all this wide expanse where the glowing fusion could not be seen under our feet through holes and cracks in the crust on which we were walking. After venturing some thirty rods upon this sea of fire, we saw just before us an open channel of seething lava, some three hundred feet wide, and whose extreme length above and below we could not see or measure. Of course there was no alternative but to beat a retreat, and we worked our way back to the place whence we started.

To many it may seem strange that any one should venture into such a place; but to a person familiar with the movements of these igneous masses, the danger is not alarming. Fused rock is heavy and of great consistency, and when left quiet for a time under the atmosphere its surface stiffens and congeals, so that I have often walked on a flow that had been liquid only five hours before. We returned to Hilo to report.

Still the eruption made steady progress toward the town, felling the forest, filling up ravines and depressions, and licking up the streams and basins of water in its way. It reached the banks of the Wailuku, and lateral arms were thrown out into the river. Again I visited the scene of action. Several ship-masters and other gentlemen wished to join me, and my two daughters begged that they also might go. The distance had been lessened to about fifteen miles, and after patient toil over rocky precipices and wearisome obstructions, we reached the flow before nightfall. A furious line of lava marked the lower end of the stream, gushing out at white heat from under the crust that covered it for miles above. This igneous stream had fallen into a stream of water, and the conflict between the elements was fierce. The water boiled with raging fury, but the fire prevailed, sending up spiral columns of steam and filling the channel. To those to whom the sight was new, it was overwhelming.

Near the margin of the flow we found a lava oven, red-hot, but not fused, and near this, on account of the cold, we made our lodging for the night. In the morning we retraced our steps to Hilo.

When the advancing stream was within ten miles of the shore, I pushed through the woods again, accompanied by one native, to the lower line of the flow. Here we found an advanced stream which had fallen into a dry wady, and was coming rapidly down to a precipice of some seventy feet, over which it continued to pour from 2 P.M. until 10 A.M. of the next day. My guide and I took seats upon the rocky roof of a cavern in the center of the channel, some distance below the lava cataract. Here we had a grand front view of the scene during the whole night. The fusion was divided by rocks into two streams, and these descended in continuous sheets through the night—where we were there was no night—filling up the deep basin below, and changing the nearly perpendicular precipice into an inclined plane of about four degrees angle. This great cavity being filled, the lava began to flow down the channel where we had established our observatory. The channel was full of boulders and very rough, so that we sat undisturbed for some time; but when the fusion began to enter the cavern on whose roof we were perched, and we heard subterranean thuds, we were admonished to seek other quarters.

As the weeks went on, I made several other visits to this lava stream—eight, I think, in all—marking its rate of progress and its varied phenomena, and concluding, with many others, that its entrance into our town and harbor was only a question of time, unless the blast of the awful furnace on the mountain should cease.

As the flood of consuming fire came nearer and nearer, the anxiety in Hilo became intense. Its approach was the great subject of conversation. In the streets, in the shops, and in our homes, the one question was, "What of the volcano?" Watchers were out keeping vigils during the livelong night. Merchants began, to pack their goods, and people looked out for boats and other conveyances, and for places of refuge to escape the impending ruin. Every house near the lower skirt of the forest was evacuated, and all the furniture and animals removed to places of safety. Our inland streams were choked, and the river which waters our town and supplies ships was as black as ink, and emitted an offensive odor. The juices of vines, and the ashes of thousands of acres of burnt forests containing charred leaves and wood came into these streams, and the smell of pyroligneous acid was strong. By day the smoke went up like the smoke of Sodom. By night the flames arose and spread out on high like a burning firmament. We thought we could calculate very nearly the day when Hilo would be on fire, when our beautiful harbor would be a pit of boiling fury, to be choked with volcanic products and abandoned forever. What could we do?

The devouring enemy was within seven miles of us, his fiery lines extending two miles in width. Already had it descended on its devastated track fifty or sixty miles, persistently overcoming every obstacle; the little distance remaining was all open, and no human power could set up any barriers, or arrest the oncoming destroyer.

All knew what we could *not* do. Some one said: "We can pray"; and I have never seen more reverent audiences than those that assembled on our day of fasting and prayer. No vain mirth, no scoffing, no skepticism then. Native and foreigner alike felt it was well to pray to Him who kindled the fire, that He would quench it.

On the 12th of February, only a few days after this, a party of fifty or sixty foreigners was made up to visit the eruption, then about six miles from the town. A United States frigate with her commodore was in our harbor, and seven or eight whale-ships. Visitors were also here from Honolulu, and eight wives of ship-masters were boarders in the town. It was a great muster; the cavalcade of ladies and gentlemen included the commodore and his suite, lawyers, judges, sheriff, merchants, ship-masters, etc.

A way had been opened for horses through the thicket by natives hired for the occasion, so that we might ride nearly to the margin of the flow.

The morning on which we started was radiant with beauty; and as we advanced, natives, catching the inspiration, turned out in troops, and it was supposed a hundred joined us.

We met in an opening in the forest, some distance from the main stream, but opposite an active flow of lava that had shot ahead down the channel of a rivulet. A number of the company desired to see the main flow in its breadth, and with these I proposed to advance two or three miles, while those who remained were to follow a trail which the natives would open, and prepare a camp near the margin of the stream. We returned about sunset and found the camp demoralized. The party had pursued the trail as directed, but at sight of the glowing fires which were rushing down in volume had taken fright, turned back on their track and fled deeper into the forest.

The commodore retreated at discretion, ordered his horse hastily, vaulted into the saddle, and taking one or two of his officers sped down the hill, out of the woods, over the rocks and through streams and mud, never halting until he had reached the shore.

The frightened ladies and children wandered here and there, bewildered in the forest, and it was midnight before the stragglers were all brought into camp. Most of them were then so terrified that they could not be persuaded to approach nearer to the burning river; but those who were reassured and ventured to join the party of observation were well repaid. Through the energy of a ship-master, a fine topsail canvas tent had been set up on a high bank of the water-channel overlooking a deep basin, into which a cascade was falling from a height of thirty-nine feet, and our position commanded the channel for half a mile. The fiery stream, perhaps seventy-five feet wide, filled the whole channel and drove the boiling water before it, burning the bushes and vines and ferns along the banks as it approached the fall. Down plunged the molten lava, moving like a serpent into the depths of the basin, covering the whole surface with enormous bubbles. A dense steam which rolled upward in convolving clouds of fleecy whiteness floated away upon the wind. Sometimes the glare of the fire would so fall upon the cloud of vapor as to produce the appearance of flame mingled with blood, and again the quivering and dancing of countless prismatic colors. By break of day there was not a drop of water left in this basin; the space was filled with smouldering lavas, and the precipice, which had reared itself at an angle of 80°, was converted into a gently sloping plane. A large slab of lava crust was tilted, and stood as a monument of the accomplished work; the flow ceased, a little red-hot lava was seen amidst the smouldering heaps of rocky coal, and from that day the fearful flood did not come another foot toward Hilo.

This was six months after the commencement of the eruption on the mountain. Above this pool, where the action ceased so suddenly, was the broad river of one to two miles wide which supplied the flow; and this also ceased to move toward Hilo, at the same time leaving a breastwork of indurated lava some twenty-five feet high across the whole terminus of the stream.

But what is most marvelous, confounding our geology, is the fact that for nine months longer, or until November, 1856, after the arrest of the flow toward our town, the great terminal furnace on Mauna Loa was in full blast, sending down billions of cubic feet of molten rock in covered channels, and depositing it near the lower end of the stream, but without pushing beyond its breastworks. This lava gushed out laterally along the margins of the stream, or burst up vertically, rending the crust, throwing it about in wild confusion, or heaping it into cones and ridges a hundred feet high, as monuments of its fury. I have mounted some of these cones, finding them cracked from base to top in fissures six to eight feet apart, but so firm that I could walk to their summits and look down in the seams on the right and left, and see the red-hot lava glow like burning coals in a coal-pit, sending out deadly blasts of acid gases.

At many points for miles above the terminus, pools, lakes, and streams of liquid fire were scattered over the square miles of *aa* and immense fields of *pahoehoe*, boiling, seething, and flowing during the nine months that followed February 13th. During all this time the water of the Wailuku was so discolored, and so offensive in taste and smell, that ships refused it, and it was disused by the residents—and in some of the lovely woodland rills the water became black like ink.

During this eruption Prof. J. D. Dana wrote to me requesting that I would ascertain on how great an angle of descent lavas would flow without breaking, as some scientists affirmed that a continuous stream could not flow down an angle of more than five degrees. I took pains to measure accurately on one of my excursions, and found lava flowing continuously on declivities of from one to ninety degrees. I also noted that our Hawaiian volcanoes send out streams of such perfect fusion that they will run like oil down any angle, and even cleave like paste to an inward curve of the rock and form a thin veneering upon it.

Another question arose: Can a lava stream flow for many miles longitudinally upon the surface, without being fed by vents or fissures from below? Of course no one will dispute the fact that fusion pouring down a steep mountainside will rush for miles with such rapidity that it can not cool in its descent so as to stop its progress. But can it push forward over broad fields of almost level surface? I have answered this question thus:

1st. On ascending the mountain to view an eruption I see no evidence of deep fractures until we are more than two-thirds the way to the summit.

2d. Where there is an opening extending down to the fiery abyss below, there will, I think, always be a column of mineral smoke ascending to mark the spot, so long as action continues. This is true of Kilauea, and it is also true of all the eruptions I have observed. We see continuous volumes of smoke ascending from the terminal crater on Mauna Loa, and others near the terminus of the stream where the fusion is gushing out from under its hardened surface. The smoke at the fountain is mineral, while that below is from vegetable matter. These two kinds of smoke are distinguishable by the smell; and the mineral smoke is nowhere continuously emitted along the line of the lava stream, however extended that may be; it is characteristic of the lava-source.

3d. I have often surveyed, for distances of five to twenty miles, the ground upon which eruptions were approaching, and have seen the burning floods come on, covering today the ground on which I traveled yesterday, and consuming the hut where I slept. Their manner of progress is so familiar to me that it is difficult to see how I can be mistaken in thinking that our longest lava streams maintain themselves wholly from the source, and are not fed from fissures beneath their course.

This eruption of 1855-56 gave us an example of the law of compensation. Repeated efforts had been made to open a road for horses through the great central forest of Hawaii. It is probably a moderate estimate to say that ten thousand days of native labor had been expended on the enterprise. But the road was abandoned long ago, after having been carried about ten miles from the shore, and in a few years it was covered with jungle. This eruption consumed the forest to within a mile of the lower skirt of it, and a bridle-path has been made to the flow, and upon this hardened stream animals have been taken through an opened passage to Waimea and Kohala. With proper effort a convenient road might be made upon this lava-field, so as to shorten greatly the distance to the western side of the island.

As before mentioned, surface lava exposed to the atmosphere crusts over before running very far, unless it is moving with great velocity, as down steep descents. This process of refrigeration so protects the liquid below that it flows onward at white-heat, it may be, until obstructed, when it gushes out on the margins, or bursts up vertically. On plains where the movement is slow the obstructions are more numerous and the force required to overcome them is less; this accounts for the lateral spreadings, the upliftings and the thousand irregularities which diversify the ever-changing surface of the lava-flow.

22

The Eruption of 1868 from Kilauea – The March and April Earthquakes – Land-Slips – Destruction of Life and Property – The Lava stream Bursts from Underground – The Volcanic Waves of August, 1868, and of May, 1877.

FROM time immemorial earthquakes have been common on Hawaii. We have felt the jar of thousands. Most of these shocks have been harmless. A few have broken a little crockery, cracked plastering, and thrown down stone walls.

But on the 27th of March, 1868, a series of remarkable earthquakes commenced. Kilauea was unusually full and in vehement action. Day after day from March 27th and onward, shocks were frequent, and growing more and more earnest. At 4 P.M., April 2d, a terrific shock rent the ground, sending consternation through all Hilo, Puna, and Kau. In some places fissures of great length, breadth, and depth were opened. Rocks of twenty to fifty tons were sent thundering down from the walls of Kilauea, and massive boulders were torn from hillsides and sent crashing down upon the plains and valleys below. Stone houses were rent and ruined, and stone walls sent flying in every direction. Horses and men were thrown to the ground; houses tilted from their foundations; furniture, hardware, crockery, books and bottles, and all things movable in houses were dashed hither and thither, as of no account. It seemed as if the ribs and the pillars of the earth were being shattered.

I was sitting, as at the present moment, at my study-table, when a fearful jerk startled me, and before I could arise, a jar still more terrible caused me to rush for the stairs, and while going down, such a crash shook the house that I supposed the roof had fallen.

Going out of doors, I found my wife standing at a distance from the house, watching with an intense gaze its swaying and trembling, while the ground rose and sank like waves, and there was no place stable where hand or foot could rest.

When the shocks intermitted a little, I went upstairs to witness a scene of wild confusion. A large bookcase, seven feet high by four wide, with glass doors, and filled with books, lay prostrate on the floor near where I had been sitting, with the glass broken into a thousand pieces.

My study-table, eight feet long, and loaded with large volumes, was thrown out from the wall into the center of the room, with one leg broken square off, and the books and papers scattered on the floor. Another bookcase, fastened to the wall, was rent from its fastenings and thrown out near the table, and three of the sleepers which supported the floor were broken by the fall of the case.

The shaking continued all night, and most or all of the Hilo people spent the night out of doors, fearing to remain in their houses. Some said they counted a thousand shocks before morning, and so rapid were these shocks, that the earth seemed to be in a continuous quiver, like a ship in a battle.

But the heaviest blows fell on Kau, the district lying south of us on the other side of Kilauea. There the earth was rent in a thousand places, and along the foothills of Mauna Loa a number of land-slips were shaken off from steep places, and thrown down with soil, boulders, and trees. In one place a slide of half a mile in width was started on a steep inclined plane, till, coming to a precipice of some 700 feet, on an angle of about seventy degrees, the vast avalanche, mixing with the waters of a running stream and several springs, was pitched down this precipice, receiving such fearful momentum as to carry it three miles in as many minutes. Ten houses, with thirty-one souls and five hundred head of cattle were buried instantly, and not one of them has been recovered.

I measured this avalanche and found it just three miles long, one-half a mile wide at the head, and of a supposed average depth of twenty feet.

At the same time the sea rose twenty feet along the southern shore of the island, and in Kau 108 houses were destroyed and forty-six people drowned, making a loss of 118 houses and seventy-seven lives in that district, during this one hour. Many houses were also destroyed in Puna, but no lives were lost. During this awful hour the coast of Puna and Kau, for the distance of seventy-five miles, subsided seven feet on the average, submerging a line of small villages all along the shore. One of my rough stone meeting-houses in Puna, where we once had a congregation of 500 to 1,000, was swept away with the influx of the sea, and its walls are now under water. Fortunately there was but one stone building in Hilo, our prison; that fell immediately. Had our coast been studded with cities built of stone and brick, the destruction of life and property would have been terrific.

This terrible earthquake was evidently caused by the subterraneous flow of the lavas from Kilauea, for the bottom of the crater sank rapidly hundreds of feet, as ice goes down when the water beneath it is drawn off. The course and the terminus of this flow were indicated by fissures, steam, and spouting of lava-jets along the whole line from Kilauea to Kahuku in Western Kau, a distance of forty miles, and I have found foldings and faults in several places.

During these days of subterranean passage, the earth was in a remarkable state of unrest; shocks were frequent, and it was asserted by trustworthy witnesses that, in several places, the ragings of the subterranean river were heard by listeners who put their ears to the ground.

On the 7th of April the lava burst out from the ground in Kahuku, nine miles from the sea, and flowed rapidly down to the shore. The place of outbreak was in a wood on one of the foothills of Mauna Loa. Travelers bound to Hilo came up to this flow on the west side, and were not able to cross it, but were obliged to return to Kona and come *via* Waimea, a circuit of one hundred and seventy miles. A fissure of a mile long was opened for the disgorgement of this igneous river, and from the whole length of this orifice the lava rushed up with intense vehemence, spouting jets one hundred to two hundred feet high, burning the forest and spreading out a mile wide. The rending, the raging, the swirling of this stream were terrific, awakening awe in all the beholders.

Flowing seaward, it came to a high precipice which ran some seven miles toward the shore, varying in height from two hundred to seven hundred feet, and separating a high fertile plain, of a deep and rich soil on the left or eastern side, from a wide field of *pahoehoe* hundreds of feet below on the right or western side.

Before the flow reached this precipice it sent out three lateral streams upon the grassy plain above, which ran a few miles, and ceased without reaching the sea. But the larger portion of the igneous river, or its main trunk, moved in a nearly straight line toward the shore, pouring over the upper end of the precipice upon the plain below, and dividing into two streams which ran parallel to each other, some hundred feet apart, until they plunged into the sea. These streams flowed four days, causing the waves to boil with great violence, and raising two large tufa cones in the water at their termini. They formed a long, narrow island, on which they enclosed thirty head of cattle, which were thus surrounded before they were aware of their danger, and it was ten days before the lava was hard enough to allow them to be taken out of their prison. During this time they had no water, and were almost maddened by the smoke and heat. Several cattle were also surrounded on the upper grassy plain, where they were lying down to ruminate or to sleep.

The owner of the ranch, with his wife and a large family of children, was living in a pleasant house surrounded by a wall, with a fine garden of trees and plants, near the center of this beautiful grassy plain, and while sleeping at night, unconscious of danger, one of these lateral streams came creeping softly and silently like a serpent toward them, until within twenty yards of the house, when a sudden spout of lava aroused them and all fled with frightened precipitation, taking neither "purse or scrip," but leaving all to the devouring fire. The lady was so overwhelmed with terror that had it not been for her husband on one side and another gentleman on the other, she must have fallen and perished in the lava.

The family, crossing a small ravine, rested a few moments on a hill near by. In ten minutes after crossing the ravine it was filled with liquid fire. Their escape was marvelous. In a few minutes the house was wrapped in flames, the garden was consumed, and all the premises were covered with a burning sea.

A little farther down this green lawn was the hut of a native Hawaiian. As the fiery flood came within fifty feet of it, it suddenly parted, one arm sweeping around one side of the house and the other around the opposite side, and uniting again left the building on a small plat of ground, of some three-quarters of an acre, surrounded by a wall of fusion. In this house five souls were imprisoned ten days with no power to escape. All their food and water were exhausted. Small fingers of lava often came under the house; it was a little grass hut, and they were obliged to beat out the fire with clubs and stamp it with their feet.

Piles of burning scoria were heaped around this house, as high as the eaves, and in some places within ten feet of it. I afterward visited this house, and found its inmates alive and rejoicing in their deliverance.

A little further on, and this lava stream came near the ruins of a stone church, which had been shaken down by the earthquake of April 2d. The walls were a heap of ruins, and the roof and timbers were piled upon the stones. Again the flood opened to the right and left, swept close to the *debris* of the church, and united again below, leaving all unconsumed.

The same earthquake demolished a large stone church in Waiohinu, the central and most important mission-station in Kau, and so rent the house of the pastor, the Rev. John F. Pogue, that he, with his family, fled to the hills, and soon after left the district to return no more. Other homes also were left desolate, the terrified inmates seeking abodes elsewhere.

On the 14th of August, 1868, a remarkable rise and fall of the sea commenced in our harbor, and continued for three days. The oscillation, or the influx and efflux of the waves occupied only ten minutes, and the rise and fall of the water was only three to four feet. What rendered this motion of the water remarkable was its long continuance, and the short intervals of the rise and fall with no apparent cause.

Another volcanic wave fell upon Hilo on the morning of the 10th of May, 1877. From a letter written by my wife* I copy the following extracts descriptive of the event: "A chilly, cheerless night shuts down upon a day that has had no parallel in kind in my previous experiences. I was just rousing from quiet slumbers this morning, not long after five, when heavy knocking at our door hastened me to it. There stood Kanuku, almost wild with excitement, and so breathless she could hardly give form to the words she poured forth; but I gathered their substance. A volcanic wave had swept in upon the shore; houses were going down, and people were hurrying *manka* (inland) with what of earthly goods they could carry.

"We hastened to the beach. People on foot and on horseback were hurrying in all directions; men with chests and trunks on their backs, women with bundles of bedding and clothing under which they staggered, grandmothers with three or four year old children on their shoulders, and mothers with little babes, all in quest of safety and a place to lodge their burdens. Arrived at the foot of our street what a sight we beheld! Houses were lifted off their under-pinning and removed a fathom or more—some had tumbled in sad confusion and lay prone in the little ponds that remained of the sea in various depressed places. Riders at breakneck speed from Waiakea brought word of still more complete ruin there; the bridge, they said, was gone.

"We walked on toward the Wailama. Then a shout, and we looked back to see the waves rising and surging landward, so we dared not linger, but turned on our track, for a better chance of escape should the sea again overpass its bounds.

"People wading in water where their homes had stood half an hour before, gathering up goods soaked by the brine, and begrimed with mud, men in wet garments who had had to swim for their lives, and women with terror in their faces caught up the refrain of a death-wail that reached our ears from the region of Kanae's place, and the word flew from lip to lip that old Kaipo was missing. Asleep, with Kanae's babe

* Mrs. L. B. Coan.

pillowed near her when the wave came upon them, she had wakened, and hastening out of the house found herself in deep water. Holding the little one above her head, she had courage and strength to keep it safe till the mother swam for it, and then, no one knows how, the old woman was swept out to sea, and hours after, the body was found at Honori.

"About nine o'clock, the rain which had come in infrequent light flurries before, began to pour in earnest, and has fallen in such pitiless inclemency through the day, that it has added to the discomforts of the poor, homeless wanderers, and to the general gloom that hangs over our little town.

"Mr. Coan has been out much of the time here and there with words of sympathy and comfort. Rebecca Nakuina told me the natives said they were safe wherever he was. One poor old man came to our door and asked in most pathetic tones if it was true that Mr. Coan had said that at noon there would be another and heavier wave, and went away comforted when assured that he had not.

"A large barque at anchor in our harbor was tossed about most marvelously at the very mercy of every efflux and reflux wave. For hours she writhed under this restless tossing, one moment pointing her prow toward Puna, and the next in the opposite direction, running back and forth the full length of her cable, like a weaver's shuttle, sometimes careening so far that we feared the next moment to see her on her beam ends, and then struggling to right herself, and for a little recovering her usual position, only to repeat these movements.

"May 11th. The birds sang and the sun shone this morning, as if there were no sorrow here. But it was a great blessing that the day was fair; the sunshine was needed for heart-warmth and for drying what of clothing and household effects had been collected from the mud and slime in which they were found.

"We went over the same ground on the nearest beach that we visited yesterday, only to realize more fully the wild havoc that had been made.

"What shall I say of what we saw on the other side of the bay! If I tell you that Mr. Coan was bewildered, seeing no familiar object by which to get his bearings, so that he exclaimed: 'Where are we!' you will understand something of what destruction must have gone on there. But unseen it can not be realized, the dreariness and desolation of a little region that was so late one of Hilo's prettiest suburbs. Not a house standing on all that frontage. Waiakea bridge had been carried a hundred rods or more from its abutments. Even the little church had been set back some two hundred feet, tolling its bell as it went, while the *luna's* house that before nestled under the shade of the pride of India trees on the grassy bank had borne it company, and fallen into shapeless ruin at the very side of the almost uninjured church.

"At this spot the people began to gather about us, so sorrowful in their homelessness, that their voices and ours choked as we exchanged 'alohas.' Some of them led the way to a hut, too small to be a shelter, but under whose low roof we found a mother sitting by the corpse of her little one that the waters had not spared to her. Close on one side, an old man lay groaning with the pain of fractured ribs and a broken leg, and on the other side, a heap of something, I could hardly tell what at first, lifted a battered head to tell us how he had been thrown upon the rocks and they had bruised his skull.

"An Englishman's escape from death seems wonderful. We visited him and found him suffering greatly, but able between groans and gaspings for breath to tell us something of his experience.

"'I got caught, sir,' he said. 'I should have escaped if I hadn't gone back after my money; when I came downstairs the roller had hit the house, and before I could get out of the door, the house had fallen upon me. I was dreadfully bruised, and you see, sir, as the wave took the house inland, it kept surging about with me in it, and getting new knocks all the while.' And what of the money—was it saved?' 'Oh, no sir, it all went, six hundred dollars. It was all I had, and I am stripped now and I'm past working, seventy-seven years old.' Kneeling by the poor man, Mr. Coan offered an earnest prayer. We left him feeling that he was very likely past working much longer.

"Five lives have been lost; twenty persons are more or less injured. Forty-four dwellings are demolished, and one hundred and sixty-three people left homeless, their means of procuring sustenance snatched from them. Had the wave fallen in the darkness of the night, many more must have perished. Daylight revealed the almost silent approach of the danger, and most had time to flee. I am thankful, if it must happen, that this has occurred before our going down to Honolulu, so that Mr. Coan is among his people to comfort and direct them. Only a few Sabbaths ago he preached a sermon on laying up treasure where thieves could not break through and steal. Who thought then of *this thief?*"

Deep sympathy was awakened in our whole community for those who suffered by this calamity. Food, clothing, blankets, were given in abundance. The report of the disaster spread over the islands, and help came from every quarter. His Excellency John Dominis, Governor of Oahu, and Her Royal Highness Lydia Dominis, the king's sister, were commissioned to come to our aid with the donations from Honolulu. A judicious distribution of money, clothing, lumber, etc., was made among the people, and thus encouraged they went cheerfully to work, and in a few months most of the losses were repaired; better houses were built, and the sufferers seemed more prosperous than before.

They now annually commemorate the 10th of May by a religious festival and a thanksgiving offering to the treasury of the Lord.

23

The Eruption of 1880-81 – Hilo Threatened as Never Before – A Day of Public Prayer – Visitors to the Lava-Flow – It Approaches within a Mile of the Shore – Hope Abandoned – After Nine Months the Action Suddenly Abates – The Deliverance – The Mechanism of a Great Lava-Flow – An Idolater Dislodged – Conclusion.

ON the 5th of November, 1880, our latest eruption from Mauna Loa broke out at a point some 12,000 feet above sea-level, and a few miles north of the great terminal crater, Moku'aweoweo. The glare was intense, and was seen at great distances. Brilliant jets of lava were thrown high in the air, and a pillar of blazing gases mounted thousands of feet skyward, spreading out into a canopy of sanguinary light which resembled, though upon a larger scale, the so-called "pine-tree appendage" formed over Vesuvius during its eruptions by the vertical column of vapors with its great horizontal cloud.

Meanwhile a raging river of lava, about three-fourths of a mile wide and from fifteen to thirty feet deep, rushed down the northeast flank of the great dome, and ran some thirty miles to the base of Mauna Kea. This stream was composed mostly of *aa* or scoria. Its terminus was visited and well described by our townsman, David Hitchcock, Esq. This flow hardened and ceased; but a stream of *pahoehoe* or field lava was now sent off to the southeast, toward Kilauea. The roaring furnace on Mauna Loa remained in full blast. Down came a third river of lava, in several channels, flowing in the direction of Hilo. This divided itself in places and reunited, leaving islands in the forest. This stream crossed the flow of 1855-56, followed its southeast margin, and fell into our great upland forest in a column from one to two miles wide. There was the sound as of a continuous cannonading as the lava moved on, rocks exploding under the heat, and gases shattering their way from confinement. We could hear the explosions in Hilo; it was like the noise of battle. Day and night the ancient forest was ablaze, and the scene was vivid beyond description. By the 25th of March the lava was within seven miles of Hilo, and steadily advancing. Until this time we had hoped that Hilo would not be threatened. But the stream pursued its way. By the 1st of June it was within five miles of us, and its advance, though slow, was persistent. It had now descended nearly fifty miles from its source, and the action on Mauna Loa was unabated. The outlook was fearful; a day of public humiliation and prayer was observed, as during the eruption of 1855. But still the lava moved onward, heading straight for Hilo. One arm of the stream was now easily accessible on its northern margin, and two more were moving in the deep jungle so far to the south that visitors had not the time or patience to penetrate to them. It now began to appear that should these streams unite no trace of Hilo, or of Hilo harbor, would remain. Some of our people were calm; others were horror-stricken. Some packed up their goods and sent them to Honolulu or elsewhere, and some abandoned their houses.

Visitors to the stream were now frequent; and the crater on Mauna Loa was reached, on a third attempt, by the Rev. Mr. Baker, of Hilo. Were I twenty years younger, I should have been on the mountaintop also, but my time to climb such rugged heights is past.

The northerly wing of the stream now hardened, clogging the channel in which the lava was taking its way toward the center of our town. But this check gave additional power to the southeast wing, so that on the 26th of June, a fierce stream broke out from the great lava pond and came rushing down the rocky channel of a stream with terrific force and uproar, exploding rocks and driving off the waters. Hilo was in trouble. We were now in immediate danger. The lava, confined in the water-channel of from fifty to a hundred feet wide, advanced so rapidly that by the 30th of June it was not more than two and a half miles from us, threatening to strike Volcano Street about a quarter of a mile from Church Street, on which I live, and to fall into our harbor about midway of the beach. The stream was fearfully active, and the danger was now close upon us. From the town we could walk up to the living lava in forty minutes, and back again in thirty. A hundred people would sometimes visit it in a day. Its roar, on coming down the rough and rocky bed of the ravine, was like that of our Wailuku River during a freshet, but a deeper and grander sound. Explosions and detonations were frequent; I counted ten in a minute. The glare of it by night was terrific. The daily progress of the flow was now from one hundred to five hundred feet.

When I visited the stream on the 18th of July, I saw a scene like this: Troops of boys and girls, young men and women, were watching the flow. They plunged poles into the viscid lava as it urged itself slowly onward; drawing out small lumps of the adhering fusion, they moulded it, before it had time to cool, into various forms at will. They made cups, canes, vases, tubes, and other articles out of this molten clay, and these they sold to visitors and strangers at from twenty-five cents to a dollar or more for a specimen. All went away with fresh spoils from the spoiler. An artist was there, who had taken sketches in oil; and the photographer has been upon the spot. Our town was now crowded with visitors from all parts of the Islands, from our Princess Regent, sister of the king, then absent, to the least of his subjects. Many spent entire nights upon the banks of the lava river.

Just in front of one of its branches a stone wall five feet high was built, in hope of protecting the great Waiakea sugar-mill, for which this arm of the flow was heading. It was not a broad or heavy arm, but it was followed up by a column of fusion which no engineering could turn aside. This small advance stream came within a yard or two of the wall, paused there, and fell asleep in its shadow. At a single point the viscid mass, about two feet deep, struck the wall. There it rested a little, until, being supplied with fresh lava from behind, it heaped itself up against the barrier, poured over it, and then stiffened and solidified. It now hangs there, a sheet of vitreous drapery, marking the limit of the flow in that direction. Judge Severance dug a moat around the Hilo prison, with an embankment seven or eight feet high, hoping to avert the necessity of a general jail-delivery; but any considerable body of lava of course defies every obstruction. We made no preparations, however, for quitting our house.

The flood came on until all agreed that in two or three days more it would be pouring into our beautiful bay. On the 10th of August it was but one mile from the sea, and half a mile from Hilo town. On that day, nine months and five days from the outbursting of the great eruption, when hope had perished in nearly every heart, the action began to abate. The raging flood, the steam, the smoke, the noise of the flow were checked; and in a day or two the great red dragon lay stiffened and harmless upon the borders of our village. The relief was unspeakable.

On the 13th of August I visited the flow for the fifth time, and felt radiating heat, but saw no more liquid lava. But the great pall of the eruption lay upon the land for fifty miles. I estimate that the lava stream covered a hundred square miles of mountain, forest, and farmland, to an average depth of twenty-five feet—enough to cover the State of Connecticut to a depth of six inches. No exact measurements, however, have yet been made.

I may add a word upon the curious process by which this lava flow, like others, has made its way over so great a distance from its source. The average slope of Mauna Loa is seven degrees; but this is made up of secondary slopes, varying from one to twenty degrees. As the lava first rushes down the steeper inclinations it flows uncovered; but its surface soon hardens, forming a firm, thick crust like ice on a river, and under this crust the torrent runs highly fluid, and retaining nearly all of its heat. In this pyroduct, if I may so call it, the lava stream may pour down the mountainside for a year or more, flowing unseen, except where openings in the roof of its covered way reveal it.

When the molten river reaches the more level highlands at the base of the mountain, it moves more slowly, and sometimes spreads out into lakes of miles in diameter. The surface of it soon hardens; the lavas below are sealed within a rigid crust that confines them on every side. Their onward progress is thus checked for hours or days. But as the tremendous pressure of the stream behind increases, the crust is rent, and the liquid lava bursts out and gushes forward or laterally for a hundred, five hundred, or a thousand feet or more, as the case may be. The surface of this extruded mass cools and stiffens in turn, again confining the living lava; then, with the pressure from behind, there is a fresh rupture in the confining shell. While the lava is held in check as I have described, the uninitiated visitor will pronounce the flow to have ceased. But it is only accumulating its forces. The lava presses down from the source, until suddenly the hardened crust is ruptured with a crash, the lava moves forward again, and a new joint is added to the covered way. Thus overcoming all obstacles, the fusion is kept under cover, and moves forward or laterally in its own ducts for an indefinite distance. It may flow at white heat in this way for thirty or forty miles and reach the sea at a distance of more than fifty miles from the mountain source.

By virtue of this pressure from behind, and of its own viscidity, the lava may even be propelled *uphill* for a certain distance, if the outbursting rush of lava be directed upon an upward slope. The lava thus grades its own path as it goes seaward.

Five or six miles inland from our town there nestled, some twenty years ago, a quiet hamlet. There was a schoolhouse in the place; and the land produced taro, potatoes, bananas, and other fruit-trees. The scenery was of enchanting beauty. But the population passed away; and of late years only one house remained on this lovely spot. Its occupant was reputed an inveterate heathen. He belonged to the ancient class of native physicians or medicine-men. When the burning flood struck the forest behind his house, he is said to have hoisted his flag in front of the slowly advancing lava, and to have forbidden it, in the name of the ancient gods of his race, to pass that flag. But onward came the flood, regardless of the edict. From time to time the heathen doctor was compelled to remove his flag to the rear, planting it nearer and nearer to his house; and at last the lava expelled him and his friends, and rolled over house, garden, and field, leaving a grisly pile of black lava over all. One circumstance in the case was curious. The lava stream surrounded a single kalo-plant, growing on an islet of eighteen inches in diameter, and on another one twice as broad, a single banana plant. They have survived the heat and are growing finely, the only green things left in the garden from which the idolater was driven.

It is time to bring these imperfect sketches to a close. The foregoing pages have been written among interruptions and anxieties, but they make some partial record of a life preserved by its Giver in many scenes of danger and crowned with many blessings. And among its chief blessings I would recognize God's goodness in granting me precious partners in my lifework. My second marriage, October 13, 1873, was to Miss Lydia Bingham, daughter of the Rev. Hiram Bingham. This faithful helpmeet is the strength and support of my age. But for her suggestions, and her patient labors in copying the manuscript of this volume, I should not have undertaken, at my time of life, the task of writing it.

As I lay aside the pen, our anxieties have passed away. If again, while I remain, the rocks should melt and flow down at the presence of the Lord, again we "will look unto the hills whence our help cometh."

HILO, *15th August, 1881.*

INDEX

Made in the USA
Las Vegas, NV
31 July 2024

93195197R00134